PENGUIN BOOKS

# THE LUCKY COUNTRY
### DONALD HORNE

Donald Horne is of the generation that came to maturity at much the same time as the modern Australia he writes of in *The Lucky Country*. He has benefited from many years of analyzing public affairs, notably as editor of the Sydney *Observer* and, later, the *Bulletin*. Since writing the first edition of *The Lucky Country*, he has written *The Permit, The Education of Young Donald, God is an Englishman, The Next Australia* and *But What If There Are No Pelicans?* He lives in Sydney but he has travelled a great deal—through Australia's neighbours in Asia and the Pacific, and also in Britain (where he lived for five years), and in the United States.

He is married, with two children.

D1380392

DONALD HORNE

# THE LUCKY COUNTRY

PENGUIN BOOKS

Penguin Books Ltd, Harmondsworth, Middlesex, England
Penguin Books Inc., Baltimore 11, Maryland, U.S.A.
Penguin Books Pty Ltd, Ringwood, Victoria, Australia

—

First published in Penguin Books 1964
Reprinted 1964, 1965, 1966, 1967, 1968, 1970, 1971, 1974

—

Copyright ©Penguin Books Australia Ltd, 1964

—

Printed in Australia for Penguin Books Australia Ltd
at The Griffin Press, Adelaide
Set in Monotype Baskerville

—

Registered in Australia for transmission
by post as a book

# CONTENTS

CONTENTS

# PREFACE TO THE SECOND EDITION

## *Writing on the run*

'I HAVE no doubt that Horne's little outburst will have been forgotten by the end of the summer', said one reviewer of the first edition of *The Lucky Country* in December 1964. This prediction did not prove to be true. *The Lucky Country* has already sold more copies than any other book of its type and now this revised edition has been prepared, with revisions and a number of supplementary sections. Why have so many Australians bought it? Perhaps what attracted a lot of people to it was that the tensions of Australia in the 1960s seemed to take it over as it was being written (perhaps making it a better book than the one first planned); it brought together most of the present frustrations and conflicts of Australians; people can disagree with some of the views of events given in it and nevertheless agree that the right problems have been set.

To write a book on the run, trying to describe a society as it moves, can be more demanding than to write as if a society were all of a piece, standing still and unchanging: but since the static approach is bound to be wrong one must plunge into the mess of conflicting social trends and hope for the best. It is the privilege of historians – not contemporary commentators – to know how things ended, and therefore what they were. *The Lucky Country's* concern with topicality – with what it's like to be *now* – may give some wrong emphases. To take one example: in writing about the tensions in Australia between puritanism and paganism I did not know what tenses to use. Past? Present? Future? All three (not to mention some of the more ambiguous tenses) would be accurate if related to different regions, different activities, different kinds of people. But this fine work is not necessary. (Probably it is not possible.) The main thing is to describe Australian paganism and Australian puritanism as two conflicting trends and to suggest that paganism is now having more victories than puritanism. There are the same kind of uncertainties in describing conflicting trends in Australian attitudes towards the British, towards technological style and towards 'Asia' (three themes taken up in the book). One cannot get the tenses and emphases right because the whole thing is changing shape. However Australia – more exactly, the younger generations in Australia – seems to be moving towards less provincial, more talent-oriented, more Asia-conscious attitudes. One recognises that unpredictable events can intervene that could make Australia move towards these attitudes at a smarter pace, or move away from them, or move off on another tack altogether. One prediction in the first edition – that we are also moving towards a comparatively less prosperous Australia – has already received some confirmation. What effect will that have?

Even if some social survey of supernatural scale and efficacy could fix an exact description of a society for one day of the year there would be even greater confusion than we now enjoy. We would have the whole mess in front of us and we could probably make nothing of it. Societies, like people, are always in a state of ambivalence, even in prevailing behaviour and attitudes: everyone of us holds beliefs and attitudes that contradict each other; our behaviour, in turn, often contradicts our beliefs – and itself. People change their 'natures' from one situation to the next. I have not bothered to argue this point in *The Lucky Country*. It seemed obvious that one could say, for example, that Australia is an egalitarian country and also say that there are differences within it: that there are economic injustices, inequalities of opportunity, snobberies. It can be both true that Australia is an egalitarian country and true that it has snobberies. I have bothered to make this point here because there is now a vogue amongst some Australians for suggesting that, because there are inequalities in Australia, it is not an unusually egalitarian country. On the contrary, despite a decline in egalitarian rhetoric, *in some of the things that Australians really care about* – in the general tone of people's relations to each other (at work, for example) and in access to pleasure – there is evidence that Australia is becoming *more* egalitarian than it used to be. And anyone who cannot, with his own sensitivity, detect the differences in tone between deferential societies such as those of Britain and Japan and that of Australia must be suffering from atrophy of the senses.

In writing about one's own country – with a sense of its present tensions – one is likely, by inference, to be unfair to it, in that one exposes situations in it that are also common to other countries, or to the general human condition. *The Lucky Country* is probably unfair in this way. However every time one makes a point about Australia one can't have a roll call of nations to see how Australia scores by comparison. This question of fairness must at times be left to the good sense and experience of the reader. From his own knowledge he can make his own comparisons. (One visitor suggested that Israel was the most illuminating place to compare Australia with!) In one sense no country except New Zealand can be compared with Australia: these are the only two 'western' nations that, strategically, are part of Asia. (What happens to Australia cooks New Zealand's hash too.) It is this special characteristic of Australia – that it is a dependent, second-hand, second-rate 'western' nation, *that happens, strategically, to be part of Asia* – that makes one unfair to it: Australia may have to be 'better' than other countries (for example, Belgium or Canada) that are also dependent, second-hand and second-rate. And since Australia is one of the world's most prosperous and stable smaller nations and dedicated to its material well-being there seems little point in self-congratulatory comparisons of it with – in this sense – unluckier countries of roughly the same population. Australians can scarcely congratulate themselves that they make up a more prosperous and stable nation than South Vietnam, Afghanistan, Sudan, or Peru.

Here the relevant comparisons are with countries like Sweden and Switzerland; and, according to the rules, Australia comes off increasingly badly in these comparisons, so far as its economic climate is concerned.

Excluding expatriates, the further away from Australia *The Lucky Country* is sold, the more people seem to think it *praises* Australia; an American wrote to me to say that he had finally decided to migrate to Australia after reading *The Lucky Country*. Australians, however, take it to be highly critical of their own country. And so it is. But not of ordinary Australians; it is the elites of Australia who are criticized: in revising the book I have added to this criticism, not modified it. That the people who run things in Australia are not much good is not news to anyone who reads books about Australia (although it may be one of the special features of *The Lucky Country* that it has gone into such terrible detail on this question). However what will not be found in this book is the stock defence of Australian elites: that they cannot help being what they are because in an egalitarian country the elites are *necessarily* second rate and *necessarily* reflect what is taken to be the mediocrity of the people. This fashionable view gives a fashionably gloomy cast to predictions about the societies of the future. However the Australian experience does not necessarily give support to it. It would seem more likely that it is the *provincial* nature of Australian elites that is the main reason why they are so second-rate, rather than the general egalitarian tone of Australians' relations with each other.

The central concern of the book is a general description of Australia. The *Lucky Country* theme is really a subplot. It comes and goes. *Overall* this book is not polemical: no single point is being driven home all the time. Nor is there any singleness of approach. A country can be looked at from a number of different points of observation. I have tried six of them, one after the other. The first chapter offers two quite different overall 'images' of Australia. The second looks for similarities amongst Australians. The third looks for differences. The next two chapters are concerned with the effects on Australia of its relations with Britain, the United States and 'Asia'. The next four chapters look at Australia another way: in social sections – businessmen, unionists, politicians, and so forth. The last chapter is concerned with the subplot. This difference of approach is deliberate, I did not want the whole thing to fall too pat.

### Revised edition

The first revised edition was revised throughout and also enlarged to include some new, or partly new sections. In Chapter 3, *Women, Migrants, Underprivileged, Wowsers,* and *Catholics* were either new or expanded. In Chapter 4, *Provincial Australia* was new and *A Republic?* was slightly expanded. In Chapter 6, *Men of business* was new. In Chapters 7 and 8 more than half the material was new. Chapter 10 was slightly expanded. An index was added.

### Second revised edition

The second edition was revised factually throughout to take into account developments in 1966 and 1967, particularly those that followed the departure from power of Sir Robert Menzies, Mr. Arthur Calwell and Dr. Soekarno.

### Third revised edition

There is a new chapter at the end of this edition, summarizing the main changes in Australia since *The Lucky Country* was first written. The rest of the book has also been revised.

# PROLOGUE

*Peopled from all over Asia*

WE were on the terrace of the Carlton Hotel, drinking whisky and looking down on the glare of Hong Kong. My Chinese host was discussing the White Australia policy. 'Be careful of the Chinese,' he said. 'We are the most intelligent race in the world. If you let too many Chinese into your country they will take you over' ... In Taipei I was in the Foreign Office drinking coffee with a Chinese official. I told him we often wondered what the Asian students in Australia said about Australia when they returned home. 'You invite Asians into your country to study?' 'There are about twelve thousand at present.' 'Twelve thousand! Why don't you tell people about it?' ... At lunch at the University of the Philippines we were talking about Australia's reclassification as an Asian country in ECAFE. The Filipino beside me said: 'Why do you remain a monarchy? Asians distrust you because you are a monarchy. You should declare yourself independent of Britain and become a republic. We are all interested in Australia. It is a huge continent. In a hundred years' time it will be peopled from all over Asia.'

I came back from a trip to the Far East early in 1963 and decided that Australia was worth a book. In the future it might be of interest to know what the huge continent was like in those early days in the nineteen sixties before it was peopled from all over Asia. Then I went overseas several more times during the year; this seemed to make it possible to evaluate my own country all over again – in the disorder of other people's reactions to it.

In Fiji colonial officials said how hard they found it to arouse interest in their colony in Canberra. In Honolulu a girl, half Japanese and half Hawaiian, who did a night club act as a Tahitian dancer, asked: 'Is Australia as comfortable to live in as it is here in America?' In Singapore. beside a swimming pool at the Goodwood Park Hotel a Malay began his conversation by saying that some of his best friends were Chinese and then questioned me about the political influence of the Chinese merchants in Sydney. In Bangkok I was questioned on land reform in Australia and the conditions of its peasants. In Hong Kong the second time, over dinner, an Englishman attempted to toast Australia for keeping out Asians; he thought it was the last bastion of civilization in the East. In Tokyo when I said to a Japanese that many Australians now considered themselves to be Asians she said: 'No, that is wrong. Australia is in Oceania, not Asia. You are civilized like us.' She then said she would like to come to Australia for the ski-ing. Back in Manila, at lunch beside Lake Taal, a young Filipino reminded me of the expulsion from Australia of the Filipino Sergeant Gamboa. 'But that happened in the nineteen forties.' 'Ah no, Mr Horne, I remember it. It happened last year.'

In Delhi there was talk of how the Indo-European races must combine against the Chinese, of how 'old empire countries' like India and Australia had so much more in common than new arrivals like Ghana. At a private beach in Alexandria two Lebanese who were thinking of migrating to Australia said that 'the niggers' (meaning the Egyptians) did not come to this beach. 'How do you treat your niggers in Australia?' 'The aborigines? Oh we're beginning to give them citizen rights now.' 'You can't give niggers civil rights. I won't migrate to Australia.' In Athens a young Greek nodded towards the Acropolis. 'This is all the past. We all love Australia here. Australia is the future.' In Rome an Italian senator dismissed Australia: 'Ah, you have no communist problem there.' In Berlin an anti-communist expert on communism told me that China was not aggressive towards 'The West'. When I replied that China was undoubtedly aggressive towards 'The East' (including Australia) there was agreement. In Frankfurt, in a chance encounter in a beer garden, I was asked about the Australian philosophy of life. When I explained it: 'So you are all existentialists there!'

In England, returning to the village where I lived for a while, there seemed to be in the electric appliances, bathrooms and bingo games something of a touch of Australia. In London an editor said that when England abandoned the monarchy the Royal Family would probably migrate to Australia. In New York a friend explained that for American intellectuals Australia did not exist. 'Even a Zionist would have more interest in you if you were an Egyptian. There is no image of Australia in America and there will not be until the intellectuals create one.' At two cocktail parties I was several times addressed as 'you English'. In San Francisco, where they were holding the mayoral elections, the maid just did not believe me when I tried to explain that in Sydney we did not hold our mayoral elections at the same time as they did in San Francisco.

Except for those places where it is still seen as a migrants' opportunity and a hope for the future, the world is not very interested in Australia – mainly because its intellectual life is second rate, and it is intellectuals who cast images of the world (however much other kinds of people then purvey them). Much of its public life is stunningly bad, but its ordinary people are fulfilling their aspirations and this is a rare thing for ordinary people to do; they have developed a style that provides a greater potential than is at present being drawn on; in some ways Australia is a 'newer' country than the U.S.A., casting images of the future that the U.S.A., with its conventions of inequality, cannot yet do. Australia may be something of a mirror to the world of what the world is likely to become if it does not blow itself up. The possibility that the world should become like Australia would profoundly alarm most cultivated people in the world; but there is solace for them in the fact that Australia may be about to undergo – or is already undergoing – changes, perhaps revolutionary changes, that are introducing those diversities without which – for the few anyway – life can become almost intolerable. Interest is added to this process by the reflection that if change does not proceed fairly rapidly Australia in its present form may cease to exist.

# 1. THE AUSTRALIAN DREAM

*Innocent happiness*

THE South Sydney Junior Leagues Club, 558a Anzac Parade, set in a suburb of what may be – in certain senses – the most democratic city in the world, would still be described in some countries as a working men's club. It has a membership of thousands of men and women of only average weekly wage who arrive by bus, taxi or private car to play its 'pokies' – the poker machines before which members stand or sit, their glasses of beer beside them, and pull levers to win an average of several thousand dollars a day. The club makes a *profit* of hundreds of thousands of dollars a year from its pokies after expenses are allowed for, and puts this money into bars, restaurants, a swimming pool, squash courts, steam rooms, gymnasia, bowling alleys, a roof garden (glassed in, with $120,000 worth of air conditioning), a small library, and a nursery. There are dances four nights a week (two are held simultaneously on Saturdays), $52,000 worth of floor shows a year, a car park, six tennis courts and 'the most beautiful billiard room in the Southern Hemisphere'. The general tone is of suburban good taste – vases of gladioli, goldfish tanks, parquet floors, pastel colours, light wood furniture and an aboriginal mural pay tribute to the cultural standards of the women's magazines. People dress as they please, men in shirtsleeves and shorts, or suits; women in party dresses or stretch pants. The club represents the Australian version of the old ideals of equality and the pursuit of happiness: that everyone has the right to a good time.

In outward form, and as far as ordinary people know or care, Australia is the most egalitarian of countries, untroubled by obvious class distinctions, caste or communal domination, the tensions of racialism or the horrors of autocracy. Taxi drivers often prefer their passengers to sit with them in the front seat and sometimes tip them the small change. A person who doesn't like ordinary people to think they are as good as he is, or to enjoy some of the things he enjoys himself, will not like Australia. The spirit of fraternalism permeates the nation. Sometimes the substance of an accompanying equality is missing; there are still inequalities of wealth, power and opportunity, but the ordinary people have won – or had delivered to them – a profound and satisfying ideological victory. Australia is a nation that for a large part accepts the ideology of fraternalism.

There are underground tensions of snobbery or power but these are almost unknown to the mass of the people. Whatever kind of a bastard the boss might be, he usually rolls up his sleeves and looks like one of the boys. Usually he does not outwardly contest the belief that those who work for him are as good as he is. Ordinary Australians no longer envy their bosses, although they may hate them or pity them. They attribute success to good luck or sharp conduct (thereby providing a more accurate view of success than most) and to them the economic advantages of getting ahead (they do not detect any social advantages) sometimes seem too slight to be worth the trouble. Ordinary Australia is not a society of striving and emulation. Ordinary people are not concerned with the ways of the rich or the highly educated. What they want they can usually get – a house, a car, oysters, suntans, cans of asparagus, lobsters, seaside holidays, golf, tennis, surfing, fishing, gardening. Life assumes meaning in the weekends and on holidays. In the ocean cities Australians can live the life of the Mediterranean or the South Seas. To some they seem lazy. They are not really lazy but they don't always take their jobs seriously. They work hard at their leisure.

Australia has one of the highest per capita national incomes in the world; there are more cars and TV sets for its population than almost anywhere; there is the largest rate of home ownership in the world; there are more savings accounts than people. Even these figures do not give an idea of Australia's economic equality. Not only are very rich or very poor people rare; the average income is not just a simple average, it is also close to the typical income.

As Australians line up at the polling booths in schools and halls at election time most of them do not know that Australia, which has been enjoying manhood suffrage and the secret ballot since 1860, was one of the first to show that society could survive what was then attacked as the triumph of 'selfishness, ignorance and democracy'. There are less than a dozen countries like Australia that, throughout the century, have been ruled efficiently by stable democratic governments that have been accepted by a vast majority of the people as legitimate.* As in these few other countries, the opponents of a government in Australia (except for the small Communist Party) are not prepared to use any except democratic means in their attempts to replace it. And there is so *much* political democracy in Australia. Less than 13,000,000 people, but there are six State Governments and a Federal Government – altogether 13 legislative chambers (including the upper houses), more than 700 politicians, about 80 Government Ministers. And the system of compulsory voting at elections, with fines for non-attendance, makes the 'donkey vote' – the vote of those who just vote down the list from top to bottom – a factor in political planning. And the system of preferential voting (in which every candidate for the one position must be voted for in order of preference with preferences being distributed until one candidate has a majority) encourages a 'fair go' for minority parties that pesters the bosses of the two major parties.

Social stability is high: Australians are too easy-going to become fanatics and they do not crave great men. People count on orderly reform to right whatever they consider to be their wrongs. It is part of the nature of Australian government to juggle things around, to avoid sharp issues

* Apart from military occupation, only the United Kingdom, the United States, Canada, the Low Countires, the Scandinavian countries, Switzerland, and New Zealand pass this test.

so that questions of final judgement do not suddenly arise. Even Australian nationalism – once strong – is now so hesitant that it no longer achieves self-definition. No one any longer tells Australians who they are, nor do they seem to care. They have their families, their leisure, they know what to do with their lives. *They* seem to know who they are but their easy-going definitions of themselves do not meet the fashions of intellectual or political rhetoric so that when Australian writers or politicians speak of their own people they often speak falsely, or with contempt. Whatever opinions Australians express personally, ordinary Australia is now a more tolerant country than it used to be. The mass of the people have available to them as full a range of civil liberties as a mass of people usually wants except, paradoxically, in the field that interests them most: having a good time. Generally, authority is despised. Politicians and government officials are distrusted and the police are often hated, although there is more unconscious acceptance of authority – perhaps indifference to authority – than Australians recognize. There are displays of aggressive individualism, although fewer than there used to be. But the aggression often springs from the feeling that someone else is being aggressive. Normal friendliness can be quickly resumed.

The remarkable openness of manner impresses – and sometimes appals – those who are used to social stiffness or deference. Truth is sometimes blurted out with a directness that can disgust those who come from more devious civilizations. A cult of informality derived from a deep belief in the essential sameness and ordinariness of mankind reduces ceremony to something that is quietly and self-consciously performed in a corner. Australians are self-conscious if they have to take part in ritual. Their wartime armies must have had the lowest saluting rate in the world. The only really national festivals are Anzac Day, Christmas and New Year. Anzac Day is the Festival of the Ordinary Man; Christmas the Festival of Family; New Year the Festival of the Good Time. Other holidays are just days off – except for people of religious conviction. On Anzac Day, commemorating the landing of Australians at Gallipoli in 1915, in every town in Australia ordinary veterans in very ordinary clothes march down the streets (many out of step), go through a brief ceremony and then many of them go and get drunk. There are themes of death and sacrifice: but the appeal of Anzac Day is as an expression of the commonness of man (even death is a leveller), of the necessity for sticking together in adversity. It is not a patriotic day but, as Peter Coleman said in the *Bulletin*, 'a tribal festival', the folk seeing itself as it is – unpretentious and comradely.

Australia is not a country of great political dialogue or intense searching after problems (or recognition of problems that exist). There is little grandiose ideology and politics is usually considered to be someone else's business and a dirty business at that. For many Australians, playing or watching sport gives life one of its principal meanings. The elements of loyalty, fanaticism, pleasure-seeking, competitiveness, ambition and struggle that are not allowed precise expression in non-sporting life (although they exist in disguise) are stated precisely in sport. The whole business of human striving becomes a game. In 1950, Bertrand Russell said that Australia pointed the way to a happier destiny for man throughout the centuries to come; 'I leave your shores with more hope for mankind than I had when I came among you.' In 1886, J.A. Froude said of Australians: 'It is hard to quarrel with men who only wish to be innocently happy.' On an Australian beach on a hot summer day people doze in the sun or shoot the breakers like Hawaiian princes on pre-missionary Waikiki. The symbol is too far fetched for Australian taste. The image of Australia is of a man in an open-necked shirt solemnly enjoying an ice-cream. His kiddy is beside him.

## Nation without a mind

Why write a book about such a happy country? One reason is that in some ways it is not so happy: one can learn something about happiness by examining Australia – its lingering puritanism, the frustrations and resentments of a triumphant mediocrity and the sheer dullness of life for many of its ordinary people. Another reason is that it is a matter of some general interest – of considerable practical interest to Australians – whether Australia will be able to maintain its happiness; have the conditions that led to so much success also weakened adaptability and slowed down the reflexes of survival? Another reason is that – in a sense – Australia has not got a mind. Intellectual life exists but it is still fugitive. Emergent and uncomfortable, it has no established relation to practical life. The upper levels of society give an impression of mindlessness triumphant. Whatever intellectual excitement there may be down below, at the top the tone is so banal that to a sophisticated observer the flavour of democratic life in Australia might seem depraved, a victory of the anti-mind.

This is not a special plea for the comfort of intellectuals. And there will certainly be no argument against 'affluence', the satisfaction of ordinary appetites by ordinary people. I shall accept as *given* the attitudes to life of most Australians (although they are not all my own preferences). One then asks: Is it possible in a modern society to preserve all the prosperity and happiness of a nation that is so strongly inimical to ideas? There is another part of the question: Is Australia really inimical to ideas? Or has there been something wrong with the ideas presented to it?

Even if the world were not to make demands on Australia – and Australians often seem to assume that since they leave the world alone it should do the same by them – the prosperity of the country might diminish compared to other countries. Throughout the world the basis of material prosperity in the future is likely to lie, for the first time in history, with clever, educated people. The need to build up a certain kind of cleverness will cause great social tensions in all industrialized countries; but especially in Australia, where cleverness can be considered un-Australian. Except in those few fields where it has a history of enterprise

Australia has not been a country of great innovation or originality. It has exploited the innovations and originality of others and much of its boasting is that of a parasite. As a transplanted society, it has had sufficient working similarities with the societies from which the innovations came to be able to exploit them with only a margin of inefficiency. But as the technological revolution passes into its new forms Australia may be left behind. It may not understand what is happening, or have the skills to implement new techniques. The present very great tendency for overseas firms to buy up Australian firms may accelerate. Australia could end up as an economically colonial country again – in manufacturing industry it is not far off it now – with foreigners managing its main economic affairs.

Australia faces an amazing number of other challenges. As Barbara Ward wrote in the *New York Times*, although each of these challenges is not in itself unique, no other 'western' nation has had to face so wide a cross-section of the mid-century's typical dilemmas. One might add that, because of its history, Australia may also be uniquely unaware of the nature of challenge. To list these challenges – and they are another reason for writing this book – is to list most of the principal headings of the way the world talks now: the collapse of European colonial empires; the emergence of communism in Asia; the lack of stability in the new states; the development of anti-racialism and of anti-colonialism; the pressures of underprivilege and of over-population; the surplus of temperate foodstuffs; the problems of maintaining growth in a sophisticated society; the problems of developing a physically 'have-not' country.

Australia merits sympathy for providing an encyclopaedic study of the main dilemmas of the mid-century. Until it has much greater strength – and ultimately that would seem to depend on a huge increase in population – there is nothing much it can do about some of its problems, except hope for the best. But it moves very slowly in doing anything about *any* of its problems. There are no great debates, there is little effective public discussion. The men in power do not seem able to excite first their own imaginations and then those of others into becoming familiar with these challenges. The government does not seem capable of getting a far from incompetent bureaucracy on the move. There are few 'new men' gathered together in the precincts of power to re-visualize the images of the nation so that change may become possible. The men at the top, the tribal leaders, are not in training for such a set of awkward situations. Their imagination seems exhausted by the country's achievements. Their own ideals – those of a more modest and earlier Australia – have been met and there are few people to whom they will listen to tell them that those ideals are now obsolete. Those who are now successful hold conventional wisdoms that belong to the first chapter of Australian history, a chapter that finished somewhere in the mid-twentieth century. There is no longer in Australia a generally accepted public sense of a future.

It is as if a whole generation has become exhausted by events, a provincial generation produced in a period when mindlessness was a virtue, the self interest of pressure groups was paramount, cleverness had to be disguised, quick action was never necessary and what happened overseas was irrelevant. In some ways the study of contemporary Australia is a study of that generation. It was not a generation that allowed a place for the kind of extraordinary man who can see the new shapes of the future – or the present – and enjoy challenge, living life at a fuller pitch. There is little of the sophisticated political discourse that can refresh politicians; there are few channels for an intellectual breakthrough; in the universities (with exceptions) clever men nurse the wounds of public indifference; government officials are exiled in Canberra, away from the people they govern. A society whose predecessors pioneered a whole continent now appears to shun anything that is at all out of the ordinary. The trouble is that, by Australian standards, almost everything that is now important is out of the ordinary.

# 2. WHAT IS AN AUSTRALIAN?

### *The first suburban nation*

MOST Australian writers seem to find it impossible to come to grips with their own people. They caricature their fellow countrymen or idealize them for qualities most of them do not possess. There is no Australian Orwell, searching for the temper of the people, accepting it, and moving on from there. This failure to take Australian life seriously leads to a hollowness and hesitation in attitudes: since the realities of Australian life have not been written about in detail they do not exist for the bookish; what they see of Australian life seems somehow unreal and perhaps temporary. They feel betrayed by their own people.

This betrayal can take different forms. As if they were a foreign elite trying to run a rebellious colony, the London-oriented Australians laugh at the 'Australian accent' or say of someone 'he's very Australian': to them Australians are a crude and 'uncultured' lot. Those who cling to the Australian rural myth consider the fact that four out of five Australians live in towns to be a betrayal of one of history's trusts. Some of them still act as if Australians were not mainly a suburban people; they shut their eyes and imagine a race of laconic country folk. Those who still maintain the 'working class' myth hate 'affluence', the young people who most strongly symbolize it, and the dwindling away of the old 'working class' rhetoric. The bohemians and rebels attack 'suburbanism'. Indeed 'suburbanism', one way or the other, is likely to be the target of practically all intellectuals. And since most Australians live in the suburbs of cities this means that intellectuals hate almost the whole community. It is a fact highly inconvenient to national myth-making that Australia is probably the most urbanized nation in the world.

Few Australians have realized that theirs was one of the first modern suburban societies. By the third quarter of the nineteenth century Australia already possessed one of the highest proportions of city dwellers in the world. Australia may have been the first *suburban* nation: for several generations most of its men have been catching the 8.2, and messing about with their houses and gardens at the weekends. Australians have been getting used to the conformities of living in suburban streets longer than most people: mass secular education arrived in Australia before most other countries; Australia was one of the first nations to find part of the meaning of life in the purchase of consumer goods; the whole business of large-scale organized distribution of human beings in a modern suburban society is not new to Australians. There is no Australian city that is yet really an urban city with a varied and lively centre in which many people live and to which others congregate. Sydney's King's Cross area, with its 100,000 people, is the most densely populated area of any 'Western' city in the world but Sydney does not yet possess a really sophisticated city life, although it is beginning to imitate one. Detailed recognition of the essentially suburban character of Australia has been slow, partly because old myths have remained virulent and partly because special factors in Australia such as the almost pantheist love of outdoor activity have muddled the pattern of what — according to overseas authorities — 'suburbanism' is supposed to be.

It is hard to imagine how one can understand Australia unless one approaches sympathetically the life most Australians lead and the values they follow. For instance, Australia is an extraordinarily stable society. The self-satisfaction that is so often attacked is one expression of this stability. Australians seem to know what they want and it includes a house (with an average of five to six rooms) set in its own garden, a considerable amount of privacy, domestic comfort and an involvement in family life. There is a strong materialist streak in Australians: they like things that are useful to them in their homes and they will work overtime to buy them on hire purchase. They have a strong philosophy of how lives should be led. You save money and get married; you pay a deposit on a house and furnish it; you hope your children will lead a happier life than you have led; you plan your retirement so that you will enjoy it; and when you die you leave your house to your children so that it can be sold and the money used to help pay off the mortgages on their own houses. To ordinary Australians life has its seasons, there are propagation and replacement. Perhaps it is the acceptance of this not unusual view of life that offends.

The 'home' occupies as central a position in Australian life as land in a peasant community except that it is disposable after death; there can be an equally strong sense of family, except that as children become adult the family group dissolves, the children go their own way. As well as the verities of home and family, Australian life has many acceptable forms of companionship, often a craving for rest and solitude, and an extraordinary identity at times with the elements. Within this context the entire range of human comedy and tragedy has its play. Births are celebrated, the dead are mourned, desires fulfilled or denied. The profusion of life doesn't wither because people live in small brick houses with red tile roofs. It is the almost universal failure of Australian writers to realize this that causes them either to caricature Australian life, or to ignore it and move into what Robert Burns described in *Dissent* as 'the ragged fringes of social life and human consciousness.' As Burns says: 'Australia's novelists, the very good as well as the quite frightful, belong in the cluster of those who regard the actual circumstances of daily life as a sort of bead curtain which must be clawed aside before the writer can drink deep at the bar of truth and fulfilment.' Almost all Australian writers – whatever their politics – are reactionaries whose attitude to the massive diversities of suburban life is to ignore it or condemn it rather than discover what it is.

In earlier periods of Australian city life there was considerable difference between gentility and vulgarity. The vulgarity came from the 'working class' of the big cities: it was pictured as happy-go-lucky, hard-drinking, hard gambling, matey, thumbing its nose at the cissies and snobs in the lower middle class suburbs. It was a non-possessive shiftless society of rented houses and sparse furniture, companionable, reckless and concerned with the expressions of toughness. This picture reflected some of the primitive virtues: a man did not tolerate injury, he rebelled against authority and sometimes might take harsh revenge. He was seen to reflect the verities of human history – a real man, not a suburban creation – as C.J. Dennis saw Ginger Mick:

'To fight and forage ... Spare me days! It's been man's leadin' soot
Since 'e learned to word a tart an' make a date.
E's been at it, good an' solid, since ole Adam bit the froot:
To fight and forage, an' perfect 'is mate.'

Such types did exist, but to identify them with all wage earners is romantic. And it should be remembered that when the collarless cavaliers of corner pub and back alley got home from this rollicking man's world of booze and two-up they might slobber with sentiment over their wives and kids but if they were in a bad mood they might bash them up. They constituted a self-centred male aristocracy following its way of life at the expense of others. For a number of reasons – greater prosperity, slum clearance, increased education, a greater growth of white collar workers (now more than half the work force) – this class is vanishing, although there are still plenty of individuals who display its characteristics (usually minus the physical brutality), by no means all of them 'working class'. And the assertion of toughness and masculinity is still an outstanding characteristic of many Australian men, along with an exclusion of women from their social life.

What is sometimes still not realized by those who attack 'suburbanism' is that the entire gentility-vulgarity confrontation is out of date. The gentility is going, too. The existence of a substantial body of people who valued sobriety and hard work was long suppressed by the myth

makers; now it is overstated. New generations are denying
the old proprieties and stuffiness. The genteel have been
vulgarized, the vulgar made more gentle. People now enjoy
themselves more in the same kind of ways. Drive around
one of the big cities in the weekend when people are getting
ready to pursue happiness and you see, especially among
the young, that they even dress the same. The cult of the
informal has extended to the once genteel; and kindliness is
softening the once brutal. Now brutality or social stiffness
are more a matter of personality or of family than of class.
A new style of life is developing that is less rigid. It is wrong
to describe it as an extension of the 'middle class' way of
life. This way of life is itself being destroyed. The mass of
young Australians (about half of the population is under
twenty-five) seems to be becoming more the same – in some
new way that is still mysterious.

## Fair go, mate

There is a whole set of Australian characteristics summed
up in the phrase, 'Fair go, mate'. This is what happened in
Australia to the ideals of Liberty, Equality and Fraternity.
As might be expected, in the transmutation these ideals
have been knocked about. But the whole thing cost no lives
and it is ingrained in the texture of Australian life. If the
outside world will allow it, it seems to be there to stay.

The general Australian belief is that it is the government's job to see that everyone gets a fair go – from old age
pensioners to manufacturers. A fair go usually means
money. Australians see a government – which they both
trust and despise – as an outfit whose job is to help them
where they need help. This attitude of expectant distrust
involves a great deal of semi-legalism; governments hand
over to semi-judicial tribunals like the Arbitration Court,
the Tariff Board or the Repatriation Tribunals much of the
business of distributing 'fair goes'.

With such a calculating approach to government there is
little of either State-worship or State-hate. The State is just

a lot of other Australians who are assumed to have gone in for politics for reasons of self interest but who are expected to ensure that the self interest of others is also secured – otherwise they should be sacked. They are managers doing a job. This cut-and-dried attitude distresses those who call for leadership and the kind of statesmanship that attempts to stir people up and prompt them to unpleasant action that is said to be for their own good. Others are distressed because it is not the kind of attitude that involves eternal struggle against the State. Much of the rhetoric of liberty is missing in Australia yet governments are checked and balanced by most intricate means and attempts to extend their power are often frustrated. Australians are often accused of being indifferent to freedom, of being submissive and potentially authoritarian; this seems a harsh judgement to make on the ordinary people. If the criticism is to be made it should be directed against the intellectuals; they are the ones who are normally expected to fight the forward battles of freedom. So far as political freedom is a matter of institutions and of ingrained attitudes and not merely of words the position is that Australia politically is one of the most free countries in the world. Democratic procedures are part of national life; there is a distrust of authority; men prefer the self interest of comradeship or family to the demands of the State. Puritanism excepted, ordinary life in Australia for ordinary people has been more free than, until recently, it was ever believed possible. Australia was one of the first countries in the world to show that this could be so. It is – in some fields – not for an excess of power but for a lack of activity that governments might be criticized in Australia.

Fair-goes are not only for oneself, but for underdogs. Even in international sporting matches Australians have been known to switch from their own side to that of a gallant challenger. Australians love a 'battler', an underdog who is fighting the top dog, although their veneration for him is likely to pass if he comes out from under. At work – among the unambitious – the feelings for underdogs runs very strong. Covering up for an incompetent mate is the usual things as long as he is considered to be trying and not simply 'bludging'. There is a feeling that 'triers' should not suffer because of their inadequacies. Thus in education concern for underdogs has played an important role and the tone tends to be keyed to the less gifted. Concern for unemployment far exceeds self interest. It is considered unjust that those who can least look after themselves and who bear the least responsibility for decisions should be the first and usually the only ones to suffer when governments or business firms blunder or change their minds. Australians do not like to think of other Australians being out of work (they are in fact one of the most fully employed peoples in the world); throughout the long rule of the Menzies governments threats of unemployment seemed to be the one thing that might unhorse the old survivor. However there are blind sides in Australian kindness to underdogs; for instance, lack of imagination and curiosity blinded them to the misfortunes of the aborigines, and there is a decline in interest in social services.

There is little public glorification of success in Australia. The few heroes or heroic occasions (other than those of sport) are remembered for their style rather than for their achievement. The early explorers, Anzac Day: these commemorate comradeship, gameness, exertion of the Will, suffering in silence. To be game, not to whinge – that's the thing – rather than some dull success coming from organization and thought. Since Australia is a commercial society there are many slick operators in Australia and those who admire them. Like other peoples Australians can say one thing and do another. But even here it can sometimes be the brazen rogues who do things with dash who are admired rather than those who are merely clever or organized.

The concept of fair-goes is of some significance in estimating Australia's adaptability and its reflexes of survival. It is essentially a non-competitive concept, a demand for protection, an attempt to gain security and certainty.

Whether it is an underdog in a factory or a top dog demanding tariff protection the feeling is that justice lies in a guarantee of existence. To fight for existence in an open market must be avoided although one may use legal or other lurks. Even the system of arbitration between employers and unions has some of this quality: the parties are not left to fight it out for themselves. I am not arguing the merits of this: it is a common human demand to want to feel safe and a sensible one if it works. But the concept of the fair-go has no international currency. Its wide acceptance in Australia sometimes renders Australians naïve when faced with nations who do not share their kindnesses.

The doctrine of fraternity, still largely meaningless in most countries, has received great ideological attention in Australia. It is just possible to live in Australia without realizing this. A man who doesn't use public transport or taxis, doesn't bump into people in the streets, or ask the way, or come into contact on anonymous terms with ordinary people may not hear the word 'mate'. There are other men to whom its use is as ordinary as 'comrade' to a communist.

In the narrower sense 'mates' are men who are thrown together by some emergency in an unfriendly environment and have become of one blood in facing it. In this sense its use is strongest in the unions and in the armed forces. Mates stick together in their adversity and their common interest. Mateship of this kind is not a theory of universal brotherhood but of the brotherhood of particular men. However the emphasis on adversity can lend a suggestion of theatricality at a time when there is not much adversity: a mate situation of this kind can become paranoid when mates all get drunk together and express their suspicions of a conspiring world.

There is a wider, but still exclusive sense, in which mateship is simply comradeship within a male fraternity. There is a socially homosexual side to Australian male life (of a 'butch' kind) that can involve prolonged displays of toughness in male company. Men stand around bars asserting their masculinity with such intensity that you half expect them to unzip their flies.

There are many pressures to conformity. This is not un-expected from a civilization that has been suburban for such a comparatively long time. Opinion studies carried out by Ronald Taft showed that the Australians tested put greater emphasis on observing conventional manners than on expressing one's individuality and preferred superficial but correct social relations to deep and intimate ones. The same opinion studies applied to a sample of Californians showed that the Americans were less likely to endorse conventional manners than the Australians. Australians like people to be ordinary. One reason might be the inability to imagine a way of life different from one's own. For instance, talking about sport, money and motor cars takes up so much of male conversation – indeed it provides a *lingua franca* between income groups and gives reality to the convention of equality – that sometimes to engage in a conversation it is necessary to have mastered these topics. Not to have done so is not to be a man. Interests run so evenly throughout the community that not to share them is to be an outcast. To be different is considered an affectation.

There are pressures to conformity in the concepts of 'sincerity' and 'consideration'. For 'sincerity' one can sometimes read 'stupidity'. Sometimes to be clever is to be insincere: 'I know you're wrong but I can't work out why.' And to be 'considerate' is not necessarily to be kind; it might simply mean not to unsettle conventions of behaviour. Cross-question an Australian on what she means ('consideration' is mainly a woman's word) and ultimately you are likely to unearth a complex of resentments against difference. A considerate person is one who fits into the majority pattern, follows the rules.

On the other hand – apart from the interventions of the puritans – Australian society has a great degree of public tolerance. People don't care about what goes on unless it directly confronts or interferes with them. This is just about as high a degree of public tolerance as one can expect from a community: not to go out of one's way to interfere with others. Tell an Australian about something nasty that's happening in another suburb, or another street and he may express a harsh opinion about it and then conclude that it takes all sorts to make a world. He doesn't start a reform movement. It's no business of his. Some critics profess to find Australians intolerant because they use rude words about migrants. But all over the world people attack other people. Perhaps this draws more attention in Australia because the climate is so professedly egalitarian. When it comes to action, Australians usually don't care. There have been few significant protests against migrants. Almost all acts of interference in any field of Australian life are inspired by the puritans and activated at the top. There are no significant mass movement fanaticisms. It is only when a difference stares them in the face that ordinary Australians become truculent; and then only in a personal way.

The concept of the essential humanity of all men is a noble one and – as long as it also allows for difference – it is also a shrewd assessment. But it needs slicking up in Australia to include a few kinds of people other than those who live in one's own suburb. Where it still flowers quite splendidly is in the openness of manner of Australians, and their informality and friendliness. The marked openness of manner sometimes offends as roughness. Sometimes it *is* roughness – the old feeling for the boisterous and robust or the anxiously male. But sometimes it is a directness that is nothing more complicated than honesty. London-oriented Australians can often be 'taken in' by people who display the mannerisms of English gentleness and politeness (but are really quite fraudulent), while they deplore the crudities of direct men. (Directness, of course, can also be fraudulent.) The Australian way is to distrust extreme politeness. 'Eh!' says the Australian. 'What's *he* after?'

The social servilities of work places are lessening. Life for ordinary people in offices used to be more stiff and more outwardly authoritarian than it is now. The long established cult of informality is now increasing. Power is still

there but it becomes devious, wears a more friendly smile.
And for most of the community, out of working hours, life
is now more relaxed, more freed of the vexations of social
forms and ceremony than older societies could have
imagined. It is a leisurely life, usually unworried by status.
The outward democracy of life in Australia represents a
successful revolution. If a Russian aristocrat of 1917 could
see photographs of Australia in 1964 he might assume that
it was here that the people had taken over, not Russia.
So, in many of the forms of social life, they have. And good
luck to them.

Max Harris says in *Australian Civilization*: 'Mateship
became an attitude to human relationship, an easy readi-
ness to strike up contact with fellow human beings in a
warm and casual way. This often strikes outsiders as evidence of vulgar over-democratization ... In fact the Australian has a rough but ready capacity for immediate
affection, a quality which, oddly for an Anglo-Saxon breed,
he shares with some of the Mediterranean people'. Australians like to establish a person-to-person basis. In the
cities they can display a traditional country hospitality to
visitors, even strangers. One of the many perplexities involved in the visits of Australians to England lies in the
frustration of not receiving the same immediate hospitality.
Since Australian friendliness often lacks knowledge of social
forms and ceremonies it can sometimes seem so strange as
to be taken for rudeness, usually for the one reason: that
most Australians are bereft of feelings of difference; they
think that all people are the same, that what is good for
oneself is good for anyone else. Their openness and friend-
ship-seeking is based on this belief. They seek similarity
where often it does not exist – even among themselves.
They reach out for the essential humanity of man but the
apparatus with which they do it is too primitive for the
task. They retreat into suspicions.

## Having a good time

To understand Australian concepts of enjoyment one must

understand that in Australia there is a battle between puritanism and a kind of paganism and that the latter is beginning to win. Old cries about dullness and crudity are still kept up by men who reached their conclusions about Australia in the 1930s and after going to all that trouble are not going to change their minds now. But things are changing – at different paces and in different ways in different parts of Australia. A lot of Australian life is still restricted by the killjoys. But it is improving.

Until these improvements began in the 1950s the story was that Australians took their pleasures solemnly, like true Anglo-Saxons. The gaiety of the Chinese or continental Europeans were not found in their cities. For many decades puritanism – bizarre in the sunshine of Australia – seemed to stifle Australian society. In most states hotel bars shut at six; liquor was not allowed with meals; betting was illegal; there were no social centres in the suburbs; the loss of the old working-class gregariousness was not replaced with new forms of companionship; the community was almost completely philistine towards the intellect and the arts; there were few good restaurants; Sundays were dismal; book banning and other forms of censorship flourished; a woman's place was in the home. Here was a country of indolent climate, general prosperity and a philosophy of happiness; it was a wonderful set-up for choice and indulgence. Yet life was dismal and such public enjoyment as occurred often degenerated into rowdiness. A pall of ennui spread over the suburbs at night and at weekends. There was all this life to lead and nothing much to lead it with. Apart from the pleasures of family life three main diversions were open to the people – drink, sport and money.

To drink became one of the tests of manliness among those who rejected at least some of the standards of puritanism. For ordinary people it was a brutal pleasure – jostled in austerely equipped bars, dazed by the bedlam, gulping beer down and perhaps later spewing it up. But some of its special significance may have come from its puritan context. Australians have never been quite the nation of

bars, social clubs, restaurants and hotel entertainment break through to a more companionable life; and women participate more openly in the pleasures of life. None of this has been achieved by political protest. Australians have remained sufficiently puritanical to be ashamed to take seriously some of the matters about which they are most concerned. It has been a matter of unorganized and unideological social pressure, probably coming from causes such as a continuing decline in puritanism, the demands of migrants for a life more like the one they are used to, the increasing number of Australians who travel overseas, and the changes in generations. One has only to look at the young to see the difference between them and the older generations. They are more open in their enjoyment, more poised, more easy in mixed company. They seek more variety. They may be about to turn sport worship upside down, treating outdoor activity as a pleasurable diversion rather than a nation-building institution. They may not care to win the Davis Cup or the Tests. They seem to prefer the individual performances to the team game – surfing, skin diving, ski-ing, archery.

Despite the puritanism that seeped into Australia through the Protestant sects, the Evangelical wing of the Church of England, the Irish Catholic Church, the Protestant Ethic (for businessmen) and the Nonconformist Conscience (for political leftwingers) there has been a counter-balancing paganism among ordinary people. When the waves are running right and the weather is fine the crowds at the beaches are doing more than enjoying themselves: they are worshipping the body and feeling identity with sand and sea and sky. Breaking through the disciplines of organized sport, people amuse themselves as they wish in outdoor games or relaxations that express a belief in the goodness of activity and nature. There has long been this element in Australia of delighting in life for its vigour and activity, without asking questions about it. It has received considerable literary expression as an unquestioning (and anti-intellectual as well as anti-puritan) hedonism, often with implied nature worship. It may be the philosophy of living of the young. When young men strap their malibu surf boards (cost $70 to $90) to their cars, drive off to the beach and command the breakers all day they seem to move into a life that is more Polynesian than puritan. In *Quadrant* Hugh Atkinson quoted a 'Surfie' as saying: 'I dunno, it's hard to describe. When you're driving hard and fast down the wall, with the soup curling behind yer, or doing this backside turn on a big one about to tube, it's just this feeling. Yer know, it leaves yer feeling stoked.'

It might be relevant to look at the life of the South Seas to throw some illumination on life in Australia, instead of the almost exclusive comparison with the United Kingdom and parts of Western Europe (ignoring Mediterranean Europe) with an occasional glance at the U.S.A. Desmond O'Grady wrote in the *Observer* of the sense of deprivation suffered by European migrants. 'They feel they are living in a void because the suburb has no organic relationship to the city. Those Italians who are disappointed because they feel that they do not belong, that they have not reached the centre of Australian life will go on feeling disappointed because there is no centre. Once they realize there is no centre and they couldn't care less about it, they'll have been assimilated.' Yet the place to send migrants so that they can feel they belong is to the beach, one of the strongest centres of gregariousness in the ocean cities. Australians do not sit at pavement cafes to watch the promenade. They go to the beach, sun themselves and surf, and watch the promenade there. They still look at people, but the people have most of their clothes off. Here a young man can show his prowess in the water to his peers and the women of his tribe, his existence stripped down to what he alone feels and sees (which isn't much); his father may be in the men's quarters telling stories of war, of fishing, or of sporting ritual; others may be sailing or looking to the garden. There is also in Australian life some of the craving for quietness and slow reflection. A man likes to sit in the sun and say nothing, do nothing and think very little. On holidays Australians like to retreat to shacks or even tents beside the water, and enjoy the primitive.

The desire for simple pleasure, so strong in Australians, still plays no part in the official view of life; presumably this is one of the reasons for the spuriousness and boredom of official statements. It may not be possible for a political party to campaign about the things that people really care about – more roads to the beaches for instance – but a party that can begin to imply its acceptance of enjoyment as part of Australian life might find itself attracting votes, especially among the young, who are liberated from some of their parents' guilts.

## Give it a go

The scene is the Domain, Sydney's Sunday afternoon orators' corner. The speaker is shouting at the crowd: 'Tell me this! What is an Australian? I say what *is* an Australian?' Someone in the crowd puts up his hand. 'An Australian is a lazy boozer.' The crowd laughs. That's it. We must poke fun at ourselves. Or is it poking fun at ourselves? What's wrong with a lazy boozer? Australians get bored with serious talk unless it is expressed in the most laconic terms. By any standards public oratory is appalling: the usual style is to speak as if one is not interested in the subject. Enthusiasm and rhetoric are likely to be treated as ratbaggery. A usual form of social intercourse is 'chi-acking', pulling someone's leg. This kind of act might sometimes go on for minutes in the most complicated way. With some people it is now a considerable art. It is a form of affection convenient for a people who distrust senti-mentality and are likely to sniff around a florid phrase like a dog sniffing a bait. Australians don't want to be taken in by words and they are suspicious of public emotion. They seem to prefer their public occasions to be as dull as ditchwater; no one will take them seriously that way.

On this most pervasive and important national character-istic Max Harris said in *Australian Civilization*: 'The modern

Australian, in so far as he thinks about the world at all, does it in an offhand unsentimental way, without self-pity or self-assuredness. From the minor daily exigencies to the Eumenidean events, there is no purpose in making a fuss … Human relationships (the mateship hangover) are pretty sacred, but most aspirations and ambitions are "bullshit". This cynicism-beneath-purpose feeds our notorious philistinism, but it also prevents blind individual egocentrism. The Australian finds it difficult to go in for consistent self-delusion. In his moments of serious thought he sees an awful lot of bullshit in the world. He can identify, recognize and make short work of such bullshit as comes within his experience. Unfortunately he extends it to those experiences and phenomena with which he cannot cope. But within a given critical range there is dry intelligence, good sense, a good-humoured resistance to all pretensions and over-valuation … the Australian is cynical and self-denigratory towards himself as well as towards the world he sees around him. He is always having a shot at his own bullshit. Normally the Australian is "sending himself up", even when he appears to be boasting. As with the Scots, it is difficult to tell when the Australian is "fair dinkum". It's not very often.'

This deeply inlaid scepticism is a genuine philosophy of life, a national style determining individual and group actions. Its influence can be detected throughout Australian society. It may be the most pervasive single influence operating on Australians. It has much to its credit. A sceptical people like the Australians is more likely to achieve change organically than by cataclysm: things move along more or less comfortably in their own directions, without the horrifying personal disasters of more catastrophic societies. And it is surely in the interests of freedom that the normal posture of Australians towards authority is one of ridicule. In the Australian armies men were brave and resourceful in action, but off duty many were Good Soldier Schweiks. They were in the army to engage the enemy, not to engage in military 'bullshit'. The very lack of any definite nationalism, of statements on who Australians are and where they stand in history, cannot be wholeheartedly deplored in an age that has seen so much horror and cruelty unleashed in the name of nationalism. History has resounded with ceremony and ideology that has almost always been 'bullshit'; in the end the common man copped the lot. From this process Australians try to stand apart. Even promises of material advantages are treated sceptically. At election time Australians take pleasure in looking gift horses in the mouth. Excessive promising is said to help lose elections in Australia. Bosses of all kinds lament lack of discipline but as far as the ordinary Australians are concerned they can go jump in the lake. Intellectuals lament the unadventureousness of Australians but they can jump in the lake too. Considering the quite preposterous nature of many ideas intellectuals put up this reaction is not necessarily stupid. In general one might agree with the ordinary Australian: most of what is pumped out of the word factories is 'bullshit'.

Combined with this scepticism is a sense of the practical that is interested in material things and, within a narrow range, prepared to experiment with them. The scepticism of Australians is not a reactionary conservatism: it is a caution in relating action to words. The high material prosperity of Australia would not have been possible in a completely unadaptable society. Scepticism does not stop Australians from at times suddenly making quite drastic changes. Once they accept a change they are all for it. They seem to have very little sense of continuity with the past, and changes, when they occur, occur suddenly and with little regret; the past is all over and done with.

They are a largely non-contemplative people who often like the thought of action and the future; that they do not engage in action more often or think of the future in more detail seems to come from a narrowness of imagination, the product of scepticism: they have a limited view of the possible but if something new is demonstrated as being possible – and this demonstration often takes place in a more innovatory country overseas – then they accept it. Good-oh. The Yanks can do it. We'll have a go at it too. What they find it difficult to do is to imagine the new for themselves. And they have no class in their own country which regularly does this for them.

Despite this lack of imagination, Australians – oddly enough – can be skilful improvisors. Impelled to action, Australians cheerfully 'give it a go'. They try something to see if it works, pretty sure that it will. There is almost a cult of optimistic improvisation, of the slapdash and the amateurish; it may even be an extension of the cult of the informal. Procedural patterns and conceptualization are so ramshackle that some parts of the country's institutional structure seem to be held together with safety pins and bits of string. Suggest to an Australian that you spend some time investigating a practical problem in detail and outlining rational procedural patterns and you bore him stiff. 'She'll be right,' he will say. 'We'll just give her a go.' Talking too much about what you are doing is 'bullshit'. It's best to get on with the job. (The phrase 'she'll be right' can strike terror into the hearts of people who are trying to run things in Australia. What it can mean is: 'Don't worry about it. Just let us muck it up for you and leave us in peace.' It is a phrase of unreasonable confidence – like the merely polite Chinese 'Yes', which can mean, 'No, but I don't like to say so.')

The scepticism of Australians produces many weaknesses as well as strengths, especially since it has penetrated many areas of power in the community. A passion for improvisation leads to slapdash attitudes that may become increasingly dangerous in a technological age; it includes distrust of the expert. Scepticism can combine with the egalitarian dislike of cleverness to oversimplify even the simplest issues. Like all optimists, Australians are stupendous simplifiers. As practical minded optimists they can get away with their dislike of discussion of even practical issues because most of these issues are clarified for them overseas. Their main job is to improvise an adaptation of overseas ideas in conditions that are not very competitive. But these cheerful simplifications will work only as long as Australian society is sufficiently similar to the societies from which the ideas come – and only as long as it is not called on to provide ideas for itself.

Scepticism reacts against imagination of even the most down-to-earth kind. Yet imagination is not merely making things up; it can also lie in discerning the shapes of problems, in probing new areas of the possible. For scepticism to oppose this type of imagination, as it does in Australia, is simply to defend conventional stereotypes. It is not really prompted by a sense of reality but by a particular form of illusion. Australian scepticism, as an expression of optimistic nationalism, can sometimes be naïve.

Faced with odd conduct, Australians ask: 'What's in it for him?' Such a view of life can strip calculating self interest of its fancy clothes; but it does not allow for the irrational, the element of craziness that may be a more important element in affairs than rationality. Themselves calculating, materialist and optimistic, Australians find it hard to accept that quixotry, pessimism, spirituality, desire for defeat, boredom, love of rhetoric or of risk, of wielding power for its own sake – all ratbaggery these – may often impel action. In the narrow shaft of clear, bright sunlight where Australians think, there is little room for the view in which we all just seem to bump around in the shadows with little understanding of what it is all about. Australians think they have life taped.

## Racketeers of the mediocre

There is more concern with gaining and manipulating power – more conspiracies and private bastardries – than ever appears in assessments of Australia. It is here that one of the real divisions in Australia occurs – between the mass of the people who pursue innocent happiness and those who attempt to gain the multiple satisfactions of power and ambition. Of the latter, those who seek power openly and openly enjoy it may now be in the minority. These are the men who established careers by pushing on with Napoleonic onslaught, Men of Will, with an eye for an opening and the ability to mass their resources to exploit it. They are often impelled by an un-Australian craving for excitement and achievement, for getting things done. They used to be common enough in Australia, but now they are confined mainly to business and even in this field their numbers are declining. One of their difficulties is that, society having become more complicated, success now demands detailed staff work as well as determination to exploit weakness and although Men of Will can learn to use intricate staff work, in Australia they have been slow to do so.

Men of this kind are sometimes dismissed by their rivals as too crudely 'Australian'; and there is now something of a reaction against them from a new generation of 'smoothies'. They must inevitably be more devious than they appear to be but there is an openness and directness about them that fits the style of the ordinary people. However a new kind of ambitious Australian is now apparent who is not straightforward in anything; he learns to conceal his ambition and to follow it deviously, under an egalitarian disguise. Especially in the middle generation, he can become as tricky and deceitful as you are likely to find. And if he is not impelled by cravings for achievement (that is to say, to get something done), but by the desire to possess power and at the same time to be liked, when he treads softly into some area of power he may not be impelled to use power for some external end, but to play with it for its own sake and to follow this secret vice into its darkest mysteries.

At the top, whatever the subterfuges, the practice of power is often inefficiently authoritarian. Men who do not understand originality or professionalism do not delegate efficiently (although they may use delegation to pass the buck): they hold their positions. They are impatient with the time taken to be expert, lack comparative standards and are uninterested in ideas. They dominate. Unlike the

Men of Will, whose decisions, though perhaps arbitrary, nevertheless form some kind of public law, they may dominate silently and capriciously – meaninglessly.

Many of the weaknesses of ordinary Australians are those likely to be found in a people anywhere. It is a sign of how deeply populist much Australian thinking is that when someone wants to criticize Australia he criticizes not the few who run it, but the mass of the people, as if the genius of the nation resided exclusively in them and only spontaneous generation on their part could affect reform. This habit conceals the fact that, while ordinary Australians have many fine and some quite exceptional characteristics, the present elites in Australia are mostly second-rate. Many of the nation's affairs are conducted by racketeers of the mediocre who have risen to authority in a non-competitive community where they are protected in their adaptations of other people's ideas. At times they almost seem to form a secret society to preserve the obsolescent or the amateurish. Yet they are very Australian about it. Characteristics that may be admirable or at least harmless in ordinary people if they permeate the areas of power may be dangerous. The passion for fair goes can then become a whingeing demand for fair goes for privilege; those who want to make money run to the government or one of its agencies with a sob story. The passion for improvisation can mean that standards are of the 'she'll do' kind and there is impatience with slow detailed preparation or professional procedure. The passion for scepticism can produce a suspicion of discussion, a tongue-tied lack of practical imagination, a mindlessness in decision and discourse. The passion for egalitarianism may combine with the passion for scepticism to hide and often frustrate talent.

The demand for mindlessness can be so pervasive that able men deliberately stumble around with the rest less they appear too clever, and therefore too 'impractical'. Within Australian institutions there is a great deal more subtlety in personal relations than the image of the simple unsophisticated Australian allows for. Much energy is wasted in pretending to be stupid. To appear ordinary, just like every-body else, is sometimes a necessary condition for success in Australia. When this is merely a disguise it can frustrate talent but not suppress it; unfortunately, all too often it is not a disguise.

The elites of Australia sometimes guard their power with a lack of interest in talent that is more open than in almost any other democracy. In this atmosphere even to attempt precise, detailed and orderly statement can sometimes excite ridicule; it is an assault on the conventions of a country whose elites often live by the rules of other people's thumbs. To be expert and adopt professional standards can be to put a man in the second grade; to argue reasonably an affectation; to take a realistic interest in the present an impertinence; to attempt to project the future a confession of impracticality. The cleverness, conceptualization and procedural skills that go into running things in innovating countries is 'mere theory' to many of the masters of Australia.

In this atmosphere cleverness and talent can become devious but still survive in some lower key. What often perishes altogether – in the bureaucracies of business or of government or in the universities and in such intellectual communities as exist – are originality, insight and sensitivity, the creative sources of human activity. In an imitative country no one has to be creative; the creative person is likely to be confronted with distrust – not perhaps in science or the arts, but almost everywhere else. It is as if the masters of Australia have inherited a civilization whose rules they do not understand.

With their distrust for Australian originality and their ignorance of the world the men who run Australia often have a peculiarly narrow view of ranges of the possible. For them, to appraise potentials is to decide to do little more than continue what is now happening. The 'rebels' in Australia normally do not appraise the possible at all; they simply express wishes. But those who profess to be practical often lack the great talent of practicality: the ability to seek out to the outermost limits of the possible. The potential for change within the ordinary people of Australia is great; it is their misfortune that their affairs are controlled by second-rate men who cannot understand the practicality of change, who are, in other words, 'conformist'. It is not the people who are stupid but their masters, who cling to power but fail to lead. Employers find the Australian people lazy; politicians and government officials distrust them; intellectuals hate them. Yet with different leadership, the Australian people might display a proud record. As it is their contempt for those who run their affairs is more than a mere expression of Australian egalitarianism: it is an accurate assessment.

# 3. SENSES OF DIFFERENCE

## *Eleven cities*

FIRE, air and water ... these are the elements of Sydney: the fire of the sun, the freedom of the air, the challenges and diversions of thirty-five beaches on the Pacific and the waters of Port Jackson, Broken Bay, Pittwater, Botany Bay and Port Hacking. Those who see only miles of suburban streets leading away from ocean, bay or river see the form of Sydney but not the way it sees itself. Sydney dreams of surfing, fishing, sailing, swimming in calm bays, lying stretched out in the sun, absorbing heat into the marrow. And it is now at long last taking on some of the *feeling* of a great city, the first city in Australia to do so. After London, Paris and Berlin, Sydney is now as big as any city in Western Europe and bigger than Madrid, Rome, or Vienna. In American terms, it is about the same size as San Francisco. Its peculiar flavour is of anarchic difference. Its getting-on-for three million people have broken their guidelines. There are no accepted forms in Sydney; it is anonymous; just people following their pursuits, indifferent to others. Sydney does not acknowledge a 'Society'; there are merely claimants to position, who can, if they wish, achieve positions by self acclamation. There are no standards. For a quarter of a century politics in New South Wales were conducted with a Tammany lack of policy, a matter of deals and pressure groups unadorned by rhetoric and of little interest except to the participants. Sydney's indifference to what others do has achieved tolerance without ideology. In Sydney you see more Asians than in any other Australian city but people seem to take no notice one way or the other. It is Melbourne that speaks up for conscience. But it is also in Melbourne that there can be scare campaigns against migrants. Sydney has dozens of migrant communities where English, at most, is only a second language; but there is no public criticism of migrants and there are no scare campaigns. No one cares. Sydney is indifferent to itself, and to the other capital cities. The other capitals are self-conscious and always aware of Sydney. To people in Sydney this is surprising.

Four hundred and fifty air miles south-west of Sydney, Melbourne, capital of Victoria and, with about 2,400,000 people, second in population to Sydney is seen as more 'English' than Sydney – not the England of London and the South, but of Manchester and provincial business. The top of its society coagulates into a recognizable pattern; there is still a significant club life, with the outward forms of gentlemanliness. You walk into a Melbourne club and, unlike Sydney, you see who's running the place. Melbourne's streets lead down not to a Harbour, as in Sydney, but to the huge, ugly Flinders Street Railway Station. And a winter obsession with Australian Rules football seems to help Melbourne people make the adjustment that is so difficult to make in Sydney: what is there in life without sunlight? People are said to be milder, less aggressive in Melbourne than in Sydney; they are also said to be more cliqueish and group-conformist. Even social groups are inwardly quarrelsome in Sydney, but it is easy to move between them. In Melbourne groups are more friendly within themselves, but interact less and suspect outsiders more. Melbourne is more outwardly puritan than Sydney. Melbourne has been described by Billy Graham as one of the most moral cities he has even seen and by Ava Gardner, when she was there to star in *On the Beach*, as a fine place to make a film about the end of the world. Melbourne worries about its crime rate. Its intellectuals consider themselves more devoted to ideas than Sydney's pragmatic lot, and, in general, it accepts itself as a more cultured city than Sydney but this is not so. Its intellectual life is different – that's all. Melbourne knows more about the management of money than any other city in Australia. It is the home of much of Australia's big business. In Sydney many rugged individualists make a lot of money and English visitors, used to tolerating almost anything as long as it pretends to be something other than itself, see Sydney as a city of crude and newly gained wealth. (It is in fact the centre for Australia's oldest rich.) But while money talks a lot in Sydney it does not talk in one voice. In Melbourne it does – in a provincial gentleman's voice, blended with social conventions and respectabilities. At the top Melbourne provides what is left of an Australian 'Establishment' – a particularly pompous and obsolescent Establishment. It may be that Australia's obsolescence is most effectively perpetuated by the Melbourne Establishment. Until recently, all four political parties were led from Melbourne.

Brisbane, capital of Queensland, about a third the size of Melbourne, and as far from it as Istanbul is from Rome, is a city with its jacket off and its sleeves rolled up, hot, languorous, at times sensuously indolent – generous in tropical flowers, beer, hospitality, dominated in politics by Catholics for a quarter of a century, now by the Methodists. (The brothels have been closed.) It is the least capital of Australian cities, least in self-importance. To the tropical north, in the sugar ports and the cattle country and the developing mining and industrial areas they do not look to Brisbane. They want a separate North Queensland State they can run themselves. The big firms in New South Wales, Victoria and South Australia see Brisbane as just a branch manager town, a city of also-rans. Brisbane is a man's city – matey, slow to change and a bit rough around the edges.

Adelaide, capital of South Australia, about as big as Brisbane and as far from it as London is from Lisbon, is in conflict with itself. The accepted picture was of a gracious city of wide boulevardes, grass squares and stone colonial buildings, set out on the grand scale; of men of property and family running affairs in a gentlemanly way from behind the green shutters and cedar doors of the Adelaide Club; of a community established without the 'Irish element' or the 'convict strain'; assured, in control of powerful interests, but puritanical and dull; dedicated to civic pride, high business ethics, good works, good taste. This picture was attacked by some as a façade for political gerrymandering and a cynical and conspiratorial social conservatism. However this may be, the undeniable criticism of the accepted version of Adelaide is that it is now out of date. Adelaide has moved into the technological age. Despite the tradition of conservatism it is a go-ahead place where industries migrate. Much of it is now noisy, dirty and confused; people now work there who may not have heard of the old families, and the new class of managers and experts provides a new social force. And – despite the gerrymander – the Labor Party finally gained power in Adelaide. Compared with their own past relations to each other, Brisbane falls backwards, Sydney falls apart, Melbourne moves forward to stay where it is, Adelaide goes ahead.

Perth, capital city of Western Australia, is about as far from Adelaide as London from Leningrad, about as far from Sydney as Saigon from Tokyo. It is separated from the rest of Australia by thousands of square miles of desert and scrubland. Perth is the most isolated city of its size in the world. Set near the Indian Ocean it is as close to Cocos Island as to Sydney. Its people did not want to join Australia at the time of Federation; the migrant gold miners forced them to. It is the centre of a world in which much of the southern part is fertile with light seasonal rain and the northern part is in the wet-dry rainfall belt but most of it is one of the driest lands on earth. The State Perth governs is ten times as big as the United Kingdom but contains only a million people. Perth is relaxed, hospitable, a world of fishing, backyard beer parties and nice gardens. It works as hard as it can but takes it a bit easy when the sun flares in the summer sky. It distrusts the 'East'. (In Adelaide they distrust the 'East' but Perth distrusts Adelaide, too.)

The next largest city in Australia is not Hobart, Tasmania's capital, (with less than 150,000 people, Hobart is eighth on the list) but Newcastle, whose expanding southern edge now lies only about 50 miles from the

expanding northern edge of Sydney. Sprawling around the
shallow, silting port where coal from the Hunter Valley
fields is loaded, its skyline formed by a significant part of
Australia's heavy industry, dominated by the government
and opportunities of Sydney and the great heavy industry
business complex of Melbourne, Newcastle is now struggling
to achieve the character of a more mature city. Its tone is
set by old families, steelworks managers and local professional leaders. To the south of Sydney, Wollongong, seventh
largest city, site of the biggest steelworks in the British
Commonwealth, is not yet so ambitious. Wollongong is a
mystery thrown up from the puzzles of industrial change.
Building and rebuilding are conducted with twentieth
century technique but in a goldrush muddle. Wollongong
is a series of settlements spread along the coast rather than
a city. The central part of this agglomeration is still a one-
street town. People from 40 or 50 nations make up Wollongong – in the steel works migrant labour runs as high as
50 per cent. It is by far the most frontier-like of Australia's
bigger cities, spreading and sprawling to God knows where.
In the less than 150 miles of coastline, that encompass
Sydney, Newcastle and Wollongong live about a quarter of
the people of Australia. Sydney has broken the bounds of
definition; Newcastle is attempting a new definition;
Wollongong is creative disorder. It may be in this turbulent
area where, on present trends, there will be five million
people by the end of the century that much of the shape of
the new Australia will be comprehended.

Hobart started life on the frontier and then went to sleep.
It was one of the earliest convict colonies and a roystering
whaling port. Then it stood easy. A ten-mile stretch of blue
water lies in front of it and a dark blue mountain crouches
behind it, covered with snow to its foothills in winter.
Streets of old colonial houses in yellow stone will remain
and the town slips so quickly into the port that ships seem
to be anchored in the streets. Those who play this kind of
game say that its people are more reserved and cautious
than the mainlanders. It is now being jerked into modernity

with new buildings, and so forth but has not yet known the kind of new development that now shakes Sydney, Melbourne, Adelaide, and Wollongong. Existence is said to be somewhere between small town serenity and small town vindictiveness. Mainlanders think little about Tasmania and foreigners want to know who owns it.

Canberra, although the national capital, is still smaller than Hobart, and it has some characteristics of a town rather than a city, although it is the centre of the administrative power game. It is not primarily a political town. Except for political party meetings (which can be decisive) and parliamentary sessions (which are now of little importance) the quilt of Australian politics is patched together all over Australia, not in Canberra. Canberra is an administrative garrison, beautified by parks and gardens, laid out across a plain that is ringed with hills, a power complex of officials isolated from the Australian people. Their pressures on the politicians – perhaps the strongest single force in government – are not usually informed by that feeling for the texture of national life that might come from living among the people one governs. In their judgement of the possible they can be out of date. They must live on memories of what the Australians seemed to be like some years ago. There is the world of government buildings and the world of small quiet houses set in garden suburbs; for some there is contact with a diplomatic community (of very uneven quality) or with members of the Australian National University; there is the kind of entertainment and cultural life one might expect in an intellectuals' garden suburb.

Before the Second World War Darwin was a left-over from Joseph Conrad; it was a sleepy, half-Asian port, debilitated by a century of almost entire failure to do anything with the Northern Territory. It was a gambling, drinking town of pearl buyers, trepang fishermen and crocodile hunters, sprawling in the heat beside the Arafura Sea. In 1942 Japanese bombers blew most of it away and some of its people looted what was left and drove off towards the desert. Now it is a town of neat houses on stilts.

Government officials make up half its population. They administer 600,000 square miles of territory where 40,000 'whites' (most of them government employees) still experiment with development and cannot yet report their success. Darwin is a very different sort of administrative garrison from Canberra; it is still a town where 'grog parties' set the tone. A lonely man might still sneak off to some rusty iron shanty and get an aboriginal woman for a bottle. It is hot, only 12 degrees south of the equator and in latitude a little further from Hobart than Khartoum is from Rome; its long wet season sometimes drives men mad; in the dry season buffaloes have broken into the golf course. The integration of part-aborigines proceeds, the integration of full aborigines moves more slowly. In its long history of fiasco, of the ruin of a hundred schemes, three definite hopes now stand out for Darwin and the Territory: the breeding of cattle, the encouragement of mining and the development of Australia's first genuine and broadly based multiracial society.

Broken Hill is not the administrative centre of anything except itself. It is a city of only 30,000, out in the hot, dusty west of New South Wales. Silver, lead and zinc are mined there. Broken Hill is run by its trade unions and so far as Broken Hill is concerned the Barrier Industrial Council is stronger than the State of New South Wales. 'Badge Show' days are held to check on financial membership of unions and prices in shops are controlled by industrial action. If a price is considered too high the shop is declared 'black'. The miners have even boycotted beer to keep prices down. The Barrier Industrial Council owns the morning paper and is prepared to declare 'black' firms that don't advertise in it. Purchase of this paper is compulsory for all unionists, even if there are several of them in one household or if they are migrants who cannot read English. When women marry they are given three months to resign from their jobs. Broken Hill follows its own laws and ignores the rest of Australia.

These sketches of the eight largest cities in Australia, and of Canberra, Darwin and Broken Hill are not meant to be taken too seriously – and I hope my bias in favour of Sydney is obvious. They are examples of the kind of things that Australians say about their cities and, like the rest of this chapter, they are provided as a qualification to the generalization of the previous chapter. However it may well be that whatever differences there are between the Australian cities are differences within a range of similarity. The two main theories about Australians (minus migrants) are that they are all the same and that they are all different. Both theories are true. A grog party in Darwin, a backyard party in Perth, a King's Cross party in Sydney have different forms but may be versions of the same thing. The laconicism of a Brisbaner may be much the same as the reserved manner of a Tasmanian. It is one of the miracles of Australia that, despite the extraordinary differences in the settlement and development of the nation, its people are so much the same.

## The bush

About 58 per cent of Australians live in capital cities, and another quarter in sizeable towns. Little more than 15 per cent live in conditions that could be described as rural; of the work force only 8 per cent derive their living directly from the land (this figure has declined from about 15 per cent in the late nineteen forties). Even in Alice Springs the old rural values are threatened. Set in the centre of Australia, where the dust sometimes clouds the air for thousands of square miles, a place where aborigines have been massacred, still a place where men can die in the desert, a centre for radio school and radio doctors in the 80,000 square miles of Australia of which 'the Alice' (population 6,000) is the centre, Alice Springs is suburbanizing itself for the tourist trade. As tourists drive by in air-conditioned buses they still see the white sands of the dry Todd River, ghost gums on its banks, run through the town like a forgotten dream. But they also see modern hotels, motels

and stores and well-kept gardens that would grace a
suburb in Melbourne.

In picturing an Australian country town one projects
one's own memories. My memory is of a town of 3,300
people, in the Hunter Valley, hilly and scattered with pepper trees. On the golf course, in the brittle brown grass
there are dried cow pats and the crows cry with anguish as
they circle in the sky. Out of town there are the white bones
of cattle; houses are wooden and simple; sprinklers keep
the lawns green unless there is a drought, when the sprinklers are turned off. Each house has water tanks that are fed
by guttering from the corrugated iron roofs. From the
verandah one can look across the brown valley to a few
stubbly old hills. The town has an established social rain-
bow ranging from the big landowners whose properties
surround the town, through the small gentry, the lower
middle class and tradesmen to the railway workers and a
small community of miners. New ideas in its shops reflect
ideas of a little time before in Sydney. There is also a litter
of old shops reflecting ideas almost everyone has forgotten.
One wonders how they kept going. Catholics worship in
a spired church on a hill and are considered a race apart.
Methodists worship in a brick chapel in the main street and
are considered low class. Presbyterians worship in another
church with a spire on another hill and seem to get by.
But it is in the Gothic-type Church of England on the river
flats that the main Anzac Day service is held before the
ceremony at the War Memorial. One wonders why the
man who seems so important when he carries the cross before the Rector on Anzac Day is also the man who delivers
the gas bill. There are light romantic novels or war adven-
tures to read at the School of Arts and in the wooden
schoolroom shaded by weeping willows, on the side of the
creek, one learned that one was lucky to be an Australian.

The schoolroom has been pulled down and the whole
memory is thirty years out of date. But even then the traditional rural values were declining. There were differences;
it was more placid to walk to work, sometimes across

paddocks, than to catch an electric train and people went home for lunch; there was less entertainment to buy than in Sydney (country people were said to 'make their own fun' more than city people); speech was a little slower; and there was more sense of social difference. But on the whole the people in country towns were mainly a slowed down version of those who lived in the suburbs of the cities, although they may have thought they were different. Of the Australia my grandfather used to tell me about, the Australia he discovered when he ran away 'to get his colonial experience' and joined a gang of drovers, they knew no more than I did. They had never made damper in a campfire. All of that was some other time, the dream time, when a man could walk into a settlement with a swag on his back and start a town.

Even in the Kimberleys, 100,000 square miles in the tropical north of Western Australia where less than 5,000 'whites' and part-aborigines live and pioneer families control cattle runs as large as medieval kingdoms, now that there are plans for doing something with the millions of acres of fertile virgin soil that lie between the Ord and Fitzroy Rivers the plans include building new towns that will look like neat little suburbs stuck out a thousand miles from nowhere. In more ordinary country towns there are Rotary, Apex and Lions Clubs, the Masons, Returned Servicemen's League clubs with poker machines, bowling clubs, golf clubs. The repertory societies put on West End successes of ten years before; the pops are played on the local radio stations; an increasing number of towns have TV; and people with suburban good taste serve salad in wooden bowls. In the country towns of some size you are now likely to find the typical 'night out' dishes of the cities – seafood cocktail, filet mignon – as well as the traditional steak and eggs.

I do not think that the values my grandfather used to talk about any longer exist in any significant form although one can still detect them in some individuals and families. They were the values of incorrigible individualism,

perhaps preserved from the eighteenth century, more aristocratic than democratic: simple honesty, carelessness of the
opinion of others or the effect on oneself of one's own actions;
a driving, almost obsessive sense of independence and hatred
for any cohesiveness including even the natural cohesiveness of friends thrown together by the hostilities of physical
or social environment; and a belief that disagreement is
beneath argument – one just walks out. Values like these
sent men off on their own and – in the material sense –
ruined or made them. They implied a rebellion against
destiny and this may be why they are still found most significantly among some of the old landowning families who
can afford to reject new values without losing their
overdrafts.

What still exists in the country, out of the towns, is the
fascination that any farmer anywhere in the world finds in
his animals, his crops, the weather, the seasons, the markets
– the feeling that those who live on the land have for the
land, that goes beyond love and becomes knowledge. It is
the world of worm drenches or stickfast fleas, of saffron
thistle or pasture improvement, of shooting hawks or reading pamphlets on copper deficiency in cows. There are the
haunting landscapes of Australia – the great herds of cattle
drifting across vast, shadeless plains, glaring with heat;
and the hot, pale sky. There is the long, slow, monotonous
spread of the wheat farms; the scrubby, boulder-dotted
paddocks of failing cow cockies; the deep green of the cane
fields, with low white clouds scudding in from across the
reef; the neatness of the fruit-growing irrigation districts;
the lonely houses and rose gardens of the 'old families';
and the mad struggle against destiny beside swamps,
deserts or ravaged hills.

There are the bleak little townships on the western
plains, a dozen or two houses, a pub, a post office, a police
station, a store, a school, where a dusty stock route makes
do for the main street and a mob of goats grazes on the
Common. Or the little townships near the sea, set in gullies
where the bell birds sing.

In this Australia they distrust the smart alecs in the cities and towns. They have a liking for difference in personality, for 'characters', some of them half crazy, whose doings can fill in hours of yarning over a beer. There can be suspicion and scepticism, and a demand from governments for a 'fair go', but there is a much greater sense of individual judgement and individual responsibility than in the cities. In some sleepy backblock, hundreds of miles from anywhere, there can be more feeling for the demands of the world outside Australia than might be found in a whole suburb of a coastal city. Whether the Japanese are buying wool or the Chinese wheat or the Americans meat is a matter of immediate importance. Although there is cheerfulness it is the cheerfulness of people who acknowledge the possibility of catastrophe – from flood, fire, plague or drought, or the collapse of markets. There is not the gentle optimism of the suburban Australian, although there can be gamblers' dreams. There can be open-hearted co-operation, or hatreds of blood-feud intensity. Except for the rich, the chances of having a good time are quite different from those in the cities and there is a constant dribbling away of the young. The rural dwellers of Australia have another distinguishing characteristic: they actually live in 'The Bush'. The mythic landscapes of the writers and painters are home to them. They are also becoming familiar to those city dwellers who take their long service leave on an air-conditioned bus tour, photographing the myth with their new cameras and perhaps noting its height above sea level, if there is a tourist signpost nearby. This kind of information comes in useful when showing colour slides.

## The wowsers

Churches no longer matter very much to most Australians. Although 89 per cent of the population still claims religious adherence when it fills in a census form (34.8 per cent Church of England, 24.6 per cent Catholic, 10.2 per cent Methodist, 9.3 per cent Presbyterian,) private surveys suggest that as many as a quarter of Australians will admit to not having any religious belief. Church attendance is less than in the United States and church attendance of non-Catholics is less than in the United Kingdom. Of 770 army recruits surveyed by a Church of England team only 19 per cent could write out the Lord's Prayer and only 21 per cent could identify the three Persons of the Trinity. Only half knew what was being celebrated on Easter Sunday.

Australians still like to use their churches for marriages. Almost all marriages are celebrated in church, but as K.S. Inglis suggests in *Australian Society*, this may be a habit left over from Nineteenth Century culture, rather than any indication of religious adherence. In disposing of their dead, Australians have a bet each way: they like a clergyman to perform the ceremony but they prefer a funeral parlor to a church as the place of service. Non-Catholic Australians show a greater preference for cremation than any other people in the world. (And Australian women may be, proportionately, the world's largest users of oral contraceptives.)

If the conversation turns to religion (it is often considered bad taste to talk religion) there may form misty memories of Christian belief, principally those associated with the Golden Rule, which becomes an expression of mateship. In whispers of immortality there are concepts of a fair-go: hell has been abolished as unfair to underdogs. If there is a happy eternal life it's for everyone. Belief in the salvationary role of Christ is no longer strong and the concept of evil is un-Australian: one must look for the good in people. The instincts of puritanism still remain; having a good time, especially among older people, can become an extremely ambivalent matter. And the sexual morality of the Churches is still accepted doctrine, although statistical information* and ordinary observation suggest that practice falls short of official precept. Belief in the dignity of

* About a quarter of first births appear to have been conceived before marriage and nearly seven per cent more are illegitimate.

man, in the human potential and in the value of human life is almost universal. The official beliefs of Australians are essentially humanist and those parts of Christianity that fit this belief are retained.

While about half the Catholics go to church regularly (and a third of the Methodists) only about one in seven professed Anglicans and Presbyterians are still regular churchgoers. The non-Catholic churches are now often stripped of almost all except the most vague doctrine. Religion becomes a mysticism, offering comfort and reassurance. The prevailing emphasis, in the Australian fashion, is often on practical matters: doctrine is unimportant. Young executives immerse themselves in the practical affairs of a parish – with money raising gimmicks, church attendance figures, and so forth – as they might otherwise immerse themselves in the affairs of a bowling club. Mother's Day becomes a religious occasion. There has been a small liturgical revival, confined mainly to clergymen and a few sympathetic laymen, but, generally speaking, in practice, Protestantism has been drained of almost all serious intellectual and moral content. Seriousness might keep people away from church.

It should be recognized that there has long been opposition to religion and 'bible bangers' amongst Australians. When Christian practices challenge other beliefs they have often come off second best. When Anzac Day (the Australian folk festival) is commemorated on a Sunday the protests of the churches are likely to be met by the counter claim that Anzac Day is more important than the churches. To many Australians it is. The beliefs associated with Anzac are more Stoic than Christian.

In fact to many Australians religion becomes important only when it stops them from doing something they want to do. This blockage occurs principally in the form of the Nonconformist Conscience, expressed in the person of the 'wowsers'. The Nonconformist Conscience has been a significant factor in the development of Australian liberalism: Michael Rowe suggests (in *Quest for Authority in Eastern*

*Australia 1835-1851*) that as early as the middle of the nineteenth century the dominant Australian view of life was already that everyone must become a good, wise, prosperous and responsible citizen. In this development the Protestants played an important part – first in helping to contest the attempt of the Church of England and the landed gentry to impose the patterns of England on Australia and then in exhorting the poor and oppressed to stop their boozing, put on their stiff collars and set themselves up in small houses in the suburbs like good Christians. The Temperance movement (which, as in England, became their principal form of social pressure) was also a movement against poverty and social unbalance but as these evils diminished and its sense of general social uplift languished it became a narrow obsession with forms of enjoyment. In this it was joined by some parts of the Irish-influenced Catholic Church who – in the Irish style – gave expression to parts of the English Nonconformist Conscience. Catholic 'wowsers' were less likely to inveigh against drinking and gambling than Protestant 'wowsers' but they led the field in inveighing against any except a particular use of sex.

It would be hard to exaggerate the traditional importance of 'wowsers' in Australia or, more generally, of the strong Australian urge to restrict the activities of other people. Before the Second World War (which may have been the beginning of their end) 'wowsers' ideologically held most of the field: they attacked drinking, gambling, smoking, divorce, women's fashions, sport on Sundays, modern verse, contemporary novels, living in flats, working mothers, and lipstick. Subjects such as contraceptives and sexual deviation were so taboo that they were not even attacked. The 'wowser' vote was considered to be of political significance and, between the two wars and into the 1950s there was no loosening of control on matters such as hotel trading hours and off-course betting. Since then the 'wowsers' have been in slow, disorderly retreat. However it is worth remembering that in the mind of even the most libertarian Australian there often still lingers a little of the conscience of the 'wowser'.

## Catholics

Perhaps the single most important issue connected with religion that remains with Australians as a whole are questions of Catholicism and anti-Catholicism. This has been one of the divisive issues in Australia. Traditionally there was an entrenched Catholic community, mostly of Irish origin, that flourished with a sense of alienation to a largely hostile environment.

Anti-Catholicism has not been as overt as it was in the nineteenth century when fear and hatred of Rome led secularists and Protestants to combine to secularize the State and education; those who have not grown up in Australia do not now always detect the significance of anti-Catholicism and it is now at last declining; but bitter distrust of the Catholic Church is part of the system of beliefs of most older non-Catholic Australians. It was nurtured by some of the Protestant clergy; it was an article of faith among many intellectuals (anti-Catholicism is the anti-semitism of the intellectuals); it was a matter of considerable importance in the lower levels of many government departments; there was an anti-Catholic bias in a significant section of the Liberal Party; many business leaders were anti-Catholic; it was a very important factor in the struggle for the Labor movement. Often the Masonic Lodges impelled anti-Catholicism. In the business world, in government departments and in the political parties Masons often took the lead against Catholics; in retaliation lay Catholics, through their own secret society, the Knights of the Southern Cross, a pseudo-Masonic outfit with special handshakes, passwords and ritualistic mumbo-jumbo, used self-protection against what they believed was a powerful and bitter enemy; this increased the suspicions of the Masons. How all this began no longer matters. It was self-perpetuating, with each side in opposition because it believed the other was plotting against it.

This antagonism has been an important impulse to action in Australia; the rival secret societies have had some of the influence secret societies had in pre-communist China.

Indeed a great deal more of the affairs of Australia are carried out in an underground of conspiracy than most people realize or anyone can describe in detail. Perhaps the outward tone of discussion is so idealistic that it is only in secret that the realities of power can be contrived. Whatever the reason, the minority of Australians who are concerned with power enjoy plots and get a kick out of dirty work.

Anti-Catholicism was usually based on the assumption that the Catholic Church was a monolith, a press button affair in which the Pope or the Cardinal or somebody put a message on the line and all Catholics obeyed it. This belief had been perpetuated by a number of pieces of evidence: there was no doubt that parish priests had influenced some of their parishioners on matters that went far beyond defined dogma; it had often been the Catholic style for Catholic spokesmen to imply a greater unity and therefore a greater strength than existed and for Catholic publications to discourage discussion; Catholics had held disproportionate power in the Labor Party (and, one might add, they had been disproportionately weak in the Liberal and Country parties); Catholic schools often encouraged their pupils to enter the public service; where there were Catholic power systems they favoured Catholics. However none of this was to prove that the Church was a monolith. The very structure of the Church was pluralist, with each bishop responsible to Rome and the Cardinal merely a bishop who, if he was to exert influence over other bishops, had to do it by democratic means.

Although there are conspiracies of Catholic laymen the entire Church was not a single manipulable conspiracy. Witness the suggestion that proportionately more Catholics than Protestants voted against the referendum to ban the Communist Party. There is some anti-clericalism among churchgoers and about a third of Catholics seem to be non-churchgoers. The traditional support for Labor (as many as 75 per cent of Catholics may have voted for Labor until the 1950s, when the Labor Party split) has been taken as evidence of conspiracy but there are more subtle explanations. It is true that Catholics obtained control of many Labor Party machines but it may have been the Labor Party that used the Church, rather than the other way around. By capillary attraction personal influences extended widely amongst Catholics and traditional voting patterns developed. There is no doubt that this pleased the clergy and that some of them helped the party bosses; but they didn't seem to get anything very much for the Church out of it all.

There had been some intellectual vitality in parts of the Church and a growth of lay influence. This movement began in Melbourne in the 1930s with the formation of the Campion Society, the first (if crude) significant lay intellectual breakthrough; Catholics became more prominent in the teaching staffs of Universities than they used to be (although they do not yet occupy a proportion of positions equal to their numbers in the general community); Australian Catholics have graduated from Oxford and Louvain, making their mark in the universities and within the Church; some of these new kind of Catholics developed their ideas in 'little magazines' (of high standard) in their effort to develop friendly dialogue in a free pluralist society. The tensions of this emergence produced some Catholic intellectuals who were seriously concerned with serious issues, keen-witted and looking at life with the vigour of people trying to work things out in a new way.

All this laid the ground work for the revolution in attitudes set loose by the Second Vatican Council. When Rome beckoned even the greatest opponents of change became apostles of liberalization. Catholic clerics are now emerging from their ghetto and engaging in dialogues on TV and changes in church services seem to be proceeding more swiftly in Australia than in most other countries. Whatever the outcome of its present tensions, the Catholic Church in Australia will never be the same.

This sudden pragmatic acceptance of change is itself very Australian. In general the strongly *Australian* character of the Catholic Church in Australia is not always recognized.

The emphasis on practicalism, on money-raising and organizing; the frequent impatience with subtle intellectual undertones; the States Rightism and factionalism; the social conformism; the practicalism of lay bodies such as the Knights of the Southern Cross (usually too non-doctrinaire for anything beyond business conspiracy) ... all of these are Australian characteristics.

What is 'un-Australian' about the Church is that it still instils a belief in the Church's universal teachings. Catholics are provided with a much more complex set of attitudes to life than other Australians. They are expected to learn these and make them part of their lives. Normally Australians no longer go through such a discipline. To Catholics life can still seem not necessarily easy and optimistic. The public manifestations of these beliefs were trivial: the obsession with contraception, divorce, mixed marriage and sex were all that most non-Catholic Australians understood of Catholicism. Manning Clark reached more profoundly in *Australian Civilization* when he wrote: 'The Irish also brought to Australia their conceptions of Christ and the Holy Mother of God. The former is difficult to characterize in words ... while Russian thinking was concerned with the presence of the ideal of the Madonna as well as the ideal of Sodom in the human heart, the Irish believed the saint and the larrikin lived in the one man. The Irish Catholics also knew what they were not: that they were not those upright, honest, ambitious, successful men the English were always holding up to them as the model.'

The flavour of both Catholicism and anti-Catholicism is revealed most significantly in the question of Government aid to Church schools; a hundred-year-old debate is now ending. Secularization threw the Catholics back on their own resources in the nineteenth century and profoundly affected the organization of the Church. Only the Catholic Church set up a comprehensive system of private schools. The few other private schools are merely for those who can afford them. There are almost 2,000 Catholic schools, about a fifth of all the schools in Australia, educating a quarter of a million children. Making sure that Catholics send their children to Church schools, raising money for schools and running an intricate educational system are often the main preoccupation of many clerics in a diocese. The flavour of Catholic life cannot be understood except to a background of Communion Breakfast speeches on government aid; raffles, bingo games and other money raising activities; family obsessions with school fees; political pressures. This atmosphere helped the impression of living in a hostile society and perpetuated clannishness.

The question of State Aid to Church Schools has been one of the questions of *real politik* in Australia. As a matter of expediency, the non-Catholic Liberal Party overcame its prejudices and began offering bits and pieces of State Aid at a time when the Labor Party was as divided on this as it was on other issues. Now no election platform is without it.

## Snobs

The basic snobbery in Australia has been connected with ownership of land but despite the continuing importance of land ownership in the 'Societies' of the various States the ordinary suburban Australian is now quite indifferent to the landowning families unless they can arrange some metropolitan distinction for themselves such as winning the Melbourne Cup or being involved in a sensational divorce. So far as almost everyone in the cities is concerned a landowner is now just another man. In a survey of occupation status conducted in Sydney, landowners were given only 'B' grade social status, ranking nineteenth (between editors and heads of government departments.) Doctors were rated first in the 'A' grade, university professors second. In the town nearest his property, however, a landowner is still likely to rate at the top. In a small country town people see enough of each other for a recognition pattern to be inevitable – it may be one of the important distinctions between city and country in Australia that in the country there is more sense of status difference – and something of the ancient relationship between landed family and town still survives, although by the harsh standards of history the difference has been softened almost out of existence; the towns in which the difference is expressed are so democratic in outward manner that to some there might not seem any difference. However to those who participate in it, it is still there.

One of the most rigid institutional manifestations of this difference appears at the annual picnic races. The races have some of the features of an English point-to-point – picnicking from the boot of a car and so forth. But it is flat racing, not steeplechasing; the horses are worse; there is more drunkenness; and entry to a point-to-point is more democratic. Dinner parties at country properties follow the races (most houses arrange house parties for the occasion) and precede a dance.

The landowners of Queensland lead their own country life, so secure in their position that even Brisbane seems just another country town. In the West they lead Society – but hardly anyone knows. In South Australia and Victoria they are still integrated with other Society leaders. In New South Wales they follow traditional rituals; they still see themselves as the centre of Society but they face a lot of opposition in the tough Sydney game. Although they once led in sophistication, the truth is that many of them are now old-hat – wealthy country cousins.

Connected with ownership of land are questions of 'Family'. To most Australians such questions do not exist. Among ordinary people to be able to claim an early arrival in the colony as an ancestor – even a convict – may give some slight prestige and there are some status differences between families, based mainly on source of income, that can become important when there is a marriage between two people whose fathers earn their incomes in strikingly different ways. But the myth of unique birth and breeding – of a Family strengthened by generations of selectivity and uniquely chosen by God or Destiny to bear certain desirable attributes – is extremely weak. It can, however, become the obsession of the few. In some landed families and among those who seek social prestige there can be an intricate concern with genealogy that reaches an English exactitude. A social climber might buy some antiques (perhaps on H.P.) to suggest family background, or at least the understanding of its importance and even the most brash *arriviste* who professedly scorns Birth will clutch at an ancestor or an heirloom if he stumbles across one.

As in England, schooling can help penetration of ingroups when landed estate or 'good family' are lacking. A man makes money and sends his children to a 'good school'. Once again the mass of the people are indifferent to all this, and ignorant of it, but there is a subtle story yet to be told of the social climbing achieved through 'good schools', of the creation of sub in-groups that are little more than old school groups somewhat extended and confused by marital connexion and of the importance of 'good schools' in business. Going to a 'good school' improves a young man's business prospects (especially if he is rather dim-witted; if he is talented he may take up a profession) and there are some firms where an old school tie cliqueishness can be ruinously strong, with its English-type emphasis on the habit of command, distrust of specialists and animosity towards ideas and skills. As in England, it also has a grip on the stock exchange.

Position can be of importance in Australia. Among ordinary people there is no necessary esteem for businessmen or high officials but some of the professions – particularly medicine – have universal esteem. In the suburbs to say 'he married a doctor's daughter' gives off a social glow. This is probably the only test of snobbery in Australia that has almost universal acceptance, because professional men can also penetrate the in-groups if their wives wish them to. Esteem for professional men is not as high among the in-groups as among the outsiders but it is hardly ever realized among the in-groups how little those of them who are not professional men are esteemed. There are no possibilities in Australia of determining status by simple inspection. You can't place a man in a social scale by listening to his accent or what he talks about or by looking at his clothes or observing his manners. Ordinary people are not likely to be able to detect a 'real gentleman' with that sensory accuracy that used to be characteristic of ordinary people in England. The schools do not produce a standard product and there is no overriding code of behaviour. In-groups are formed by self-acclamation. With some members of in-groups (particularly the non-professional men) there can be a brusqueness and crudity that would exclude them from the in-groups of most other parts of the world. As with so many other forms of success in Australia, socially Top People are often not world class.

From reading the women's pages of the newspapers one can get an impression that a Society exists in each of the cities, but in most cases what is being presented is a women's Society dominated by women who organize the big charities: this has created images sharp enough for the newspapers to project and to many of those who read about it, this is Society. Society has so disintegrated in Sydney that many of those – especially the younger people – who would consider themselves in it are now happy to avoid doing almost all the things they were once supposed to do.

The women who set the standards of the social world that is reported in the women's pages are not necessarily very rich; they occupy a commanding position because their charity committees organize the kind of entertainments that only the possession of wealth once provided. To become a member of this Society is mainly a matter of calculation. To appear to be a member of it, by getting one's picture in the paper, can be easy – just arrange things so that you make a pretty picture at the races, an art opening, a first night, a gala film preview; or at a cocktail party, a barbecue, a yacht club, a wine tasting, a ball; or by getting married at a fashionable church (most of them Anglican) or a University College Chapel.

The most publicized figure in this world in Sydney came to be Mrs Marcel Dekyvere, chairman of the socially powerful Black and White Ball Committee and several others. She began writing a weekly diary in the Sydney *Sunday Telegraph*. To hold a mirror to her world, consider what this world is from a paraphrase of her diary for a busy week in February: On Sunday she went to church. The Sermon was 'I Have a Dream'. She comments: 'We must all keep our dreams, even if sometimes they don't come true. Don't you agree?' On Monday she got a Christmas card from Bob Hope whom she had met at a charity occasion in Sydney some time ago. She had lunch at the Australia Hotel and then went to the showing of an autumn-winter collection. She dined at the Chevron Hilton Hotel. 'Altogether it was a grand evening.' On Tuesday she chaired a meeting of a charity committee, went to a bible class and then mused on the fact that she was going to travel by air on a business trip with her husband. 'I suppose this modern air travel is good experience ... I have flown before ... that was thirty years ago.' On Wednesday while driving along Macleay Street she reflected that it looks 'a little like a corner of Paris'. Later she went to a preview of an exhibition of paintings. The colours were 'brilliantly beautiful'. She ended the day by seeing 'The Importance of Being Earnest' at the Old Tote Theatre. On Thursday she had a slimming treatment and bought a hat to wear in the aeroplane ('I know nobody wears hats in aeroplanes but I'm going to'). She had a charity meeting in the afternoon and went out to dinner. On Friday she admired the new air luggage her husband had given her and went to a cocktail party. On Saturday she went to the races and at night she watched TV.

## Cultural breakthrough

In literature and some of the arts in Australia there has been all the confusion of a breakthrough. The old certainties have gone and the changes are in such contradiction and of such comparative violence that contemporary detailed evaluations are worth very little. In these, committed critics often give a bleak picture; they are confused and sometimes made

73

angry by the sudden variety. What overwhelms is the activity. For a nation of Australia's type and size a lot of people are writing verse, novels and plays or painting pictures, running art galleries or little theatres, going to concerts or the theatre.

So far as public design is concerned it is no longer possible to be as universally scathing as one could once so easily be. There is still the confident amateurishness that Robin Boyd (in *The Australian Ugliness*) found amongst businessmen and as part of the national style; newspaper typographic and layout policies are designed by editors; showrooms by salesmen; suburban couples like to design their own houses and so forth. But there is now some awareness of standards – at least of fashion – although it may be only the first flickerings. Some of the new buildings that are going up all over Sydney and Melbourne are not bad; at least there is somewhat more unity and style in their glittering glass than in the nondescript Victorian buildings that have been knocked down. There are few grand visions, although in Sydney one can detect the beginning of dreams of architectural *grandeur*.

People are now interested in such old buildings as still exist, especially the few examples of colonial Georgian. Old terrace houses with filigree iron decorations have long been fashionable. The restorers are at work in Paddington as they are in Gramercy Square. There are even 'Iron Shops' that sell nothing but bits and pieces of filigree iron work. And the big new city buildings are subjects for conversation: at last people are now expressing opinions on how their cities should look. Many now spend a great deal of time and money worrying about the design of new houses – sometimes with disappointing results. Most of this trend seems an interest in the right direction. There is *change* and improvement and one cannot say this about many of the other fields of activity in Australia. With the lack of professionalism and the slow appreciation of originality the standards may fall short of desire but one can at least say that, as things sort themselves out and especially as the older generation lose control, there may be much greater concern with design in Australia than has existed since the early colonial period.

In the meantime much of what remains still looks like something slapped up in a gold rush. And the more it is nervously fiddled with, painted and prettified, the more it reaches 'The Great Australian Ugliness' described by Robin Boyd. The great dabs of vivid primary colours, the split stone veneers, the stripes, wiggles and squares of decoration, the laminated plastic – these were the first symptoms of the new Australian craving for 'taste'.

In music the boom in concert performances is now well established. In a year there are now almost a thousand separate public performances at professional level of serious music. Almost all of this is controlled by the Australian Broadcasting Commission. The A.B.C. controls all the permanent professional orchestras (two full size orchestras in Sydney and Melbourne and small orchestras in the other capitals) and engages almost all overseas musicians who tour Australia; it also provides the orchestras for the Elizabethan Trust opera seasons. The main criticism that is made of the A.B.C.'s concert policy is of its preference for the middlebrow. Australia is said to be isolated from live performances of contemporary music. In a kind of musical mateship the A.B.C. goes for the big numbers.

It is typical of slapdash Australian exuberance that there are complaints that although in Sydney alone there are now about 200 exhibitions of painting in a year there are 'only twenty top class artists and fifteen others of promise'. There is a great deal of activity. Painting has become fashionable. P.R. Departments (or the wives of managing directors) persuade firms to put up art prizes or commission paintings or sculpture. Art openings are part of the round of society women. Attendance at the Art Gallery of N.S.W. in Sydney, at a gallery-estimated 750,000 a year, is now almost four times what it was in the early nineteen forties. But the permanent collections are poorly endowed with public money and most of them are of low international standard. To acquire a thorough knowledge of painting – that is to say, to find out what all these paintings one has prints of actually look like – it is necessary to go overseas.

In the theatre, the Elizabethan Theatre Trust spends public money, sometimes well, sometimes badly; the commercial theatre has revived and there is a nest of Little Theatres. In Sydney or Melbourne at least one can usually see fairly quickly whatever is being talked about overseas, even if it is sometimes in an indifferent performance. There are fourteen theatres in Sydney, including the firmly established Little Theatres. The success of 'The Summer of the Seventeenth Doll' started demands for a renaissance in Australian drama but renaissances are hard to organize. There have been five or six good plays put on since then but this has not satisfied Australians, whose standards seem to be those of Shakespeare's London. They blame theatre managements. Others say that it is easier to obtain some kind of a performance for a new play in Australia than in many other countries. A dozen new Australian plays are likely to be presented by the commercial and top repertory companies in a year. What *is* lacking is a film industry. Although the world's first movie, *Soldiers of the Cross*, was made in Australia in 1901 and about 200 full feature films followed it in the next twenty years, for many years after the second World War the rate slowed down to less than one a year. The result was that Australians, among the greatest of cinema-going people until TV, did not see images of their own country when they went to the movies.

There are several dozen poets whose work is known to those who are interested; and – as the publication of verse goes – publication is not difficult to achieve. The number of copies printed of a volume of Australian verse is often as great as the print run in countries of much bigger population. However an Australian interested in poetry may lament that the country has *only* half a dozen, perhaps a dozen good poets – as if that were possible! As in painting, there are highly developed senses of difference and considerable talk of 'schools'; but some of this is gossip rather than literary criticism. Novels are being written all over the place, and not only by 'literary' people. About two dozen of fair standard are printed in Australia each year – others are printed abroad. Publishing is now becoming more sophisticated and there is increasing interest in Australian writing in the world publishing market. It is hard to imagine that any work worth being published is not finally published. There are about a dozen literary or semiliterary magazines.

This is not the place to attempt to evaluate all this activity. However there are things to learn about Australia in this cultural breakthrough. For example, Australians with cultivated tastes, or the desire to have them, largely consider theatre, music, and books as something to enjoy, to consume like a good meal: talk about it for a bit, then forget it. Culture is part of the enjoyment of life, part of happiness. They do not demand exclusively the happy or the fantastic; they can enjoy the sad and the real – as they enjoy 'The Summer of the Seventeenth Doll', the verse of A. D. Hope or the more melancholy Australian paintings. But they have not developed that solemn high reverence towards Art that has been the fashion since the nineteenth century. Nor have they developed very much detailed knowledge. The result is that their reactions are spontaneous, unlearned and, very largely, ill-informed.

It is also significant that there is sometimes a bustle of optimism among those who do the creating; some of their work is slapdash. There is a give-it-a-go flavour about it; a virtue is fabricated out of lack of style, spontaneity and even sincerity, as if these were art standards. Not with everyone; among some of the best known writers especially there is a much greater sense of care and responsibility than is usual in Australia – perhaps because the participants are aware of international rather than purely local standards. For most of the century there was a kind of Tariff Board approach to art and literature, a nationalism that applied purely Australian standards, as if there were some special artistic virtue in being Australian. Among some there was a desire to hoard up old traditions as if one should go on writing forever as people did in the late nineteenth century. These demands remain, but now they are being lost in the rush.

Criticism of literature and the arts is poor, and some of it extremely cliqueish. There is a lot of 'knocking' and back-biting, sometimes reflecting in-group battles and sometimes perhaps a very real frustration about what to say. It is an illusion to believe that a man must be familiar with the whole history of painting before he paints, or of writing before he writes, but of critics one might expect thorough knowledge and systematic position. These standards are often missing in Australian critics; discussion on Australian literature is sometimes better informed in the American Universities that have taken it up, than in some of the Australian Universities. In the past there has been such an obsession with rattling off the genealogies of Australian writing that there was little sense of contemporary judgement. It was like having to sit through all those early flashbacks in a saga before you could find out what had been happening recently.

These weaknesses in criticism, rather than the stupidities of the audience, may be one of the reasons why some Australian work is 'misunderstood'; it has not been sympathetically and knowledgeably explained. Criticism is essentially a task for the intellect and the weaknesses of Australian criticism may be part of the general inability to pursue prolonged, subtle and exhaustive thought. Conversation about literature or the arts often shows the same characteristics: a few snap judgements, perhaps a bit of shouting, and then you pass on to the next topic. Conversation does not flourish in Australia. It is possible to find good conversation, but you have to know where to look.

For its size and nature Australia has a vigorous cultural life, in which, amongst the second to tenth rate activity usually found in any cultural life, there has been permanent achievement, particularly in poetry and painting. For one good man to rise each generation is something; Australia has provided more than that. Australian critics often –

usually – expect too much. They show an obsessive concern with attacking the nonsense that usually surrounds art. Some of them seem to have a solitary view of art – an art without audience and without other practitioners, the peace of a man mowing his own back lawn or standing on the rocks fishing alone. Yet an audience (which will usually be partly silly) and a bustle of activity (much of which will usually be bad) are often the conditions under which good work appears. Australian intellectuals always expect too much of Australia: they demand painting without dealers, poetry without pretension, theatre without audiences. Others express genuine dismay because most Australians are indifferent to the products of their culture, as of course they are. Culture does not run to equality.

In literature and the arts one can make no demands of subject; an artist may draw his ideas from anywhere. To deny this is barbarous; to impose standards, as some Australians have done, that are arbitrarily said to be dictated by national history and tradition is simply to impose limits on the human imagination. However, while acknowledging this, it is also proper to seek for any attitudes to life that seem common to many Australian writers and artists in the hope that this may tell one something about Australia. What is first noteworthy is that in any artistically effective form the old 'class-conscious' democratic spirit has gone. This is not surprising. Only sentimentalists or crooks could still write in ignorance of the profound and obvious changes in Australian society. But no one seems to be interested in the new forms of fraternalism of ordinary Australians; creative people don't seem interested in the mateship of the cab driver or the R.S.L. Club. Much of the old utopian humanism has also gone. There is still plenty of humanism amongst the ordinary people but it seems to have turned sour in more cultivated minds and a new sense of a future for Australia has not yet emerged to be utopian about. New Lands and New Ages are no longer fashionable, although the New Age is now outlining itself: perhaps it seemed better to the fastidious when it wasn't there. There is some of the old exuberance and robustness left, some sense of joy in living, but it is often now more muted: as the people become more joyous the poets seem to become more sombre.

There is still obsession with landscape, natural environment and myth. Some of this is as pantheistic as the ordinary people's ability to identify with their environment. Even the most sophisticated minds seem to go bush for their images of innocence: to some poets and painters the desert seems to be the Australian symbol of hope. There is little urban literature that deals with ordinary Australians as if they were observable human beings. Usually if an artist looks at the ordinary people he turns on them and savages them or invents romantic substitutes. However there are many haunted images of melancholy or despair, gestures of dismay or disillusion. Paradise has been lost and artists are disappointed.

Literature and the arts in Australia no longer represent the moods and attitudes of the community, except unconsciously and in distortion; they show a remarkable lack of interest in the people. To say this is not to criticize either artists or people but to suggest that the sense of alienation and disappointment felt by so many writers and artists is something of their own contrivance. There are exceptions. One of these is to be found in the paintings of Russell Drysdale. As Max Harris said in *Australian Book Review*: 'There is alienation in Drysdale's canvasses ... the loneliness is expressive of self-containment, of a kind of inner quietness ... Drysdale feels, as does every bush dweller, complete identity with the landscape. This identity, the belongingness of man and environment, is the rich and rewarding return of the condition of Australian loneliness. In terms of European thought, "loneliness" is a word of purely tragic impact ... Drysdale's paintings are interpretative exercises in this beautiful man-and-environment oneness ... the "essence" of Drysdale's figures is not threatened, but assured, contained, enduring.' In the Australian sense of reserve, the sudden desire for quiet, there can sometimes be not shyness but a sense that this is all there is: man and his environment. It's not what all the books promise, but there's a pattern in it; and an interest in it; and it's all there is.

## Women

It is both true and untrue that Australia is peculiarly a 'man's country'.

In access to occupational opportunities and professional or public position Australia is quantitatively no more a 'man's country' than any other 'western' society. That is to say that it still *is* a man's country, but no more so than in comparable countries. In *Women in Australia* Norman Mackenzie showed how the distribution of women in the Australian labor force was remarkably like that in other developed industrial societies. Indeed participation in the professions in Australia was slightly higher than in the U.S.A. or Sweden. 'But in terms of absolute numbers the differences are striking. While the percentage of women in the medical profession is slightly higher in Australia, there are merely a few hundred women doctors against more than 12,000 in the U.S. ... As numbers increase, even if the proportion remains much the same, women in a profession develop a sense of confidence and solidarity.' The numbers are not large enough to allow this in Australia and this lack of size decreases public acceptance, opportunities for specialization and the chance for women to reach the top.

Perhaps where it has been most obviously true that Australia has been a man's country is in access to leisure activities and pleasure. Until recently – in many parts of society – the cliche image was demonstrably true. At parties men stood at one end of the room and talked about sport, money, motor cars – and women. At the other end of the room women sat and talked about children, homes, undies – and men. Beer drinking, perhaps the most common form of Australian companionship, was almost an exclusively male pursuit. While the men stood up in their bars and fantasized about the women they would like to get into bed with, their wives gathered at home over afternoon tea and fantasized about new bedspreads.

As with all cliche images of this kind, there were many exceptions. In Sydney, for instance, in the vogue-forming Eastern Suburbs, both in the inner suburbs where the old-style bohemians gathered and in the richer suburbs along the Harbour foreshores where such *chic* as there is in Sydney is generated, it was known that in overseas countries women mixed with men and the people in these areas did the same. But the more important qualification to make is that the whole situation is now changing, especially among the young, but – in many ways – also among the middle-aged.

It may be that this stiffness in relations between the sexes is better described as social awkwardness rather than male dominance. Men and women go their own ways, but the men get the best of the bargain because they have more ways to go. Statistically, of course, Australia was a man's country for most of its history. During the period of settlement there were likely to be 100 men to 70 women in the towns and as many as four men to one woman in the outback: there is still a marginal preponderance of men. Perhaps the awkwardness grew up over this period and became a habit. In what might be described as more cultivated circles it might be that no one had anything much to say: in a country where the art of general conversation languishes, what could men and women talk about?

It may have had something to do with the fact that in Australia women often rule the roost. The man goes off to work and in his spare time plays with his mates. In the house he is often merely the odd jobs man, the chauffeur and the gardener. The woman sets herself high standards of housewifemanship and family care and makes a temple of her home. An American West Coast Professor of Psychology Dan L. Adler has even gone to the trouble of inventing a word, 'matriduxy', to dramatise his research findings – that more often than not, Mother is the decision-maker in the Australian home, and that Australian homes are more Mother-dominated than American homes. This research usefully confirmed something that was already evident: that the obsession of many Australian women with their homes goes beyond fashion or normal motherly concern; it represents an attempt to provide spiritual value in material things and modes of living. In a largely non-religious and non-competitive society an obsession for 'good taste' in homes, in their furniture and decoration, and in home entertainment and cooking gives life much of its meaning. (That much of the 'good taste' is bad is beside the point.)

This is often mistakenly compared with what is said to be the American concern with status. There is far too much loose talk in Australia about 'status symbols'. They exist in a crude form in the small world of ambitious men. If an Australian man wants to show off he can buy a certain kind of car, or a big house in a fashionable suburb, or try to get into an exclusive club, or go for a trip overseas. He can use his money and throw his weight around by buying symbols of power that are simply symbols of money. He may oppose 'taste' because money can't always buy it. But an Australian woman is looking for the good life, the right and satisfying way of doing things. She is not usually concerned with her husband's career; she does not use her 'home' to help him in his job, but to build a world in which she believes. She has created a much more subtle world than the man's world, not so dependent on money, a world of multiple difference.

Some of the values of this world are shown in these quotations from the women's pages of newspapers: 'The dinner party was given under the stars in a walled courtyard softly lit by storm-globed candles in black wrought iron stands' ... 'The dining room looked elegant with a soft glow from yellow candles in silver candlesticks on the sideboard, and from candlesticks flanking dahlias on the long table' ... 'City parties started last Sunday with a very lovely buffet lunch given by A and D at their Killara home with a creek flowing through the garden' ... 'For L and K, who leave Friday for a fantastic trip abroad, it's been a continuous round of *au revoirs*. Their itinerary will take in

Egypt, with a trip up the Nile, Jerusalem, Amman, Petra, the Greek Islands, the Continent, England and home via the Americas' ... 'A dinner that was just teeming with atmosphere was given by artistic L and A to say "goodbye, return soon" to R, who leaves Friday for her charming Chelsea house and pet poodle Buttercup' ... 'For originality of ideas you can't beat D and C who gave a simply super St Valentine's Day party. The red heart motif was carried out in name tags and lace-edged hearts decorated the white cloth on the buffet table. Even the jellied salad and sweets were heart-shaped' ... 'The moment the front door of the rosy pink Villa Porto Rosa is opened one has a sense of being transported to the Mediterranean coast. From its tiled floors and colonnaded balcony to the palm trees and a view of boats on the water, this house at Watson's Bay is Italian in feeling' ... 'Crisped vegetables seasoned with garlic, oil, tarragon vinegar and freshly ground pepper team in any exciting combination salad that's a winner for meatless lenten menus' ... 'Make your next party an outstanding success by serving some of the world-famous Chinese dishes'.

## Migrants – how assimilated?

Australia has managed to be an immigrant country for most of its history without even thinking about it. In the goldrush decade of the 1850s the population trebled, mainly because of migration, and even by the end of the century only 77 per cent of Australians were native born. Even now only 83 per cent of Australians were born in Australia (and of these five per cent have migrant parents). Yet, unlike Americans, Australians have not taken any pride in projecting an image of their country as a haven for the oppressed or as a market for the talents of the world. Yet they might well do so. After the Second World War Australia absorbed a big proportion of the 'displaced persons' of Europe and throughout its history it has been a society open to the ambition of immigrant talent. If entry in the

Australian *Who's Who* is any kind of a test, the proportion of migrants who achieve success is more than double the proportion of native Australians who achieve success.

The constant factor in policy has been that Australia, traditionally, has *bought* most of its immigrants. Apart from the gold rush decade and the two main periods of economic depression – in the 1890s and 1930s – most migrants have come to Australia because the Australian government has actively encouraged them and paid their fares. Before the immigration that followed the Second World War, since most of the immigrants came from the British Isles, it was assumed that once they got here it was up to them to make their adjustments to what they found. This caused many hardships. Australia is not as 'British' as it looks. However the immigrants spoke English – although not to Australian standards – and the rest was up to them.

The break in patterns came after the Second World War. Australians had got such a scare when the Japanese almost seized all of New Guinea, and bombed Northern Australia, that the 1930s slogan 'Populate or Perish' was given new meaning. It was decided to bring in from Britain and Europe enough migrants to double the annual population increase. For the first time, people who did not come from the British Isles were to be bought, along with the British.

The 167,000 'displaced persons' who came to Australia in the late 1940s and early 1950s were bought very cheaply. Most of them were penniless. They had little or no other choice. They were transported to Australia for nothing, housed in old army huts, even tents, and put to work on construction projects, mainly in the country areas. For two years they were bound to manual labour. After that, it was up to them. (Educated people with special skills – unless they cared to swing a spade for a couple of years – were not invited.) From an economic viewpoint they were a godsend. They helped to get the country on its postwar move without involving immediate expensive additions to its super-structure.

Having taken the plunge in procuring 'reffos' (who were

successfully labelled 'New Australians'), Australian governments then went on to sign migration agreements with
most of the governments of Western Europe to assist the
passage to Australia of people who had more choice in the
matter. To these were added a number of other Europeans
whose relatives brought them out here. For the first time a
large segment of the Australian population is of non-British
or non-Irish origin.

Officially there was still a narrow assimilation doctrine,
in which immigrants were supposed to 'become Australians'
in double quick time. Six migrant centres and 29 hostels
were set up to assist this purpose. Lessons in the English
language and in Australian customs were pumped into the
newcomers. Community organizations were formed. Annual
citizenship conventions (stocked with Uncle Toms) were
summoned. And a naturalization ceremony was rigged up
at which New Australians were required to swear allegiance,
among other things, to Elizabeth II – a requirement that is
not officially made of the native born.

Needless to say none of this has had the particular effects
required. Immigrants continue to make their own time in
adjusting to a new society and many of them continue with
old ways. There are about 70 foreign language newspapers
and periodicals in a couple of dozen languages and hundreds of clubs and societies in which immigrants pursue
old friendships and old enmities. In soccer, by far the
fastest-growing spectator sport, the old rivalries of Europe
are resumed by teams bearing national names, that provide
a basis for the English football pools in the English summer.
The Hungarians sit in espresso-land and still divide on the
question of the Arrow Cross. Greeks parade the streets
bearing anti-Royalist placards. (Even Greeks who have
sworn allegiance to Elizabeth II.) The Yugoslavs are bitterly
divided between Serbs and Croats (when ex-King Peter
came to Australia to visit migrant Yugoslavs the Croats
attacked him as a 'Serbian king'), and to a lesser extent
between Slovenes, Macedonians, Montenegrins and Bos-
nians. Fascist outfits like the Ustashi still exercise some

power. Most of the Eastern Europeans divide not only among themselves, but also as Jews and non-Jews.

Amazingly, no one really knows what degree of assimilation is going on. If you saw the Australian Greeks going down to the wharves at Woolloomooloo to wait for a brideship, you might say – none. If you saw a Dutch family in its home in a suburban street, as self-contained and accommodated to its surroundings as a molecule that passes from one body of matter to another, you might say that assimilation was complete. There is some evidence that a sense of community can disappear with Germans, Poles and other Northern Europeans in the first native born generation. (With the Dutch it seems to disappear with the migrants themselves.) Southern Europeans seem to lose their sense of difference more slowly, especially when there has been chain migration in which a significant part of a community in the homeland transfers itself in groups to Australia and attempts to continue its group life. Greeks may be the slowest assimilators of all.

What seems obvious is that ordinary Australians themselves have 'assimilated' to Europeans more quickly and gently than most critics of ordinary Australians had allowed for. It is true that the continuing employment boom has meant that there has been little or no competition for jobs but – whatever the reason – the immigration into Australia of European immigrants who do not speak English has worked without the tensions of America. There have not been closed areas of settlement and separate schools, or strong political groupings extending into the general community or (with the exception of the Greeks) separate church groupings. Although it has no doubt involved the many individual unhappinesses natural to migration, the post-war migration to Australia has been a reasonably happy migration, as migrations go. Migrants are not more delinquent than other Australians; in fact the crime rate among migrants has proved less than among the native born.

The old belief that Australia swallows its migrants whole and does not itself change as a result of their digestion no longer seems true. It is true that children of most migrants cease to be Europeans but in the process somewhere Australians are also ceasing to be 'Australians'. It is normal liberal thought to wish to see old national minority cultures preserved, though integrated; but what now seems to be the Australian way, in which both old and new grope towards something different, has a great deal to be said for it. Since it is extremely unlikely that Australia is going to have much of a future without continued immigration, and that the immigration might have to increase in rate and change in kind, it would seem a good idea if the 'assimilation' theory could be re-worded somewhat less arrogantly, although the old assumption that inter-marriage is desirable in a migration programme seems sensible enough. Australians do not wish their nation to be a muddle of permanent national minorities. Assimilation is best made in bed.

The effect on Australia of this post-war migration has been enormous. It has leavened the lump in Australia. It is doubtful if Australia would have got as far as it has in increased sophistication without the accelerated migration of the last two decades. In some ways this has been obvious enough to become generally accepted – in the development of small factories that have added specialist products to the Australian markets, in the development of specialist shops and restaurants, in changing taste in food and the arts.

But it is also the ambition and talent of immigrants that have made continuing Australian prosperity possible. It is true that most migrants still work in relatively unskilled jobs in manufacturing, building, and construction and that, except for the British-born, they do not yet play much part in public life. But it is also the talent of immigrants, or their unusual cultivation of talent in their children, that has helped to keep the whole show going. Almost two thirds of the research staff of the Commonwealth Scientific and Industrial Research Organization are immigrants; so are more than a third of university staffs; the children of immigrants tend more towards university courses than the children of native Australians; immigrants or their children are beginning to play an important part in some government departments; when the government wants more skilled tradesmen it now shops for them overseas. However, as the economic differences between Australia and Western Europe diminish the supply may run out.

## The Underprivileged

According to a currently fashionable method of calculating minimum basic needs, while at least 20 per cent of American households and 14 per cent of British households are in severe need, only eight per cent of Australian households live at the poverty level. This is no cause for congratulation to Australians. The structural deficiencies that cause high poverty rates in the U.S.A. and Britain barely exist in Australia. There is no Negro problem (the aborigines are equivalent to a Red Indian problem, not a negro problem) and nothing like the British class problem. There is very little slum problem and *at the bottom* educational opportunities are more equal in Australia. Employment is high; automation is not yet a grave threat to employment in Australia; and the Australian minimum wage arrangements are unique in the world.

What has gone wrong? The answer is probably that now that the more obvious miseries have been relieved in Australia the mass of the people have lost knowledge of those who are still depressed and the politicians either do not know – or see no percentage in it. Social service in Australia has now proceeded beyond the stage of grand struggle and general rhetoric and become a matter of different areas of detail. Most of this detail has not been taken up.

Treatment of widows is mean; in a country where standards of comfort and the proper raising of children are part of the real meaning of life, widows and their families are thrown from one standard of comfort to a much lesser one through no fault of their own. When a man dies a woman cannot hope to keep things as they were. She receives an inadequate pension on which there is a means test. If she earns extra money she must do so with stealth. If the inspectors find out she will lose her pension. Deserted wives are in even worse position. For six months they just do the best they can; it is only after that time that they can draw a pension.

The greatest single disaster in Australia, however, is to grow old. The single family group is now almost universal, Unless they are wealthy, heads of families may lose respect as they grow older. There is no place at the fireside for them. There are reasons why this might be so. But nothing has taken its place. The old are left to fend for themselves, or to rely on the many fine voluntary schemes that have come from the natural kindness of Australians. Old age is unhappy for all except the most fortunate but when it is accompanied by loneliness and a disappearance of all meaning from life it is doubly so. Often parents grow very old, alone, except for an occasional visit from their children. Old blind people sit in small apartments listening to the radio. Bed-ridden old people know only the kind charity lady who brings them lunch. Deserted old people rely on the landlady to keep their rooms clean and cut their fingernails.

Australians are likely to pride themselves on being pioneers in general social advance, but they haven't been as good as they think. Although for most of the century their pension schemes were ahead of the United States and Britain, they did not originate any of these ideas, and in fact, they have usually been a bit behind New Zealand. Since the Second World War their rate of advance has been slower than in the U.S.A. and Britain; they are well behind some of the more progressive smaller countries, such as Sweden (where a retirement scheme now allows for a pension providing 60 per cent of average annual income over the 15 highest paid years of a working life).

The Australian approach – except for the health service scheme – has been confined mainly to income security. It ignores the many other factors that can cause misery and the minimum incomes now guaranteed are too low, by the more affluent standards of the last 20 years. This is a matter in which simply to steal some good ideas from overseas and transplant them in the particularly favourable conditions that apply in Australia would help put Australia back where it is supposed to be: a country where there should be no external reason why ordinary people should be unhappy.

# 4. BETWEEN BRITAIN AND AMERICA

## *Lost bearings*

IT is usually said that Australia is a part of European civilization transplanted to this big south land and it now finds itself in the alien world of Asia. What can be said at once is that Australians do not yet seem to know where they are – a great deal of public discussion could still equally well be carried out somewhere in the United Kingdom. It may be worthwhile remembering exactly where Australia is. It lies south of Indonesia and the rest of South-East Asia – Malaysia, the Philippines, Vietnam, Laos, Cambodia, Thailand, Burma, a sub-continent containing almost as many people as there are in Africa. Dominating this sub-continent are the sub-continents of India and China, with more than a third of the world's population. Near China are Japan, Korea, and Taiwan (and Quemoy and Matsu) with a population about half that of Africa. To the north and east there is the South Pacific Ocean, with New Zealand, New Guinea, the Solomons, the New Hebrides, Fiji and the other islands of Oceania. And across the Pacific are the Seventh Fleet, Pearl Harbour, and the U.S.A. This is the strategic world of Australia.

It is a paradox of Australian history that as communications elsewhere in the world broaden horizons, Australia's horizons have become more narrow. Until 1941 all that mattered to Australians was Europe, and the European colonial powers that ruled Australia's world. In the early days of the settlement, not nearby people but the French were the most likely enemies; and for most of this century, the Germans. When in 1939 Australians enlisted in an expeditionary force to defend the Middle East from the Germans, everything seemed much the same as it did when their fathers landed at Gallipoli in 1915 to fight the Germans' allies, the Turks. When the Japanese bombed Pearl Harbour in December 1941 and were about to seize all South-East Asia and invade the Australian territory of New Guinea most of Australia's front line troops were 7,000 miles away. Churchill tried to stop the return of the Australian troops to defend their own country; quickly measured from the other end of the map Australia may have seemed expendable. On 27 December 1941, John Curtin made the single most significant statement ever made by an Australian Prime Minister: 'Without any inhibitions of any kind, I make it quite clear that Australia looks to America, free of any pangs as to our traditional links on kinship with the United Kingdom. We know the problems that the United Kingdom faces ... But we know, too, that Australia can go and Britain can still hold on. We are, therefore, determined that Australia shall not go.' Then, as any Australian will tell you, the Americans saved Australia from invasion (with Australian assistance) and subsequently won the war. The Japanese destroyed the old power situation in the Pacific and from the paroxysm of disorder and chaos there is a new power situation, to which Australians are – even yet – not effectively orientated.

To Australians much of this is still a dream. Names ... Vietnam, Indonesia, Malaysia ... impinge on Australian consciousness. Almost half the Australian diplomatic service is deployed in Asia. But there is still a sense of unreality. Asian names come and go in the newspapers according to external events, and they form patterns in Australian politics when they meet a party political demand. But most Australians have not gained a real 'feel' for the part of the world they live in, even if many of them now talk about it. There are names on a map, statistics in handbooks, events in newspapers, passages of voguish rhetoric; but working attitudes reveal little feeling for the texture of life in Asia and the Pacific. Australians talk of Asia as if they were still living in Europe.

## *Looking to Britain*

Despite the strong obsessional system that still marks Australian attitudes to Britain and Western Europe, to describe Australia as 'British' is wrong. 'The British' have been a kind of confederation of social classes and regional types that go under one name. These regional types and social classes were represented in Australia in a different mix (significantly there were more Irish) and the regional strains were not maintained. Only the Catholic Irish continued interbreeding and even some of them married non-Irish or non-Catholics. They have not gone on feeling as 'Irish' as many Irish groups in the U.S.A. For some time their priests remained Irish, but that has now changed. They did, however, remain Catholic, and this meant that there is a much bigger Catholic influence in Australia than in England. Other regional types married more widely; their children had no real feeling of continuity with the place their parents came from. There are still Highland Games and so on but often this is mere dressing up. According to one set of guesses the ancestry of the people now living in Australia might run: less than two thirds English, Scottish, and Welsh; less than a fifth Irish; more than a fifth other European.

This new people, the Australians, fused out of old ingredients and separated in new ways, have taken British and European history to be their history (they could scarcely claim the history of the aborigines) and have retained many of the forms of British political and social life without examining the differences. Words like 'democracy', 'monarchy', 'trades union', 'parliament', 'upper class', 'working class' and a whole terminological apparatus are used in the two countries with different meanings. Australians are not merely transplanted English. When they reach London the tens of thousands of Australians who, since the war, have migrated for a season or two to England often enjoy the theatres, the music and art shows, the natural beauties of England, its closeness to Europe, without achieving any rapport with the English. Their conversation reveals the alienation of people in someone else's country. Almost every Australian feels a sense of difference when arriving in England.

Yet a Prime Minister of Australia could take pleasure in allowing the Queen of Great Britain (also constitutionally the Queen of Australia) to make him a Knight of the Thistle, as if he were some great Scottish gentleman, and allow himself to be surrounded by those who jostled for honours with some of the energy of nobles in a petty German court in the eighteenth century. There is no Australian national anthem, only 'God Save the Queen'; 'Advance Australia Fair' merely has the status of a national song, something the natives might chant after they have made their major obeisance. On ceremonial occasions the British flag often hangs beside the Australian flag. Migrants who come from European republics have to swear allegiance to a monarch before they can become naturalized. Melbourne businessmen sit amid their brown leather and mahogany and play English gentlemen in clubs that they believe to be the same as London clubs (in which some of them would not be accepted as members). Service officers still draw their commissions from the Queen as they did in the First Settlement (although they no longer have to buy them). Until recently almost all Governors-General and State Governors were still imported from England.

I am not putting up an idealist appeal for complete rationality in human affairs. Trivialities such as those I have mentioned may still have good effects in England but the ceremonial clinging to Britain was part of the delusional structure of the people who were running Australia. It was a symptom of an inability to recognize and to dramatize the new strategic environment of Australia and the present problems of Australia. The momentum towards concepts of independent nationhood has slowed down, or stopped. Perhaps the world has become too puzzling to Australians; there are too many changes and uncertainties for them to make the final effort.

To some Australians of fifty years ago this present pause would be unbelievable. The radical position then was to be anti-British, to develop an Australian nationalism and to dream of an independent Australian republic. This represented not only the influence of the Irish, who hated England for good reason, but of the general egalitarian position. England represented privilege and wealth; Australia represented equality and mateship. The nationalism that developed was a rustic exaltation of improvisation and vigour, far too thin and old-fashioned for the needs of today; we cannot any longer pretend we are all drovers boiling our billies. When the political independence and outward acceptance of equality were achieved nationalism became confused and rundown; there might now be less positive anti-British feeling in Australia than ever before.

On the other hand the other streak in Australian life, the confidently pro-British imperialist jingoistic feeling, is dying with the older generations. Up to the Second World War the Empire still lay very thick on a certain kind of Australian. There was all that red on the map; there were the garrisons and fleets in the Pacific; England was by far Australia's greatest trading partner; and the whole romantic concept of Empire could seem more full-bodied than the thin flavour of local nationalism. It was easier to feel self-important as an imperialist than as a nationalist. It was possible to imagine that thinking about imperial issues provided a real link with them. (It didn't. It was simply Australia's role to agree with the decisions of imperialism.) Yet even those who identified themselves with the British were subject to the shocks of reality when they met the 'pommies'. Fewer Australians really liked the British than liked the idea of the British, the pomp of empire and the historical and cultural heritage to which they felt they had as much right as their contemporaries in the British Isles.

Just as the collapse of world power has at times paralysed the British it has perplexed those Australians who were born into the period of British power. Many Australians still suck wisdom from London. In the imperial days the wisdom may have been relevant to the world and Australia. Now it is the wisdom merely of an important European power. Yet the lack of strong intellectual life in Australia has meant that Australian intellectuals who like to keep up with things often – perhaps usually – fell back on 'quality' newspapers and weeklies from London. They looked at the world from London and this could mean not only that they were inclined to accept London views of what the solutions to problems were – at least in this there was a variety of attitudes – but they also accepted a London definition of what the problems themselves were, of what a reasonable person might be expected to be interested in. What they saw of Australia's world was mainly what Britain saw. Even in Australian newspapers there is still likely to be more news about Scotland in a year than about New Zealand, and perhaps not one background article on the Philippines.

Deriving inspiration from London has helped to befuddle some of the Australian 'Left' by raising issues that are of little importance to Australia. The agonizing reappraisals of 'affluence', a symptom of the decay of progressive thought in London, become fatuous when repeated in a country like Australia. The whole alienation of progressive intellectuals from 'the workers' has little to do with Australian intellectuals, although it may impress the many Englishmen who are employed in the Australian universities.

The habit of acting as if one were living in Europe is not confined to those who dream of third forces. Migrants from continental Europe, especially from countries now ruled by communist regimes, see cold war skirmishes with European immediacy. (Their children may have already inherited the gentle Australian dream. When President Kennedy was assassinated the eighteen-year-old-son of a Czechoslovak friend said to me: 'It is impossible to imagine this happening in the twentieth century.' His parents had evaded the Nazis and later the Communists. His grandfather was shot dead in his apartment by Nazis and members of the family had disappeared under the Communists.) Many Australians think a great deal more about Russia, Eastern Europe, and

West Berlin than they do about China or South Vietnam. Their training tells them to do so. This is the kind of area in their text books where most history happens. Yet there is nothing Australia can do about Russia, or West Berlin, or Europe, except to put up its hand at the United Nations and append its name to the sentiments of more powerful nations. There is a type of Australian who supports 'The Western Alliance', and holds staunch views about a part of the world in which his opinions do not matter. But he may also take a European view on Asia. Yet the Europeans sometimes play with policies on Asia as part of a game of rivalry with the U.S.A. To Australians the issues are more important than that. It is true that the future of Australia – along with the rest of the world – could be settled as a symptom of the U.S.A.-Soviet confrontation. And it is also true that the future of Australia could be settled, as it were, privately – without involving the non-Asian world. In our part of the world there is no NATO, no Common Market, no 'Western Alliance'.

Despite the realism that marked Sir Robert Menzie's policy towards South East Asia (his performance fell behind his commitments and his rhetoric) throughout the fifties and until the shocks of the Common Market debate, Menzies was more British than the British, always running several years behind London, expressing dreams of Commonwealth that had something of the flavour of progressive discussion in 1908. He still worked on reflexes learned in his youth. The debate on Britain's first try for the Common Market caused a reassessment in the Australian 'Right'. If President De Gaulle had allowed the British to enter the European Economic Community the results on Australian opinion might have produced an illuminating and useful crisis. That was why some Australians hoped that Britain would enter. Whatever the inconveniences to Australia the psychological shock of being dumped might have hastened that dramatic re-orientation, of admitting where in the world Australia really is and doing something about it, that may be a necessary condition for Australia's survival. As it is there remained a fairly general suspicion that Australia was still living on borrowed time, allowed to sell foodstuffs to Britain until Britain entered Europe.

## Looking to America

The strategic relation between Australia and the United States is obvious. This dependence on American power does not seem to arouse in Australia the bitterness it arouses in other parts of the world. From their occasional outbursts of megalomania in foreign policy one might not guess it, but Australians are used to being insignificant and relying on the power of others. They have lived in a state of such protected comfort and innocence for so long that one of their noticeable weaknesses is to have taken the power of Britain and then of America so much for granted that they often ignore the realities of power and do not take it into their calculation. Australians have lived with the recognition of American world power longer than any other nation outside the Western Hemisphere – since early 1942 when General MacArthur escaped from the Philippines to Darwin. Australia was the first country in the contemporary world to be saved by the Americans.

It is one of the few that will admit that it was saved by the Americans. It has even forgiven the Americans for saving it. Australians are helped in doing this by knowing that in the Second World War with a huge proportion of their population in uniform and a high degree of skill and courage they went as far in saving themselves as their resources would allow. This is not always true of those America saves. (Nor is it now true of Australia.) This almost unique ability to live with American power may derive some of its strength from the fact that Australia is one of the few countries in the world that has not received American economic aid. Americans can show signs of emotional insecurity when this is pointed out to them by Australians. They may not even believe it. Americans have become so used to believing that everyone in the world has drawn economic assistance from them that it seems an affront to American generosity for Australians not to have drawn on it.

One walks into a field of mystery and guesses, but it seems likely that Australia could enter into a quite massive relationship with America without generating any politically effective anti-Americanism among ordinary Australians, although there would be considerable opposition in the 'Left' of the Labour Movement. Why is this? One can only guess. One answer might be that Australians and Americans are in some ways – only some ways – the same kind of people. Exactly what the word 'American' is supposed to mean is hard to say; there are so many different Americans. Perhaps the best way of putting it is that Australians do not find distasteful the official story of what America is supposed to be. Freedom, equality, affluence, the pursuit of happiness ... these words are all right by Australians. When Australians and Americans use these words there may be more common meaning in them than when Englishmen and Australians use them. Australians accept American talk of competitiveness, even if they do not know what it means. The rhetorical expression of American idealism may sometimes leave Australians cold, suspicious as they are of all idealism. (What's in it for him?) But Australians have what they would consider to be a hard-headed respect for American material success and expertise.

Guessing about Australian 'images' of the United Kingdom and the United States is perhaps worthless, but it is irresistible. My guess would be that the United Kingdom would come out associated with the Queen, culture, dowdiness, Westminster Abbey, snobbery, the West End theatre, with swinging London as a puzzling symbol of the present. America would come out associated with electric washing machines, military strength, MacArthur, Kennedy, TV, egalitarianism. Relations with England prickle with familial misunderstandings. It's like growing away from one's parents and seeking new patterns of identity with them, looking for common hobbies and topics of interest so that one can keep up a connexion. Relations with America

are those of a young cousin to an immensely successful and
older cousin, with plenty of criticism, practically no hero
worship; it is a more straightforward relation. Australians
seek companionship from strangers, extend an open hand of
equal friendship. This can get them into a mess with the
English, with their mandarin manners. With Americans
they think they can get on with the conversation.

To a limited extent the two countries have shared the
same experiences, come to the same 'conclusions'. Or at
least there are some common elements in their histories that
cannot be shared with any European country. Australia has
been spared the brutality of civil war and racial violence;
it has not known the aggrandizement of colossal power; life
in Australia is more equal and less competitive than in
America; but there are dozens of similarities ... migration
to a new land, the mystique of pioneering (actually somewhat different in the two countries), the turbulence of gold
rushes, the brutality of relaxed restraint, the boredoms of
the backblocks, the feeling of making life anew. There may
be more similarities between the history of Australia and
America than for the moment Australians can understand.
Australian history may have been much more of a mad
explosion of power and craziness than the historians allow
for – with goblets of congealed gentility thrown out to be
collected and put in a case marked 'history'. Patrick
White's study of an explorer in *Voss* and the first volumes of
Manning Clark's new history show the possibility of inter-
pretations quite different from those of the official versions.

There are politically effective 'anti-Americans' in Australia but they should be distinguished from Australians
who are merely critical of America (as they have every
right to be). On the reading 'Left' they often draw their
ammunition from overseas matter. On the mindless 'Right'
they rely on fading memories; the Americans lack the
finesse of the British and so forth. But by far the greatest
source of criticism of America in Australia comes from
America itself, perhaps now the most self-critical society in
the world. Power Elites, Paper Economies, Organization

Men, Radical Rights, Hidden Persuaders ... these ogres marched upon Australians with such force that Australians sometimes looked for Radical Rights or Organization Men under their own beds, just as they falsely applied London criticism of Britain to Australia.

Americans – even the most influential and educated – often display an ignorance of Australia, seeing it in terms of England or in terms of America, or in no terms at all. That can wound Australians. They innocently feel that Americans should understand them better than that. Australia has not yet been satisfactorily created as an image in America, by either Australian intellectuals or American intellectuals. To many Americans it seems a dull sort of place, not interesting like Laos or Saudi Arabia. Yet given the pragmatism and relative straightforwardness of Australians, considerable communication should be possible between America and Australia. Nations never 'understand' each other, no more than groups within a nation do, or individuals. But Americans could find here some of the best friends they are likely to find in an envious world. Partly because in the pursuit of happiness for ordinary people Australians believe they are already ahead of America.

## Provincial Australia

In a sense, Australia has remained a province of Britain. It is, in a sense, now also a province of the U.S.A. (It is also, in a sense, a comparatively aging 'emergent nation'. And also, in a sense, an Asian power.)

I do not wish to push the metaphor of Australia's provincialism too far, and certainly not in the direction that London intellectuals have recently pushed it: that there is a great world of the intellect flourishing in the metropolis that the provincials cannot understand. (This in itself may be a symptom of the increasing parochialism of London.) And one must disassociate oneself from Auden's cosy snobbery: 'The dominions ... are for me tiefste Provinz, places which have produced no art and are inhabited by the kind of person with whom I have least in common ...' For some reason this has always reminded me of Arnold Bennett's patronizing entry in his diary: 'Lunched today with D. H. Lawrence, the provincial genius.' Arnold Bennett! It may not have been accident that Lawrence wrote so well about Australia and even thought of settling here. Some writers can flourish in provinces.

However what other word than 'provincial' does one use to describe a nation in which most activities are derivative and most new ideas are taken from abroad? In which the main decisions in manufacturing and strategy are dominated by overseas centres and in which vogues are usually out of date? Which not only lacks a feeling of importance in the present, but has no feeling of importance in the past? That sometimes watches the policies and trends of its twin metropolises (Britain and the U.S.A.) with more interest and knowledge than it watches its own?

There is a certain type of Australian who can be understood *only* as a provincial – unless 'colonial' is an even better word. He was brought up to believe in the 'Britishness' of pomp and destiny, in the master race philosophy that God chose the British to run the world. This belief in 'Britishness' was one of the most effective ideologies among trendsetters and decision-makers in Australia until the second world war and some of those who were influenced by it still hold power. If you were 'British' you knew who you were and what you were supposed to be doing; you enjoyed a sense of the past and a sense of the future. For these Empire loyalists, loyalty was primarily a matter of the Empire and the Monarch. Loyalty was due to Australia because it was 'British'. To the extent that Australians deviated from 'Britishness' they denied their heritage and their destiny. To distinguish between the interests of Australia and Britain was disloyal. Many Establishment men saw themselves as those who would keep the natives (their fellow countrymen) in line, keep them loyal to the Empire and the Throne – and punish them if they deviated. They were doing the Empire's job out here in this distant, unlikely place where they happened to have been born.

The old Empire loyalists, when they judged the ordinary people of Australia by what they believed to be the standards of the metropolis, found them lacking. They developed a contempt for the ordinary people of their own country. They blamed ordinary Australians for not possessing characteristics that you do not find in ordinary people anywhere – and that were also missing in most of those who make the criticism. This habit may have been one of the main reasons why, in Australia, ordinary people are blamed for not possessing elite characteristics and, why, if it is noted that the elites often lack these characteristics, the ordinary people are blamed for that, too. To despise one's fellow countrymen can be very provincial.

When British world power collapsed these older generations were left with their memories – on which they still acted. Most of the rituals of Australia still reinforce their memories. However there is obviously going to be a dramatic change in generations in Australia. For the moment the new generation may be transfixed in horror at what it sees around it: the perpetuation of burdensome fictions and the lack of self-confidence increases its sense of inadequacy and despair. But as it gets on the move it is likely to be less concerned than any previous generation with being either 'British' or 'Anti-British'.

In the past, Australia has also displayed the other side of provincialism: the boastfulness and arrogance of the liberated province, parading its very provincialism as if it were home-grown. There has been a special raciness of style that is taken to be peculiarly Australian; yet much of this 'Australian language' is simply city slang or provincial idiom or even thieves' cant brought over from England during the settlement. The whole bush ballad movement of the nineties was shot through with derivation. Even Australian egalitarianism is derived: it should be remembered that, beneath the acceptance of the deferential system in Britain, there has long been an egalitarian spirit too; mateship has been submerged ideology in Britain affecting the lives of a great number of people. When the TV series

*Z Cars* came to Australia, Australians saw part of themselves – with North Country accents. Even Australian laconicism has its derivation; it is an extreme form of British understatement. Australia is very 'British' in the sense that both societies are outwardly sceptical and pragmatic, distrusting public emotion and any complicated form of conceptualisation and systematization. The Australian 'let's give it a go' concept may be an extreme form of the British concept of 'muddling through'.

As provincials, Australians can be sceptical about a whole range of decisions that affect Australians but are made in some other country. This is one of the characteristics of provincialism: that decisions are made somewhere else. Australians are also in the position, comforting to an English-speaking nation, of being able to criticize both Englishmen *and* Americans. If some English lord came out to be Governor-General he was criticized for living like a lord. If some Texas millionaire came out to be U.S. Ambassador he was criticized for acting like a Texas millionaire. Australians criticize Englishmen by American standards and they criticize Americans by English standards. It would be smart for the British to send out Englishmen who act like Texas millionaires and for the Americans to send out Americans who act like English lords.

## A Republic?

There are many comforts in being provincial, but, given Australia's peculiar relationship to the rest of Asia, these are comforts that Australia may not continue to be able to afford. It is possible that Australia will have to begin making its own decisions in a kind of way that will be painful to existing attitudes. The extraordinarily belated recognition by the Menzies Government in the mid 1960s that Australia should again have a defence force may prove to be the first example of this process. Australia may cease to be provincial – the hard way. If Australia is luckier than this, it is still unlikely that much basis of power will continue to lie behind its relationship with Britain – either in trade, or in strategy. Where Britain was not long ago Australia's main customer it is now only its third best customer, after Japan and the U.S.A. And while Australia still imports more from Britain than from any other country, this is also likely to change. The British are still the main investors in Australia but new investment comes more from the U.S.A. than from Britain. And the British military commitment in Malaysia/Singapore is, at the most, likely to be little more than Australia's. With trade weakened and strategic protection going, what support will be left in the British constitutional connection? Australians are likely to feel increasingly foolish that their Head of State resides in London.

In a sense Australia is a republic already. The traditional British forms already run much more shallow than the more elderly Australians realize. To people who are under thirty-five, who were still at school when Singapore fell or not even born, there is no basis of power or performance or reason in the monarchy. To the migrants or the under thirty-fives – and that is now a majority of the population – the Royal Family is a novelty item, charming celebrities. Even in this role they don't seem to be pulling as well as they used to. Australia is no longer short of visiting 'celebrities'.

How Australia will become a republic, and when, is not predictable. However one knows that the older generations to whom such a change is unthinkable are going to die, and that in the younger generations there is likely to be little interest in preserving Australia as a monarchy. Merely to write the word is to invite derision. Hardly any Australian below a certain age would consider his country to be a monarchy yet that is its constitutional position. It will become politically practicable to make this break; all that is needed is some push from events, some dramatic reason for making it. No one can tell what that push might be, but it will be pushing against a lightly locked door.

Already the general tone of private discussion among those who do not hold monarchist principles but might oppose change or not urge it, is cynical and whiggish. They argue that the monarchic link is a useful fiction, divorcing ceremony from power ... or that Australia does not run to the kind of people who could be elevated into a presidency ... or that no one could trust an Australian in such a job; he might turn himself into a dictator ... or that although in theory a monarchy is absurdly obsolescent in practice this is a matter of minor importance and it may even do some good, that one should concentrate on the great issues of the day, not on minor matters such as the monarchy.

Arguments such as these are themselves symptoms of Australia's malaise. Some of them – the unimportance-of-the-issue kind of argument – are London arguments.

The British link is taken seriously by other countries, particularly in Asia. Australia is sometimes considered to be a half-sovereign state, a weird survival of the colonial age, a cunningly contrived British satellite with some freedoms, a Hungary or a Poland of 'The West', not even a Yugoslavia or an Albania. This is an irritating and dangerous reputation to bear. It is one of which many Australian diplomats are not fully aware; Asians don't like to tell them about it.

Discussion still goes on about the use of the Commonwealth as an instrument of power, directing hopes and ambitions from more realistic forms of association with other nations. Australia needs sudden shocks of re-orientation within its society that will divorce it from the largely irrelevant problems of the British, make it possible to speed necessary changes and to develop some new sense of identity, some public feeling of being a people who can be described – even if incorrectly – as such-and-such a kind of nation, and act at times as if it were so. Australians are anonymous, featureless, nothing-men. This modest anonymity reveals itself in the argument that Australia does not run to the kind of person we could turn into a president. Is Australia alone in the world in being unable to rig up its own head of state? This is backwater colonialism, nervous of its final responsibilities.

When Australia becomes a republic a President might be

appointed by pretending that nothing had really changed:
just replace the Governor-General as quietly as possible
with a President. One might think that such a dignitary
would have to be elected by the people but the Australian
political leaders might prefer to sneak him in through a back
door. At present the Prime Minister appoints the Governor-
General; he nominates someone to the Queen who then
announces the appointment. As in Russia, the effective
political leader appoints the ceremonial head of state. It
would be possible to keep this tradition going by calling
together both Houses of the Federal Parliament at stated
intervals and they could formally elect the man on the
Prime Minister's ticket. Something more ambitious might
be attempted – a national convention of State and Federal
Parliaments. This would take the president-making away
from the Prime Minister and leave the matter to be settled
by horse-trading among the country's most powerful
politicians. Direct methods of election might be opposed on
the argument that to destroy what is left of the mystique of
the monarchy might threaten the basis of Australian democracy. I doubt that this would be so.

In the meantime the appointment by a Liberal Government of an Australian as Governor-General – the first such
appointment made by a Liberal Government – was accepted
as an overdue reform and there has now even been discussion as to how the position of Governor-General might be
abolished – but without Australia formally becoming a
republic. The suggestion was that the constitutional provision that an Administrator can act with the powers of a
Governor-General in the absence of a Governor-General
could be used. The Government could simply not appoint a
Governor-General; some distinguished person could then
double up as Administrator to do the necessary signing of
documents, and so forth, but he would not perform any
public duties. This seemed a typically Australian suggestion.
It is not likely to be quite as easy as that.

# 5. LIVING WITH ASIA

## *What is Asia?*

BEFORE discussing Australian attitudes to Asia it should be
made clear what one is not saying. Among people who take
a sophisticated interest in Asia it is fairly common ground
that the term is too wide in reference for any except an
arbitrary geographical meaning. Asia is a place where half
the world lives, located at such-and-such a position on the
map. The whole concept of 'continents' breaks down when
one comes to Asia.

In the days of colonial conquest Europeans felt a difference between themselves and 'Asiatics'. There were
differences of pigment and bone structure; 'Asiatics' did
not speak European languages; they had not generated an
industrial revolution; they were heathens; they had let
themselves be dominated by the colonialists. It may have
been this fact of domination that established the differences.
Professedly Christian peoples were engaged in some
slaughter and considerable disruption and subjection; it was
inevitable that an ideological rationalization of this would
be developed. Otherwise how could the troops, functionaries
and traders face each other at church on Sundays?

Out of this guilt and the rationalization of it grew the
lunatic division between an allegedly superior 'white world'
(that was a pink and brown and light yellow and grey world
as well) and an inferior 'coloured' world. This division was
based primarily on power, not on quality of civilizations.
This power was overthrown by the Japanese. As early as
1905 they defeated the Russians. In the 1930s in China the
Japanese advanced and the Europeans retreated. In the
Second World War they ended European power in Asia.

'Asian' once had some meaning as an opposite to
'European'. With the liberation of Asia from the Europeans

'Asia' ceased to have meaning. There were no common characteristics between the races and nations that made it up. For those who find significance in the colour of skins or the shape of noses Asia is disappointing. It has all kinds of skin pigmentation; all shapes of noses. There is no pan-Asianism. There are divisions between the nations of Asia and, above all, there are immense feelings of difference between races. Race is discussed a great deal in Asia. Japanese look down on many other Asians as primitives; they are likely to find more community of interest with Australians than with Indonesians. In China, in Taiwan and Hong Kong, or in the overseas Chinese communities in Malaysia, Thailand, Vietnam, the Philippines, and Indonesia the Chinese consider themselves to be the greatest and most intelligent race, inheritors of the Central Kingdom, the true governors of Asia and perhaps the world. Filipinos hate the Chinese and the Japanese; everyone distrusts the Filipinos and the Japanese. Everyone who is not Chinese or Indian distrusts both the Chinese and the Indians. Among the Chinese and Indians themselves there are differences of race and class. To state these differences is not to criticize Asia. It simply means that the people who live there are part of the human race and display familiar human characteristics. It can become one of the obsessions of European anti-colonialists to de-humanize people who live in Asia, to idealize them as charming puppy dogs, innocent idiots. The reality is that Asians display versatility and difference more than Europeans. Pan-Africanism and Pan-Europeanism are now developing some signs of possible political reality. Pan-Asianism is not. Asia is too big, too diverse, to consider itself as an entity. It is a collection of sub-continents, themselves divided.

The physical racial differences of Asians are greater than those of Europeans, Religious differences are greater, (Buddhism in several varieties, Hinduism, Confucianism, Communism, Mahommedanism, Christianity). Stages of economic development are considerably greater. And while there is some sense of a common civilization in Europe there is *none* in Asia – except amongst those top people who are 'westernized'. 'Oriental fatalism' is a convenient dream. It comes from reading religious texts or observing depressed rural communities. One could have applied these selective tests to Europe and come up with the same conclusions. The religious dogmas of Europe, with their concern for the vanity of this world and the rewards of the hereafter have been ignored by most of those who made Europe's history. The same kind of thing happens in Asia. Ambition, conquest, enterprise are as much a part of its history as of Europe's. What happened to Asia is that the sudden burst of creative growth in Europe temporarily overwhelmed it. It was slow to realize that the world was open, the future boundless, to gain the modern sense of constantly moving into the new. But so, for a long time, did the communities of Europe, even at the time when changes were happening. Japan, where the Europeans did not suppress or distort local initiative as they did everywhere else in Asia, moved into the New Age more quickly than the under-developed European nations. The Chinese entrepreneurs in Taipeh, Hong Kong, Singapore, Bangkok, Manila are not oriental fatalists. Indian businessmen are not holy men – although the depressed rural communities in India may still be fatalistic. (Fatalism is, as it were, their only hope.) Manila bustles with sharp practice while the countryside rots – as has happened in Southern Spain, in Sicily, in Greece, and in other European countries at earlier states in their development.

Asians are not any more unfathomable than anyone else. The truth is that we are all unfathomable. Asians are unfathomable to each other. Indians cannot understand the Chinese; the Japanese cannot understand the Indonesians; the Cambodians cannot understand the Thais; and so on. Does a Balkan European understand a Western Catholic? Do Norwegians understand Spaniards? Does anyone understand the English? I read recently a book on Japanese businessmen. It tried to distinguish them from 'western' businessmen. There seemed to be something familiar about

the description ... the nepotism, the sense of family, the continued interest in military matters, the sloth ... it was also
a description of businessmen in England. Europeans
usually apply to people who live in Asia tests that are more
objective than the tests Europeans would apply to themselves. These harsh examinations can produce a sense of
Evelyn Waugh absurdity. But the same tests applied to
European institutions are likely to produce the same results.
Perhaps all human effort is absurd. If this is so, it is no more
absurd in Asia than in Europe. Dress Sir Anthony Eden and
his 1956 Cabinet up in tropical dress, move them to Vien-
tiane and have them pursue a policy against Xiengkhouana
with the ruthless ineptitude with which they pursued their
Suez policy and you have an 'unfathomable' Asian situation.

And what is European about the civilization that Australia is said to represent? Let us proceed beyond the
official handouts: Christianity, respect for human life, belief
in democracy and so on. Can we seriously describe Europe,
the continent of unparalleled slaughter and conquest as
necessarily practising these ideals? Are they really its distinguishing characteristics? This is the way people in Asia
sometimes see the Europeans: they see them as hypo-
critical conquerors and murderers.

There *is* more respect for human life in Australia than in
most countries of Asia; Australian democracy functions
without serious internal challenge; and Australians enjoy
one of the highest living standards in the world, ahead of
the Japanese and well ahead of other countries in Asia. But
this had not always been so. Australia was first established
as a miserable penal settlement where men were flogged
and hanged almost out of hand and the aborigines were
sometimes hunted like animals or poisoned like dogs. In
Tasmania they were exterminated. Australians are not far
removed from barbarisms. Perhaps one should simply think
of the Pacific as it was at the end of the eighteenth century.
Think of Sydney, Singapore, Shanghai, Hong Kong, Tokyo,
San Francisco, Pearl Harbour, Manila. These places were

about to be unrecognizably transformed. The one great mysterious convulsion of 'industrialization' and 'westernization' has thrown them all up in their modern forms. In different ways the lives of all of us around the Pacific are being affected by the same forces. And, in the test of the sense of constantly moving into the new that is the modern spirit, Australia is not the most 'modern' nation in 'Asia'; Japan is.

## The power situation

It is not a question of Australia seeking to be understood in Asia. Australians might well begin any debate on foreign affairs with the thought that there is no chance that they will ever enjoy good relations with all the nations to their north. Australia's problem is that it now exists in a new and dangerous power situation and its people and policies are not properly re-orientated towards this fact.

Asia is the place where western European colonialism first collapsed, pushed over by the Japanese. (Africa was an afterthought.) The Europeans tried to force their way back after the Second World War but their strength dribbled away in lost colonial wars, or gestures of realistic magnanimity. The romance and the rackets of European imperialism were over. National armies filled the barracks that the colonialists built and national presidents moved into the governors' palaces. For Australians this has produced a new world in which old attitudes are meaningless.

It is not surprising that a strong sense of imminent catastrophe marked Australia's initial awareness of Asia. The threat of Japanese invasion made a macabre opening to Australia's new interest in its environment and the sense of possible disaster remained as the Communists swept into power in China and, among the disorders of the nationalist revolts in the countries fringing China, there were strong movements of Communist insurgency. Then the Korean War, the Malaysian Confrontation and the Vietnam War all demanded Australian military expeditions. The subcontinent of South East Asia, to which Australia appends, remains potentially the most unstable area in the world. In this quarrelsome, insecure, unpredictable situation, what is surprising is that Australian policy developed unexpected subtleties. Out of the mess of confrontation between Soekarno's regime and Malaysia and the later separation of Singapore and Malaysia Australia, although intervening, managed to retain friendships all round. There is no other nation of the 'West' of comparable size that has had to concern itself with such continuing active diplomacy and military commitment as Australia has had to exercise since the Second World War.

In a world where racialism is now correctly classified as a disease Australia has the reputation of being racialist because of its 'White Australia' policy. Sir Robert Menzies said on British television: 'Oh, we don't call it that now.' But although there has been some minor (if secret), reform nevertheless Australia quite clearly practises immigration discrimination against every country in Asia. It encourages and subsidises migration from Europe, including the migration of those who do not speak English, yet it conducts such rigorous (and secret) tests against Asians that very few Asians get in. This is taken to be racialist by Asians and so it is, in effect, whatever its motives. It causes Australia to be distrusted by every nation in Asia.

This policy is sometimes likened, and even confused, with Australia's past ill-treatment of its aborigines. Things are improving in attitudes towards the remaining 100,000 aborigines and part aborigines but there is still truth in the statement made some years ago by Paul Hasluck: 'When we enter into international discussion and raise our voice, as we should raise it, in defence of human rights and the protection of human welfare, our very words are mocked by thousands of degraded and depressed people who crouch on rubbish beds throughout the whole of this continent.' Asians do not worry much about the aborigines. (Their treatment of their own aborigines is often worse than Australia's. Besides the aborigines are 'blacks' and there is probably more prejudice against 'blacks' in Asia, than in

Europe, or in Australia.) However, the aborigines are taken to be victims of the 'White Australia' policy and the policy is often described as an Australian 'apartheid'.

That such a suburban and unambitious people as the Australians should become one of the last colonial powers is an accident of geography. Yet the Australian administration of New Guinea, (though New Guinea is modestly described as a 'territory') has been undoubtedly colonial, however well-meaning it might seem to the innocent – and largely uninterested – minds of Australians. In the early 1960s the worst that happened to Australia were reprimands from the United Nations Trusteeship Council for not speeding up its training of New Guineans for self-government. But it seemed clear that the accelerated development towards self-government that Australia initiated in 1964, with a House of Assembly that had a majority of indigenous people, would develop a momentum towards independent nationhood for East New Guinea that would catch Australia unprepared.

Asia is the only part of the world, apart from the Caribbean, where there are both high population density and high population growth. At present rates, in forty years it will hold – if that's the word – a billion people more than all the world does today. Australia is the least densely populated country in the world – almost 3,000,000 square miles of it, sixth largest nation in area and fewer people than Holland. That a large part of it is desert, and another large part extremely arid is not believed in Asia, or considered to be relevant. To Asians, Australia is a great unexploited 'continent'. I remember facing a roomful of disbelieving Filipinos and trying to explain that although Australia could accommodate incalculably more people in its industrial and fertile areas, nevertheless a large part of it was desert. Finally, I asked for an atlas and pointed to the great blob of yellow that takes up two-thirds of Australia on the rainfall map, third biggest yellow blob on the rainfall map of the world. The Filipinos still did not believe that this was desert. They wished to believe that south of them there was a 'continent' of great richness that could provide a solution to everybody's problems. Australia should try to get itself reclassified as an island. It sounds less interesting.

There are other empty areas in Asia – Manchuria, the North and North-West Provinces of China, Sumatra, Thailand. But low population density in Australia creates animosity among Australia's neighbours because it is associated with such high prosperity. Australia enjoys almost unparelleled prosperity while in Asia there are some of the most destitute populations in the world. Australia has not the resources to play Lady Bountiful to all Asia but per capita national income in Australia is sixteen times that of Asia. Despite its internal democracy, Australia plays an aristocratic role in the society of Asia – rich, self-centred, frivolous, blind.

## Images of Asia

If the impression has been given that no one in Australia ever thinks of Asia, it should be pointed out that this is now far from true. There has been a huge shift in attitudes. Sensations burst into the newspapers, seminars are held, articles are written. But the interest is sometimes that of someone momentarily attracted to an idea: *Fascinating stuff I must find out what it's all about sometime.* There is not very much real *feel* for Asia. It is a learned lesson and people can get their lines wrong. Someone may say over his claret, 'We may only have a few years before China wins. It's not myself I'm worried about but my children.' Then over his brandy he will confound those who suggest that Australia is geographically an extension of South-East Asia by saying, 'Distances don't matter any more and geographical location is less important. Australia is part of The West.'

In the following paragraphs I have attempted some broad categorization of how Australian attitudes towards Asia can go wrong.

'*The faceless hordes.*' The lumping of all Asians together can create a mindless panic: fifty-two per cent of the world's population lives in Asia, therefore fifty two per cent of the world's population *en bloc* threatens Australia. This arithmetical method has a long history, going back well before the arrival of communism. As a common substitute for thought there is a corny poetic quality about it. *The settlers gather in the stockade and while away the night at cards, sure that with the dawn they will all be scalped by the Indians.* It is a thoroughly pessimistic view that could cause a people to bolt at a time of crisis.

'*I like Asians.*' A minority of those who hold the view that all Asians are the same seem delighted by the prospect of more than a billion identical neighbours. This belief is often associated with statements about the vitality and youth of Asians – that mock the conservatism that lays destitute so many rural areas in Asia, and the sloth that is so often the despair of Asian economic planning. I once sat through a dinner in which the speaker propounded the thesis that one Asian was as good as two Australians. He then explained that he had recently met some Africans. They spoke good English; some of them even spoke French. So one African became as good as two Asians (or four Australians). When ignorance is confronted with an Asian who does not pick his nose and can discuss affairs of the day in the tongue of a former colonial power it is likely to idealize him in terms that insult the reality of the dreadful problems of the depressed communities of Asia. Sometimes this sort of generalization becomes less of a personal fantasy and makes slightly more sense. An Australian decides that he has a favourite nation in Asia. 'I like Indians' is even more meaningless than 'I like Englishmen'. But it is a start, a beginning of the breakdown of generalities. It makes more sense than 'I like Asians'.

'*Give them what they want.*' These attitudes of extreme reverence can sometimes lead to the belief that Asians are not interested in power politics, that all they want is love, and perhaps aid. This comes out in its most extreme form in relation to China. The argument runs: the Chinese are rejected by the world; treat them as ordinary people and they will respond to this treatment, lose their emotional insecurity and display affection. This attitude was also found towards Soekarno. Give him whatever it was he wanted and he would quieten down. After all, we have to live with these people. There are many areas where Australia, by dramatizing its identity of interest with certain Asian nations, has much to gain. But this is not to suggest that the elites of Asia do not play the power game. The history of Asia is a spectacle of rampaging power just like the history of any other continent. And the attitudes of modern Asians to power are those of human beings. Some of them love it.

'*We must respect Asian opinion.*' Some Australians move into the confused ideology of non-alignment. One can express plenty of sympathy for Asian countries that profess to be non-aligned. But to some Australians there is a special virtue in non-alignment, an obvious moral superiority making self evident the truth of propositions such as that non-aligned Asian nations are better than aligned ones; or that military dictatorship in them can be excused for reasons that do not apply to aligned nations; or that what is all right in Burma is wrong in Thailand (this comparison is grossly unfair to Thailand). India was dumped like a faithless wife when it was invaded by China. It had become aligned. This approach (not widely represented in Australia outside intellectual and left wing groups) would have it that Australia will never be trusted by 'Asia' unless it withdraws itself from its alliance with America and declares itself to be non-aligned.

'*The Chinese will win.*' There are Australians of many kinds, on the Right as well as the Left, who – like people all over Asia – are fascinated by Communist China, held in the grip of what they see as destiny and anxious to accommodate themselves to the 'facts'. Some wish to make a quick quid. Others believe that China will win, that a realistic policy for Australia is to assume this and 'come to terms'. There are people in Australia who see themselves as those who 'understand the Chinese'. They hope to make the appropriate arrangements when the day comes. The 'China Lobby' in Australia – diffuse, partly contradictory, often confused – should not be underestimated.

*The anti-communists.* By this I mean not the mass of the people in Australia, who might also be described in this way, but those who would probably describe themselves as the tough-minded realists on Australian foreign policy who believe that Australia does not go far enough. Their assessment of one considerable part of Australia's future – the threat of communist regimes in South-East Asia – is often valuable and realistic. But in attitudes to Asia generally some of them show two weaknesses. Some can take the ideologies and sacred texts of Marxism too seriously; they can become so learned in dogma that they might lose sight of the monstrous but human realities beneath; they can over-intellectualize. For this reason some of them were very slow in acknowledging the Sino-Soviet split. It didn't fit into the picture. Others – or the same ones – might concentrate so much on communism in Asia that they see all communism and no Asia. For instance a friend was considering organizing a conference in Sydney of intellectuals from 'the tough anti-communist Asian countries'. No sooner had he prepared his list, with the Pakistanis on it and the Indians off it, than the Chinese invaded India. He had to cross Pakistan off ('soft on communism') and put India on ('hard line'). Then President Macapagal of the Philippines, SEATO member, hard line and Christian too, bolted with President Soekarno on the Malaysia issue. Who was hard on communism now? The committed Philippines or the officially non-aligned Malays? People who see themselves as prophets in a hostile environment can lose their sense of human absurdity and complexity. They can become doctrinaire, lose their political touch, fail to see the muddle in which human affairs are usually conducted, forget how, although issues may be important, those who are concerned with them are often clowns. The ideal position for an Australian in facing Asia is to see Asia including communism. But not only communism.

'*It's no business of ours.*' There seem to be a number of Australians who sincerely believe that nothing is anybody else's business. They feel that if Australia has nothing to do with Asia, Asia will have nothing to do with Australia. Life is a street in the suburbs where each house keeps to itself. If Australia goes poking its nose into Asia, that will only stir things up. This view can also be taken by some of those who are at other times most keen that Australia should be considered an Asian power. Australia must not 'interfere' in Asian affairs, although it seems to be all right for Asian nations to 'interfere' with each other.

'*We're all Asians now.*' This is a view taken by many young people, and I would take it myself. I think it is up to Australians to seek for similarities in Asians and mutual interests. To take our ideology of fraternalism seriously and apply it to Asians could lead to a creative awakening among Australians. But the view can become senseless if – as often happens – it does not allow for the considerable differences of Asia. And it carries obligations greater than expressions of good will. It must necessarily involve taking sides and thereby sometimes offending. Not to have supported India against China meant taking sides against India; to have professed neutrality on the issue of Malaysia meant taking sides against Malaysia. Simply saying, 'We're all Asians now', does not relieve one of decision-making; it simply begins to define the problem.

In making these categories of attitudes I have not said what the general opinion among Australians is. There is a good reason for this. No one knows what it is. All that one might guess is that overall there is confusion and a feeling of futility. Foreign policy, as Hugo Wolfsohn said in *Dissent*, is nobody's business. Public men do not make it their main field of interest. There are no long range surveys. Foreign affairs do not operate as permanent fields of political activity and study. There is 'a collection of gestures and paper schemes', of discussions that bear 'little or no relation to the problems of Australia's foreign policy.' There is insufficient institutional backing. Ministers of External Affairs do not conceptualize; little information is made available to Members of Parliament; no public or private bodies exist whose work on foreign policy has national importance.

## Racism in Australia: White Australia

The 'White Australia' policy – by its very name – was racist, however politely it has now been dressed up. It was born of the fear of Chinese migration in the gold rushes. (The *Bulletin*'s motto originally went: 'Australia for the White Man and China for The Chows.')* It also had an economic basis, particularly in the agitation against the use of cheap indentured 'kanaka' labour in Queensland, with its possibility that these South Sea Islanders might become semi-slaves. Public expression of the racist strain has become weaker and weaker; now scarcely anyone is prepared to defend the policy publicly in directly racist terms. The old platforms for racism have, one by one, been chopped down.

Behind the scenes there are still Australians obsessed with 'colour'. (A few Australians might still refer to the Chinese as 'niggers'.) The truth about Australians, as of most peoples, is that they nurture all kinds of prejudices about race, nationality and religion. But it is not necessarily of public concern that this is so unless the prejudices are put into effect in some public, fanatical way. To attempt to legislate away feelings of difference would only be successful if one legislated democracy away as well. One must recognize that it is true to say that many Australians are prejudiced against Asians. But this is not necessarily of policy-making significance. Perhaps most Australians were prejudiced against the migration of Catholics; some were prejudiced against the migration of Jews. The underside of life often smells nasty; the best one can do is to hope that the smells stay where they are. Despite prejudices against Eastern and Southern Europeans, Catholics and Jews, migration has continued and there has proved to be no public significance in these prejudices although privately they might still be strong. Except for endemic religious sectarianism Australians may be more capable of effective

* This motto had been refined to 'Australia For The White Man' when, on becoming editor of the *Bulletin* in 1960, I removed it, and precipitated some pathological abuse.

policies of live-and-let-live – whatever nonsense they talk in bars and their sitting rooms – than some may give them credit for.

There is considerable opposition to the present policy from the churches, universities and some newspapers. Public opinion polls suggest that a majority of Australians now favour some change in migration policies. Over the period of the Menzies administration – this may not have been the intention but it happened – there seems to have been a considerable easing of the more primitive fears of Asian migration. The 12,000 Asian students in Australia, with the other Asians who have been allowed into Australia, are now a feature of life in the big Australian cities. People have got used to the idea without any of the friction that was forecast. If this is so the argument that the present policy avoids racial friction becomes rather weak. It may now be possible to announce an end to the policy and replace it with a controlled encouragement of migration from Asia without arousing a crisis within the community.

This might be possible so far as the people of Australia are concerned. However it is not likely from the present ruling generation of politicians. Even if the Liberals wanted to change the policy (and there is no sign that the old hands do), they would not risk it until the Labor Party positively demanded change. Despite the wishes of some of its members the Party is not yet in that position. So politically, for the moment, that's that. It may not last like this for long. The generation still in charge in Australia will soon be writing its memoirs. One can safely predict that younger Australians are determined on change. Immigration reform is now an almost universally held belief among the university-educated, and among young Labor and Liberal supporters. In the desire to change this policy, as with many other things, there are much greater forces for change in Australia than the older or many of the middle-aged generations now realize.

Proposals for reform have been prepared by Immigration Reform Groups, consisting mainly of university people, that

for several years have operated within what would be described in other countries as opinion-forming quarters. If
reform of immigration policies proceeds calmly these
Groups are entitled to much of the praise. In the pamphlet
*Control or Colour Bar?* there is a conservative approach. It is
suggested that intake should be limited 'by the need to
avoid harmful economic competition that gives rise to social
tensions, to prevent a concentration of any racial group in
low-status employment, to avoid housing congestion and to
ensure reasonable dispersion throughout the Australian
community.' It leaves estimates of the future to the future,
but suggests that for the present Australia 'could now accept
several times the recent average rate of intake without
undue strain.' What has been done is to take objections
based on cultural homogeneity seriously and try to meet
them. In *Quadrant* two members of a Group wrote: '... this
is the acid test of the argument ... Homogeneity cannot be
equated with whiteness.' For example, there are plenty of
Filipinos in Manila who seem to meet the tests of homogeneity, even including Christian faith. Why exclude them?

Even the most liberally expressed support for easing
immigration restrictions is hedged by fears – mainly of
other people's reactions: that other Australians cannot be
trusted to behave decently; that a policy of quotas would
arouse more animosity than it allayed among Asians; that
there would be hatred of employed Asians if there were a
large scale depression. These fears necessarily breed in
ignorance because no one knows who would want to come
to Australia. It is generally assumed that Eurasians would
be pleased to come, perhaps Filipinos, perhaps rich Chinese,
especially from Hong Kong. If these were the main classes
it is difficult to see what risks of tension or destruction of
ways of life their arrival would entail. Many Asians point
out that Indians are usually happy to stay in India. Malays
in Malaya, Chinese in Singapore; if they want to migrate
they try to migrate to Britain. It is sometimes feared that
a more liberal policy might alienate Asian governments by
stripping their nations of part of their elites, who would

flock to Australia, yet this seems a matter that can be regulated by treaty. It is a matter for Asian governments, not for Australia. This fear applies even more acutely to the Asian students who are educated in Australia, yet again this would be the business of their own governments. Opposition to Asians who have been educated in Australia remaining in Australia seems indefensible on any grounds except those of race prejudice.

An increased intake of Asian elites would certainly enrich Australian life. It would help Australians to become more familiar with the world they live next to, lead to a greater versatility of approach and perhaps partly offset the fact that Australia – herself short of elites – imports a significant proportion of the teaching staff of its universities from England. This last fact may in itself help to account for the continuing serious alienation of Australian intellectuals from their own people. We may need some Japanese, Indians, and Chinese to help break up the English influence.

If Australia is to play a more forceful role in Asia the change in immigration policies must be dramatic enough to impress Asians that it *is* a change. It would seem a comparatively simple method to enter into migration agreements with Asian countries that might meet any of their own fears and that would set up clear public standards of assimilability – of language, education and working capacity. This would be an initial reform. Over a period of time these tests might be made more general so that they applied to all migration to Australia. My own view is that the future holds dramatic possibilities for Australia which may necessarily include racial change, that this is Australia's 'destiny'. It is going to happen one way of the other. It is a task that will be undertaken either by Australians, or by someone else.

## Racism in Australia: Aborigines

In the early years of settlement, despite occasional periods of reform, the aborigines were treated, at worst, as 'treacherous animals', or with the indifference that can push aside a primitive culture and trample on it without meaning to; at best, as a people who were to be protected, and therefore segregated. The treatment given to the aborigines was like that of other migrating races when confronted with an extremely weak and disorganized aboriginal society. Most of the dominant races in Asia treated their aborigines similarly; they pushed them out of the way.

To make this comparison is not to excuse present attitudes, but to place Australian settlement in a context of the whole world's savage history of settlement. There was nothing peculiarly Australian in past treatment of the aborigines, however much it should remain on the consciences of present Australians (including the 17 per cent who were not born in Australia). What matters is the position now. There is no doubt that given the affluence, skills, and professions of humanitarianism and fraternalism in Australian society, modern Australians have made a mess of restoring the aborigines to the human race.

It would take too long to summarize the aborigines' present position, because they come under different jurisdictions – in the States of Queensland, Western Australia, South Australia, Victoria, and New South Wales they are the responsibility of the State governments, and in the Northern Territory of the Commonwealth Government. (There are no aborigines in Tasmania because they were all killed.) Summary is also difficult because in all these areas there are now varying degrees of liberalization. At the time of writing Queensland is the State most backward in revising the laws that concern aborigines. However in general terms, while there are still some aborigines leading tribal lives the possibility of preserving their civilization – either as a museum piece or in respect to their wishes – seems small. As Peter Coleman put it in the *Observer*: 'Despite official claims our policy towards the aborigines has in one fundamental respect never changed. Once the idea was to kill them off; then the more humane programme was to let them die out peacefully and meanwhile to smooth their dying pillow; now the policy is to assimilate them.

But as far as the aborigines themselves are concerned the result in each case is the same. Assimilation ultimately means absorption and that means extinction. As a "nation" with its own way of life and even as a race the aborigines are still destined to disappear ... It is one of the ironies of our history that the only recompense we seem to be able to give this race for what we have done to it is to help it disappear.'

All the governments concerned with aborigines are now committed to assimilation. At a conference in 1951 of representatives from State and Federal Governments the principles of assimilation were accepted. It was restated at a similar conference in 1961 and after that there was quick liberalization in some areas. Aborigines are expected to 'attain the same manner of living as other Australians and to live as members of a single Australian community.' This should be understood by those people throughout the world who confuse treatment of aborigines with the 'White Australia' immigration policy and claim that there is an apartheid policy within Australia. The position is very unsatisfactory and there is underprivilege and in some areas there is still *de facto* segregation, but the official policy is assimilation, not apartheid and the policy is being fulfilled – although too slowly.

Most Australians (who may never see an aboriginal from one year to the next) now seem to wish them well and to agree that they should simply be considered as Australians. There is now a vogue for bark paintings and other aboriginal artifacts and concern for the future of aborigines has become an article of faith among younger educated Australians. Their actual position lies in a spectrum stretching from the few who are commercially successful and are simply Australians, to those who are trying to become so in the cities or the country towns, to those who live half-Australian, half-aboriginal lives in official 'stations' or unofficial river camps outside the country towns, to those who live in protected aboriginal communities, to those who are still nomads and desert dwellers. Although legal discriminations are disappearing – and it is a policy that this should be so – many of them have been second-class citizens (although they now all have the Federal vote), and the necessary accompaniment of paternalism, lavish expenditure on welfare and imaginative planning was not present – although over the 1950s there was improvement and there has been very considerable improvement in the 1960s.

In some areas there are a lot of petty prejudices against aborigines; in others there are not. It would be hard to legislate these out of existence. Where Australian society might be condemned as a whole is that it was slow to move in granting full rights and in spending more money. This may have come partly from theories of race, but it has come mainly from blindness of conscience and a sheer lack of imagination that did not understand that a lack of policy is itself a policy.

## Attitudes to Oceania

The refusal of Australians to recognize their environment is perhaps most startlingly shown in their almost complete oblivion to the world of Oceania: New Guinea, New Zealand; and 800 to 1,000 miles out to sea, smaller islands – the Solomons, the New Hebrides, New Caledonia; further out, Fiji; and then a string of islands right across the South Pacific, the western part mainly under New Zealand influence, the eastern part mainly French. In this part of the world Australia is a big nation. There has been considerable Australian initiative shown here, mainly by individuals; and a lot of money made by business firms. But as an Australian concept the area does not exist. Australians know more about Europe than they do about Asia, more about Asia than they do about Oceania. A country whose imagination was influenced by that of British history seems unable to acknowledge the existence of such detail.

In 1958 when the *Observer* tried to interest people in New Guinea it was accused of being obsessed. It was said to be hysterical to write: 'Here is our test of policy: New Guinea is one of the disputed territories of the world; it is one of those places where a war could break out tomorrow, and we control half of it. It could be the Alsace-Lorraine of the South Pacific: it is the possible testing point of all our policies: who – apart from ourselves – really gives a damn about it? If we took some kind of a stand on New Guinea would any one at all support us?' The answer quickly proved to be 'No'. By 1961 the Indonesia 'confrontation' of the Dutch over the future of West New Guinea destroyed Australian policy. The Australian government had long privately opposed Indonesian acquisition of West New Guinea. But after having pursued for ten years a policy that was based on nothing but wishes and diplomacy Australia gave in. The people of West New Guinea were given no chance to determine their own future; they were handed over to Indonesia and Soekarno moved on to the 'confrontation' of Malaysia.

Now that a House of Assembly (with a majority of indigenous people) has been elected in the two Australian-controlled territories that make up East New Guinea it is inevitable that – whatever the Australian Government says – a strong independence movement will form, and secure independence. The 20,000 Europeans (mostly Australians) who live in New Guinea are at the end of their period of dominance. There will be a Republic of New Guinea. As a result of a lack of imagination in Australia this New Guinea Republic will be economically dependent on Australia or on whatever support it can get from any other country. It will not possess a trained elite of sufficient numbers. There has, even at a late stage, been a typically Australian assumption that New Guinea is different from other colonies. On this question of New Guinea there are almost endless permutations of discord likely to fall on Australia's head.

Relations with New Zealand have been marked by that same graduated blindness that so often afflicts Australians: the closer a place to Australia, the less Australians know about it. Sometimes one learns more about New Zealand from the London *Times* than from Australian newspapers.

New Zealanders have attitudes towards Australians,*
Australians have no attitudes towards New Zealanders.
They can be surprised – and hurt – when New Zealanders
express their attitudes, which include expressions of
superiority. Who would expect this from New Zealand?

New Zealand's population is only a quarter that of Australia's; her imports are proportionately double Australia's;
her exports are dangerously confined to wool, meat, and
dairy products; and far too much of her trade is bound up
with Britain. British entry into the European Economic
Community would probably wreck New Zealand. Australia,
with a smaller reliance on imports, more diversified exports
and greater industrial sophistication, could survive the
strain. New Zealand needs – indeed, must have – a larger
country to attach herself to. In theory, as part of the
ANZUS alliance of Australia, New Zealand, and the United
States, she has America as an ally. Economically she is
bound to Britain. But it could be to her advantage to
attach herself strategically and economically to Australia.
Strategically, there could be an integration of defence
forces; economically, access to Australia's overseas balances
and the combined marketing of products both countries
export could assist New Zealand out of its chronic state of
international bankruptcy. Full economic union would be
contested by Australian dairy farmers, some of whom might
go down to New Zealand competition, and by New Zealand
manufacturers who might be pushed out of their own
markets by stronger Australian based firms. These are the
kind of problems that seem insuperable in Australia because
they involve change; but elsewhere in the world greater
changes than these are happening. For most of last century
New Zealand was considered to be part of the complex of
colonies that made up Australasia and at the beginning of
this century she opened discussions about joining the new

* They often see themselves as Britain's favourite among the former
dominions: Australia is gauche, noisy, belligerent, untrustworthy;
paradoxically it is also a great friendly land of opportunity and 50,000
New Zealanders live there.

Australian Federation (and was unsuccessful). These discussions could be resumed. In 1965 (largely on New Zealand initiative) the two countries finally signed a very conservative free trade agreement (covering the non-controversial 60 per cent of trade).

It would be tedious to run through the smaller islands of the South Pacific separately. But the position of many – and this will be the inevitable trend in all – is that they must move toward some form of independence. They are all tiny communities needing some special arrangement. Some of them have extraordinary problems. Australia is often their principal economic exploiter. Some administrations have turned to Australia for assistance – and have been refused.

Here is a strange island world where imagination in Australia, with New Zealand co-operation, could create new political forms, leading to the greater happiness of the people who live there – and some assurance in this of security for Australia and New Zealand. Of Australia's many blindnesses its blindness to Oceania is the most difficult to forgive. It is possible to ask the world to extend a charitable view towards Australia when faced with the perplexities of Asia. But the world might ask why Australians have not taken a more practical interest in Oceania, where they are a large nation, and capable of initiative. Before paying attention to our own calls for sympathy the world might ask what we have done for these others who need our interest and help.

# 6. MEN AT WORK

## *Men of business*

IN some parts of New Guinea there are people who believe
that Heaven is to be found somewhere in the clouds just
above Sydney and is connected with Sydney by a ladder.
Here, while the Spirits of the Dead loll in their cane chairs
and gorge themselves on the canned meat and whisky that
is served to them by the angels, God spends his time creating
consumer goods, which go down the ladder from Heaven to
Sydney and then, as ship's cargo, on to lucky people in
New Guinea.

Australians do not have this look-no-hands attitude.
They manufacture most of their own consumer goods. But
a look-no-brains attitude in endemic among some Australian
attitudes to manufacturing. The processes of invention and
innovation that are such an essential part of the Western
Mind play less domestic part in Australia than in any other
prosperous country, apart from Canada. No matter what
miracles Australians achieved in the earlier settlement of the
continent and however spectacularly successful they can be
at improvising when they are pushed to it, Australian businessmen have not proved to be very good at getting people
to think up new things to make. Instructions about how
to make new things usually come from the heavens that lie
across the U.S.A., Britain and Europe. Unlike Sweden and
Switzerland, Australia has not developed any significant
world specialities of its own in manufacture. Not only do
Australians not think things up: in their behaviour they
often show a remarkable distrust for another essential part
of the Western Mind: a practising belief in the efficacy of
competition.

Australia is a rich prize in international investment, full
of loot. Recently discovered bauxite fields show the largest

known resources in the world. Reserves of iron ore are estimated at as much as eight billion tons. Oil is being discovered in commercial quantities; reserves of coal are huge; production of lead is the largest in the world; production of zinc is the third largest; wool production is a third of the world total. Most of the manufacturing in what could accurately be described in the cliche term as a 'land rich in resources' is now under foreign control.

The only major manufacturing industry groups that are not dominated by overseas firms are steel, cement, glass, sugar and paper. Of the top 100 Australian firms at least two thirds are overseas controlled. When it is remembered how these firms then dominate their suppliers and clients it would be safe to say that most Australian manufacturing is ultimately dependent on overseas enterprise and decision. Even firms that are wholly Australian-owned usually depend on overseas patents for their ideas. The ideas behind the so-called 'industrial revolution' of the 1950s and 1960s came mainly from overseas. Nor is this the whole story. Most of the innovations in managerial and marketing styles also come from overseas and there is now a tendency for overseas firms to move direct into Australian accounting, management consulting and advertising. The success of Australian industry in most significant sectors has been that of an advanced colonial society, with overseas capital and enterprise employing intelligent native labour. Or as Neil McInnes put it in *Quadrant*: 'It is as though a part of Europe's population were being brought here so that U.S. business could supply them, more conveniently than in Europe, with cars, soap and coco-pops.'

There seems little possibility that this trend will not continue. As McInnes says: 'The degree of economic independence we have enjoyed will last only as long as coal, steel and sugar (all three mostly owned locally) remain our biggest non-rural industries. As we enter further into the new technological era, the percentage of major economic decisions taken outside Australia will approach nearer 100. Within a few years most of the upper middle class in this country will be working for organizations having head office and the boss in New York or elsewhere outside Australia or in Australian companies that are totally dependent on such organizations.' The dependence on foreigners is not limited to internal decisions. Australia's 'export drive' in manufactured goods is largely controlled by overseas decision. Overseas firms who have companies in Australia decide whether it is more profitable or more expedient to export to certain markets from Australia or from a plant somewhere else in the world. Overseas firms that license the manufacture of goods in Australia decide whether they should extend the franchise of their patents to other parts of the world. And, as in Canada, overseas companies are now tending to stifle such native research and development as occurs; if they find a good man they bring him back to headquarters.

Not that Australia has ever spent much on research and development anyway. The Australian proportion of G.N.P. spent on research is the smallest of the whole group of prosperous countries (although it is almost three times that of Ghana). This indifference to research and development goes beyond the question of foreign ownership. Australian-owned firms often just do not understand the use of research and development. Australian research findings are sometimes touted overseas because no Australian firm can be found that understands that research can be used to make money. There are many Australians who know how to conduct research; many of the best go overseas. The very idea of clever, expert men thinking up new things to do is one that is repulsive to many Australian business men: to accept the importance of research might seem to imperil their self-importance. And in such matters Australian businessmen often treat their own countrymen with the scorn that the colonialists used to treat those they exploited: you can't expect the natives to have ideas.

There is still talk of 'free enterprise' in Australia but to many Australian manufacturers this is just a lesson they have learned off by heart without understanding: the particular meaning they give it is eccentric. Often what it means is that the business man demands from the government a special protection that will help him continue to survive.

In this latter process the Tariff Board plays an essential part. It sees that those who want to make money get a 'fair go'. This Board was established in 1921 as an independent body empowered to conduct inquiries into claims by local industries to be protected by tariff from overseas competition. It was originally intended to protect young and inexperienced businesses but now everyone hops in for his cut. Once protection is dished out it usually stays. In the absence of any government plan for sustaining unemployed men over a retraining period or in assisting diversification, the political risks in allowing an inefficient industry to collapse are too great. The use of tariff protection by the textile industry, for example, has become notorious. Although there is some excellent textile production in Australia the inefficient manufacturers set the pace in pushing up the tariff to as much as 100 per cent. The average tariff is about 30 per cent.

Overall, the Tariff Board may have been a good idea. The diversification of manufacturing in Australia may have proceeded much more slowly – in parts, not at all – without the Tariff Board. The Australian domestic market is too small for really efficient long production runs (and the proliferation of models increases this problem). Total annual production in Australia of some of the big overseas-owned companies can be equal to as little as only one day's production in the parent country. In this sense, Australian manufacturers have done well. However one should not forget something that many of them would deny: most of the labour force is educated, adaptable and responsible (although not deferential), perhaps – as Galbraith suggested when he was in Australia – more adaptable at the bottom to the problems of an automated age than America's, because of its degree of education and lack of social or racial stratification.

However, while in balance it is possible to argue that the Tariff Board, despite its abuses, has acted to Australia's advantage, its existence has encouraged the gambling in business decision that has often been a feature of Australia. To many Australian businessmen the way to make money has been to grab some ideas from overseas, rush them into operation, however inefficiently, and then rely on the Tariff Board for protection. The central preoccupation of Australian manufacturing is often to kill overseas competition with high tariffs. (Many of the industries that were built in this way were later being picked off in profitable overseas takeovers. Some of the overseas investment in Australia does not start new enterprise; it just buys up a safe bet.) Under Australian conditions there was no particular need to be efficient or to worry about world standards. Many Australian manufacturers have not been concerned with building up their competitive output in a relatively open market, but with making profits by putting pressure on the Tariff Board or by collusive practices with their competitors. Often the Australian business man was mainly a 'fixer'.

Two types of businessmen in Australia provide special problems – the spare-time directors who often sit on Boards, and the Men of Will who often run them.

In Australia company directors are not usually working directors as they are in America. A survey conducted in 1964 suggested that three-fifths of the directors came from outside the firms they directed. Directors are often amateurs and there are sometimes shareouts of directorships among old school friends and fellow club members. One single school provides a significant proportion of all the main directors in Melbourne; the membership of the Adelaide Club is largely the same as a list of the main directors in Adelaide. The racket of directorships in Australia is easy enough to organize. Ownership of companies is usually so wide that an oligarchy can perpetuate itself by perfunctorily submitting lists to amorphous shareholders. Even if there is a challenge the social homogeneity of the directing classes almost always crushes it. One sees here the ossification of institutions that is sometimes a characteristic of Australia. There is a mateship, a fraternity of directors, determined to maintain things as they are in the board room. One result of this is that the interests of the oligarchies may at times override the interests of the companies they control.

The American process of top management doing its managing from the board room is rare. The main breakthroughs are achieved by professional advisers, mainly accountants or lawyers (who, in America, are more usually hired for advice than put on the board) and both these classes of persons are often almost uniquely unsuited to the business of bold decision; it is more their job to evaluate the decisions of others. When put on a company board they sometimes reinforce the board's conservatism although there have been some notable cases of accountants who have helped to keep companies going. There are of course some extremely competent directors but all too often these may sit on as many as a dozen boards, even more. There were competent directors on the boards of some of the companies that crashed so spectacularly in the early sixties; but they seemed to be too busy to supervise closely the affairs of the companies they had been appointed to supervise.

It is difficult to see how business can be enlivened without the at least partial extinction of what amounts almost to a caste system, and its replacement, as in America, by a spirit of professionalism, loyalty to firms and a desire for efficiency.

Into this cosy world there barged the Men of Will described by Robin Boyd: 'They are not the solid Australian fathers of finance and industry who are usually some ten years older and heavily conservative, nor are they the younger early-thirties men who began their careers in the atmosphere of easy mutual confidence. They are the miracle men of ambition, usually capable, always strong in will, the men who travel most, especially to America, who drive themselves and their big cars hard, who are consciously un-Australian in their attitude to work and who see themselves as the real life-savers that Australia always needed ...

All of them were born this century. The oldest finished school in the unsettled years after the First World War and the youngest had entered adult life before the beginning of the Second World War ... They are more alert to international standards, especially American standards, than any executive Australians before them, but they are still real Australians in their suspicion of original Australian ideas and impatience with time taken in polishing any idea. For they are the exceptional, active product of a depressed, disenchanted, dull period in Australia's development. They know themselves to be exceptional among their flat unenterprising contemporaries in their uninspiring school, university or apprenticeship days. Long ago they got into the habit of relying on their own resources on practically all occasions ... So they became accustomed to making the decisions all round ... Their faith in Australia has been and still is limited to their faith in themselves.'

Australia owes much to these men. Their sheer pleasure in bustle and in imposing their will on other men and their blindness to complexity drove them along in a series of gay improvisations that forced the pace. It was they who rigged up the modern look of Australia. The criticism of them is that their attitudes, once useful, may now stand in the way of further progress.

The kind of man in his fifties or early sixties who is now on top matured at a time that was so different from the present that his early experience may cripple him in facing new problems. Nevertheless he just goes it alone. He may be unable to see the importance of simple definition, to shape thinking and policy towards the future, to delegate administration, to institute planning, to encourage expertise, to sustain insight, initiative, and teamwork. The job this kind of man is trying to do all by himself is often too big for him. He may not understand the increasing range of possibilities of the technological age and the new shape of business problems: to make the benefits of scientific and technological advance available to the public as quickly as possible. Technology has produced a greater momentum

137

than the Australian concept of entrepreneurship may be able to keep up with.

Despite increasing industrialisation there is an alarming shortage of capable managers, from foremen to managing directors. The whole tone of the country is not one in which capability is much regarded and the processes of training, advancement and selection often proceed on other grounds. The spirit of practicalism has meant a relatively late start in setting up institutions for the training of managers, although interest in management courses is now growing rapidly as the 'Young Turks' of industry prepare themselves for a takeover of responsibility. Perhaps those at the top (some of them are very old) instinctively resist the creation of what might finally prove to be a victorious new social class. The difficulties into which companies get themselves do not always arise from Government stop-and-go policies: they sometimes come from the fact that no one in the top management of a firm has read a book.

*

A case can be made for saying that it does not matter if all Australian industry is foreign-owned, if expenditure on research and development remains low and if manufacturing in Australia continues to be sheltered from external competition. Conditions for ordinary people will remain quite pleasant; they will still be able to cram their houses with the artefads of the age, so why worry? What does it matter where the design for a new windscreen wiper comes from?

In fact Australia was chosen, in a Research and Development debunking discussion in England, as an example of a country for which it may be more economical to lease the fruits of modern research than to think up things for itself; the stock of scientists and engineers is small in Australia (per head of population it is only *half* that of the United Kingdom) and it is suggested that since they are in short supply they are best used in developing other people's research. The first answer to this is that the stock of scientists and engineers should be doubled. It is not only research that is weak in Australia, but development too, and there should surely at least be more spending on *that*. And if the number of scientists and technologists was increased and there were more to go round it is not necessarily always true that it is cheaper to lease ideas from abroad. Naturally, Australian manufacturing does not itself have to think up everything it wants to make, but it is worth remembering, as P. C. Stubbs points out, that licence payments can take from 1 to 5 per cent of the works cost of production of consumer goods. In a paper at the 1965 A.N.Z.A.S. Conference, Stubbs estimated that a manufacturer of consumer durables who spend $600,000 a year on licences and another $100,000 on design translation could, for this money, set up a research and development unit of 38 qualified workers and 65 to 70 assistants. And this would be only a fixed cost – it would not go up with increased sales, as licence payments often do. However, the even stronger case for native research is that Australia is particularly good at doing certain things – mainly in the primary industries – and that further spending on research, and even more on development, may strengthen this process. Its efficient steel industry and its other metal industries could also become stronger if native engineering and design could provide more things for the metal to be made into. The resources of its coal industry could be converted into economic enterprise with good research and development. This is not likely to happen while Australia continues to produce such a proportionately small number of graduates with higher degrees in science and engineering, the smallest proportion of such graduates among the prosperous nations, (20 per million in Australia, 50 per million in Britain, 388 per million in the United States.) It is difficult to see how, as technology proceeds, Australia will be able to maintain its position even in the things it is good at, without spending more money on native talent; or even how it will be able to follow out the instructions it receives from overseas.

The social effects of Australia's economic derivativeness may be even more important. It is likely to lead to a stupid society, a childish society that is self-confident with the familiar and uneasy with the unfamiliar, not capable of reacting to danger or making its own decisions. In such a highly commercialist society as Australia, in which commercialist standards permeate many other areas of power and decision-making the fact that commercial success can be gained with such small inventive talents is likely to stupefy original decision-making and thinking in general. Australians do not suffer from the old colonial belief that you do not have to work for prosperity but they do tend to believe that no one has to think for prosperity and this is likely to affect their attitudes to those many matters that cannot be decided for them overseas. If Australia were Idaho, it would not affect its future no matter how stupid it was. But it is thousands of miles from Idaho.

## Open spaces

Markets are declining for some of Australia's rural industries. After the boom caused by the Korean War the terms of trade went against Australia (in general profile they have been going against Australia for fifty years) and by the beginning of the sixties wool was threatened by synthetics, wheat by a world glut, and fruit and dairy products by the Common Market.

In advanced countries food production was constantly improving so that Australian foodstuff producers were becoming increasingly worried; Australia produced more and more food, when, as a result of its wars, the paying world was hungry but those who could pay for food were now growing much more of it themselves; the U.S.A., Western Europe (as a whole) and the advanced Commonwealth countries all had certain kinds of food surpluses; and the size of these surpluses was likely to increase; except for meat, Australia's position as a food supplier to the more prosperous parts of the world seemed in danger.

What is worrying for Australia is that the main decisions about the future of world trade in foodstuffs are largely political matters – matters of international commodity agreement, of unpredictable decisions by the controlled economies (principally communist), of equally unpredictable political decisions within other countries (such as the desire to subsidise French farmers or the American quota arrangements) and the flukes of world politics (for example, Cuban sugar). The best Australia can do is to hope that the bottom does not drop out of all the foodstuff markets at once and to encourage shifts in food production where they are possible. One rather cynical solution that has been suggested is such an increase in population, accompanied by further industrialisation to reduce imports, that Australia can eat its own food surpluses.

The other principal export – wool – would seem to have a more predictable future, yet what one might describe as the moral certainties of this $7,000 million industry have withered with the development of synthetics. For most of Australia's history wool producers looked at the future with long term assuredness, although there were many short term worries. Wool dominated Australian exports and Australian wool dominated the world's fine wool markets. Merino rams were a symbol of national prosperity and even of national integrity. Several generations of Australians were taught to venerate not lions or eagles or other aggressive symbols of nationalism; they were taught to venerate sheep. The 'squatters' whose predecessors drove off into the bush with a couple of horses, some flour and sugar, a bullock dray, a flock of sheep, and a dog, and built their fortunes from simple bark huts, lived in style and dominated much Australian life. Their empires are now subdivided.

There may be a fake scare about wool markets. If someone engaged in protein research stumbles on a way to manufacture regenerated wool fibres, wool may be done for. Presumably this will happen some day but at present, although the production of synthetic fibres now exceeds world wool production and the price of synthetics is going down it is also true that world demand for wool increases as industrial efficiency and living standards rise. The preponderance of synthetics increases, but so does the demand for blended fabrics, part synthetic, part wool, so the total demand for wool increases, even if wool occupies a smaller position in the total textile market. Australian woolgrowers should spend more on marketing and research; they should certainly pay attention to the quality of wool and standards of classing, both of which are declining; but their greatest problem is not in selling wool, but in making money out of it; that in a protected economy their costs continue to go up but they can't recoup them on the world market. There still seems to be a market for wool but it is becoming less and less profitable to grow wool. Failing wool farmers may switch to meat. Over a ten year period Australian graziers grew almost a third more wool but the price they got remained much the same and production costs increased by about a quarter. Since there was considerable inflation over this period this means that as a whole producers made less real profit although they produced more. The position has been made worse by the encouragement of subdivision. Where there was once one station there may sometimes now be as many as twelve, each carrying overheads almost as great as the original station carried.

It is just possible that overseas investors may move into the wool industry and rationalize it. Since the production of fine merino wools has been one of Australia's really significant world innovations such as an occurrence would be a considerable humiliation.

Research in the pastoral and agricultural industries is one field of research to which Australians attach importance and in which standards are of world class. However there is not enough of it. Problems queue up for the research scientists who are very good, but if there were more of them they could get more done. This is one field of specialist research where Australia makes regular contributions to world knowledge. If programmes were more lavish, specialists might be attracted from all over the world to Australia.

There should also be much more second grade research

into problems of farm management, much of it carried out in local districts. The State Agriculture Departments are under-staffed; there are not enough Agricultural Colleges; there is not enough local extension work; and not enough men on the land have received the kind of technical training that lets them apply the benefits of research quickly and intelligently. Despite the excellence of scientific work there is still some resistance to new methods, both among wealthier property holders whose lack of training or feeling of social position can sometimes impede their acceptance of the merely expert, and among less successful farmers whose lack of education and capital make research meaningless. In the dairy industry the labour force might be cut by something approaching half if all the scientific knowledge now available were used and if the far too many small holdings were rationalized.

Although about one-third of Australia lies in the tropics, little more than three per cent of Australians live there. There is one school of thought that holds that this does not matter: it is argued that investment of scarce capital and manpower in other parts of Australia would bring greater development than equivalent investment in the North; that expensive price support schemes would be necessary for northern development; that it is doubtful if there are markets for the things that might be produced in the North; that countries already producing these things are becoming more efficient at it; that real diversification of growth is unlikely in the North; that investment in tourism (Come and See the Empty Spaces) might be the most economic investment; that the reason the North is undeveloped is due to fundamental economic forces, not political neglect – it is not worth developing.

Some of these arguments have already been pushed aside by the discoveries of iron ore, bauxite, silver, zinc, lead, copper, and uranium: willy nilly this has caused development of isolated frontier settlements, based mainly on the investment of overseas capital, with Australian governments providing some of the infrastructure. Raising cattle seems a 'natural' industry for the North, now made more economic by the low costs of road trains. There are other pressures for developmental schemes to increase the cultivation of rice, cotton, peanuts, tobacco, linseed, safflower, cattle fodder. Development schemes now operate, but there is no coherence in them, nothing as imaginative as the National Reclamation Act passed by the American Congress in 1902, of which it has been said, because of the subsequent successful development of the seventeen 'irrigation states' of the American West, that it had an effect on America 'as great as the Civil War, the development of the railroads or the coming of the aeroplane.' Migration has not been keyed to the potentials of the North; the construction of beef roads has been slow. According to engineers from France-Technique there is an enormous potential for electricity production from the large rise and fall of the tides on the Kimberley coast – 'something of the order of several 10,000 million kilowatt hours per annum of continuous economic power.' (Present output of Western Australia is about 1,000 million kilowatt hours.) Schemes like this have their season.

Those who argue against development in the North base their case on purely economic calculation. However it seems morally wrong to Australians – when they think about it – that so few people live in the North and that its resources are largely unused. There is anxiety that Australia will not really have staked its claim to the 'continent' until it does something about the North; that the neglect of the North causes hostility in Asia. What is needed is a form of development that will add to Australian production, not merely duplicate at great expense what is already being done. Then an enormous amount of planning would be needed to co-ordinate migration, business plans, rural development and service industries. What Australians will not face is that if the North is to be populated it needs more than new crops to grow, more cattle to breed and more minerals to dig out of the earth. It needs more than the development of primary industry. It demands big new towns and *cities*. That is the only way to ensure a massive increase in population. 'The development of the North' really amounts to creating the second half of the nation.

## The unions

If the ambitions of an ordinary Australian union member begin to prickle what can he do? (Assume that he's not an 'extremist' or even particularly able: just an ordinary 'moderate' who would like to be a union official.) He must first learn how to talk about union business at union meetings and the more low-level and matey he can get, the better he may be trusted. He can talk about dirty lavatories, dismal lunch rooms, hot water that runs cold. He should keep a look-out for members of other unions trying to do jobs men in his union consider their right. He might pick up a working knowledge of the political slogans that are the fashion in his union, not too far ahead, not too far behind, not too 'right', not too 'left'. He will have joined his local Labor Party branch.

To become an Organizer he now has to get the votes. If he can gain the favour of the men who run his union they may do this for him. If he is a 'rebel' he may allow himself to be talked over. If he can get any support on the side from the communists he might use it. Once he is an Organizer he has to learn how to talk to managements – without much knowledge of industrial law or the conditions of the industry, or indeed of anything. If he is any good, he will learn, but it might be hard going because there's nobody to teach him. He may rely on Government inspectors and the Industrial Commissions to prop him up and do much of his work; and on intrigue to keep his position. He becomes a kind of policeman, ensuring that shops keep to awards: if he makes enough threats the employer will give in, or the matter will go to one of the Commissions. All his life he will have to keep his sails trimmed to the wind, as he follows the politics of his union. If he becomes Secretary he might gradually lose interest in union affairs, perhaps drink too much beer, and emphasize his reforming mission by dressing more untidily than his members. He might become more interested in the Labor Party Executive in his State than in his union, and get some feeling of power and purpose from this. If he's lucky someone might give him a trip to Russia or America.

This may seem a caricature. There are dedicated men in the union movement, many competent men, a few brilliant men, but the kind of man just pictured also survives, petty and conservative, and not very good at his job.

After New Zealand, Australia has had the highest union membership rate of any democracy; Australian wage earners enjoyed more paid leisure earlier than in other countries. Yet despite this most Australian unionists are normally indifferent to their unions, and do not participate to a great extent in their affairs. Hardly any attend union meetings (although job meetings are better attended), less than half vote in union elections (sometimes much less) and they are often slow in paying union dues. The greatest enthusiasm is often aroused for some 'unofficial' strike or protest when men in a shop take action without consulting the union, or in defiance of it; this kind of action can still have some meaning for them. But often the very men who are indifferent to unions may go home to their suburbs, change their clothes and play a strenuous organizational part in local clubs. Their indifference may be partly a protest against the irrelevance of union ideologies to the life Australians now lead. The unions play little part in the things modern Australians are really interested in – getting homes, raising their children, going on holidays.

Organizationally most unions are weak and amateurish. There are too many small unions trying to operate all over Australia; unions with less than 2,000 members may have to sustain six state officers and a federal office. Payment to officials is stingy and in any except the biggest unions the maintenance of expert, sizeable staffs is not possible. Many of the able men are hamstrung by the inadequacy of union resources. Too often an able but overworked secretary must muddle through the best he can, without the assistance of the kind of experts that are at the disposal of the employer and the Governments. He may spend most of his time just running the office, answering letters, preparing for meetings, submitting reports, keeping the books. Unions where the state branches are stronger than the federal executive may duplicate all the overheads that might be better centred in the executive. There is no training programme for union officials. A dislike of education and expertise ravages the union movement. Its officials are often isolated from the main forces operating in the community and out of touch with the thinking of their own members. Many of them scorn the intellectuals who would be ready to help them. They may be indifferent to the apathy of their members, uninterested in trying to fabricate some meaningful rank and file participation in the union, even by the airing of grievances. In fact many of them like their union rank and file to be apathetic. There is no 'interference' from members and no trouble in arranging re-election in an apathetic union.

If anything the calibre of union officials has declined. In the more exciting days of union history, gaining a union position was one of the few ways in which a talented young underdog could pull himself up; now he can get a university scholarship and become a professional man, or enter a business firm or a government department. And the inducement to sacrifice is less, except to the politically inspired; there is no longer a desperate situation of wage earners to which a man could feel that he could devote his life.

What keeps the show going sufficiently well to give a sense of achievement to unionists is a mixture of Arbitration and Conciliation Tribunals and occasional intervention by State Governments. This highly complex and legalistic mess is unpredictable. There are both State and Federal Arbitration and Conciliation Tribunals. The Federal Tribunal usually points the way but State governments can legislate directly. The New South Wales Labor Government had several times produced industrial legislation on the working week, annual leave and long service leave that forced the issue throughout the rest of Australia. This muddle means that a whole section of economic planning in Australia is all over the place.

And the Federal Arbitration Tribunal, said to hold more power over the conduct of industry than any other instrumentality, is simply a body of judges who make their decisions irrespective of other government policy, and are not expert in their field. In 1961 this quasi-legal, *de facto* planning authority declared: 'We are not national economic policy makers or planners.' It has no economic intelligence unit to guide it. It settles big economic questions piecemeal. There will not necessarily be any economic coherence in its three judgements. It is sometimes suggested that the only consistency to be found in the tribunal's findings is a desire to conciliate parties sufficiently to preserve the arbitration system.

Proceedings are conducted in a legalistic manner that often keeps away expert witnesses; outrageous claims are made by parties. (In the 1964 basic wage hearing the unions asked for an extra $5.20 a week and the employers offered 60c.) 'Each party to a case will endeavour to prove that expert witnesses called by the other party are incompetents, liars and cheats.' There is little discussion or probing by the judges of the expert submissions. There is some reference to sacred texts (including articles planted by either side in economic journals) and there are references to productivity that are as expert as references to astrology charts. It is almost as if a medieval ecclesiastical court took over the economic planning of Australia.

Other countries also get themselves into a mess with the regulation of wages and conditions of labour but they usually do not set up quite so many institutions to do it. There seems to be a belief in Australia that if an administrative process is wrapped up in sufficient legal trappings it will somehow or other provide a 'fair go'. The 'fair go' is as arbitrary as any other method of decision but the rhetoric associated with it suggests otherwise. Both employers and employees are cynical about this system. Collective agreements might produce more realism in bargaining and produce more good faith over settlements by both parties but to be effective they would have to be accompanied by an improvement in the calibre of union officials.

The whole system may be nearing breaking point now that an increasing number of professional groups are also using it. It is hard to pretend that there are standards by which a quasi-legal tribunal can judge what a professional engineer or a professor of Latin is 'worth', but tribunals have attempted the task, and thereby strengthened the wage spiral. When professional men in government departments are given big increases they may receive more than the heads of their departments; if the heads are given a rise the Ministers and politicians might get a rise, too. If this happens the rest of the community puts in for another rise. If the politicians can get away with it, so can they. Everybody has his fair go in turn. A real attempt by the professional and white collar associations to use all the blue collar union tactics in the arbitration system may finally wreck the system. Nowhere else in the world is there a wages system of such automatic compensation. As soon as one group get a rise every other group puts in for one. Now that men who may get rises of $2,000 a year have joined the system they may reduce it to absurdity.

There are a number of things that unions could be doing in Australia that most of them ignore. They do not usually consider providing the general social benefits for their members that are often provided by American unions; there is little discussion on joint consultation in industry, in providing experimental beginnings for the introduction of democracy in the field of life where people spend so much of their time; there is no employment policy; and only a rhetorical concern with productivity. There is something of a hoax in some of the successes that are obtained. The wage rises are sometimes illusory, when costs also go up. What unionists really want is higher purchasing power. They want this even more than increased leisure. There are already a few small awards where employers have agreed to pay a bonus week's wage in lieu of an extra week's holiday. And men of thirty who find themselves qualifying for three months long service leave would often sooner have the money.

The conservative clinging to old-fashioned small craft unions litters industry with all kinds of restrictive practices and weakens union strength by involving unions in a great number of demarcation disputes and much bitterness. Despite its proliferation and its success one of the remarkable things about the Australian union movement is its institutional weakness. Employers band together on an industrial basis; unions attempt to do so, but their effort is much less convincing. The Australian Council of Trade Unions, bargaining body for the blue collar unions (including the 180,000 strong Australian Workers' Union, which joined in the 1960s) runs on the cheap. Its officials are badly paid – and there are only four of them anyway – to handle the affairs of about a million members. Its annual income is little more than $40,000. Its power over member unions is purely diplomatic, sometimes strong, sometimes weak. In States where there is a Labor Government union leaders, through their control of the party machine, can force concessions for their members in provisions for leave, workers' compensation and factory standards. This is their greatest single strength. The rest of their gains come more from the system than from union brilliance or even strength.

To understand the Australian union movement one must recognize the importance of communists in it. The Communist Party of Australia is little more than 3,000 strong and its membership has been declining; it is a highly factionalist party, often consumed with internal struggles in which ideology and policy are thrown up as symptoms of the power struggle; it has built-in tensions between the various States and between its few intellectuals and its union activists; its voting figures in State and Federal elections are less than one per cent; its doctrines are usually so out of touch

with the wishes and attitudes of ordinary Australians as to
appear ludicrous; its adventurism occasionally throws it
completely off balance; there are some able men in it but
much of its membership is of very indifferent quality,
merely sustained by the changing certainties of party lines;
it has split into pro-Peking and pro-Moscow parties. Yet it
is a force in Australia because of its penetration of the union
movement and its subsequent influence over parts of the
Labor Party.

It shows considerable organizational skill (it has a bigger
staff than all the political parties put together) and some
communist union officials have earned their position through
efficiency. But it is not mainly through its own strength
that it has achieved success – despite its unscrupulousness
if it were faced with strong opposition it would be obliter-
ated – but through weaknesses in the situation in which it
exists. The apathy of union members, the growing gap
between rank and file and leadership, the obsolescence of
much union ideology and old-fashioned emotional 'left-
ism', the laziness and worthlessness of some union officials
(who stay in power with communist organizational support
– for a price) ... factors like these allow communist success.

In the A.C.T.U. communists have sometimes controlled
up to a third of the voting and they have sometimes controlled the voting of the 'moderates'. With their strength
they could influence the Executive and at Congress provide
most of the activity. At the 1959 Congress altogether 222
resolutions were on the agenda; they came from only thirty
affiliated unions and, of these thirty, eight were communist
controlled, and twelve were communist influenced. The
resolutions were along the same lines as those taken by the
Party in the preceding months.

The kind of atmosphere engendered by such a situation
was nicely brought out in the issue of the levies for overseas
'trips' that shook the Australian union movement. Albert
Monk, then president of the A.C.T.U., and as experienced
a survivor as Sir Robert Menzies, had established himself
as a go-between with the Menzies Government and as

part of his system of patronage he dispensed free overseas trips. The Russian, Chinese and American governments also dispensed trips. In 1956 when the idea of sending two Australians to China was raised at an A.C.T.U. Executive meeting it met opposition; but when the delegation was increased to five the idea was accepted. After that almost the whole Executive had a free trip to Russia, China or both. Monk himself went on more than fifty overseas trips. When the A.C.T.U. decided on a compulsory levy to finance reciprocal visits between Australia and communist countries the explicitly anti-communist unions revolted, and in 1961, seventeen of them, including the powerful Ironworkers' and Clerks' Unions, and the Australian Society of Engineers, were excluded from the A.C.T.U. Congress because they refused to be levied. The communists played it quietly; if the A.C.T.U. was wrecked they would lose the main 'mass organization' they could influence; a compromise was effected. This dispute was the principal concern of the union movement for several years.

The communist penetration of unions helps make reform of the Australian union movement more difficult. The communists are 'activists' in the unions. They often set the pace of action and the tone of rhetoric. The effect of this is to give a nineteenth-century flavour to union affairs that does not help in the task of re-defining the responsibilities of unions to their members. Far too much of the time of the ablest men is taken up fighting communists. And by the process in which communists and Labor Party men share the fruits of office in a particular union, some Labor Party union officials become captives of the communists and do their work for them.

# 7. MEN IN POWER

## *Who runs Australia?*

THERE is no evidence that there exists in Australia a small
clique of people – certainly not a whole 'class' of people –
who 'run' the place. When applied to a society such as
Australia in which there are so many conflicting areas of
power (and where so many of the areas of power are in any
case further fragmented into State areas of power) tight
conspiracy theories of society can be demonstrated to be
untrue. A lot of the people who make decisions in Australia
just never meet each other.

At the heart of affairs there are always uncertainties,
muddles, misunderstandings; people who sit in the seats of
power create patterns that attempt to give coherence to the
mysteries and absurdities of their own decisions; they try to
hide their confusion from other people – and from themselves. They emanate around themselves an aura that suggests that they know what they are doing. And those who
are not at the heart of affairs are also likely to create
illusions of decision (of good or evil decision, according to
taste), a mirage of rationality that makes events shine with
more sense and cohesion than events ever possess.

These mysterious processes are not a great feature of
Australian society. Many Australians see life as a muddle –
or at least a lottery – and, since the spreading of mass
consumption, they have seemed less and less inclined to see
life as a grand conspiracy, although some of the socialists
maintain this belief. They have become indifferent to how
it all works: the results seem good enough so they let it go
at that. A minority still seek conspiracies. And of course
there are conspiracies but the usual mistake is to confuse
a lot of different conspiracies with a grand conspiracy.
There are powerful Australians who devise and connive

and exert power conspiratorially; some of them know each other and many even work in together. There have been some memorable wire pullers and standover men. But as a whole it doesn't add up. It's just individuals or groups powerfully tugging here and there. The strong divisions of interest between the States, the fragmentation of Australian social life and the religious differences have so far made grand conspiracy impossible. To suggest that in Australian society there is a self-perpetuating and ideologically cohesive class that monopolizes privilege is simply ridiculous.

What one does witness in Australia is what Hugo Wolfsohn described in an article in *Dissent* as 'the institutionalization of mediocrity'. The established rhetoricians and ideology makers of Australia, whose conservative values are 'largely a third-rate imitation of the paternalistic postures of the nineteenth-century British upper class', often still set the tone for public occasions to such an extent that even public men who do not believe it sometimes feel bound to repeat this Establishment line. It is this obsolescence of public rhetoric that still holds Australia in its power, spellbound in boredom, rather than any calculating conspiracy, and one does not yet see what will replace it.

## From America – Federalism

Australia did not 'earn' nationhood by struggle against the oppressor or civil war. It could have become a nation earlier than it did, if it had wanted to. At the end of the 19th Century there was a desultory debate for 20 years as the six separate Colonies began to talk about federating. Finally there was a referendum. Sixty per cent of Australians voted in it; altogether 43 per cent of all electors voted 'yes' and on January 1 1901, by Act of the British Parliament and 'to the permanent glory of the British Empire' a federation of States on American lines was set up, with a weak central government and a strong tradition of independence among the States. Many people still living were born into an Australia where there were customs ports on the State borders and which, according to its official texts, did not achieve full status as a nation until April 25 1915, when the Australian soldiers assisted in the Gallipoli landing by storming Anzac Cove. It was as if the whole process of achieving nationhood was so easy that it was not until men died – if quite irrelevantly, and in a minor and unsuccessful campaign – that Australians felt they had earned their way into the world. This is one of the several reasons why the Anzac legend has been such an important element of belief among 20th Century Australians.

Although Australia took its federal structure from the U.S.A., with a House of Representatives and a Senate, and a federal court that interpreted a written constitution, the six Colonies had already taken from Britain the system of parliamentary government and the workings of the federal court have been different. Australia's nation-building was not marked by that 18th Century concern for the rights of man that is entrenched in the American Constitution. Perhaps some of the rights of man flourish more in Australia than in the U.S.A. but the rhetoric of natural rights in Australia has been weaker (Australia has been more concerned with the rhetoric of democracy than of natural rights) and there are no liberal guarantees written into its Constitution. Because the Australian Constitution is a terse and extraordinary uninteresting document that does not hold any great truths to be self-evident, its High Court has not been able to play the same role as the American Supreme Court. The only clause that really allows a great deal of interpretative work is Section 92, which guarantees free trade between the States.

Regional interests and loyalties are even stronger among Australians than among Americans – in that in social life they exist almost without challenge. Canberra is a poor thing compared with Washington and there is no great metropolis like New York that sets many of the nation's vogues. There is no generally acknowledged central city in Australia where the important things are believed to happen and it seems better to be. Not only – in certain senses – is

Australia a province of two external powers. It is itself made up of six provinces that do not between them acknowledge that one metropolis is somehow more important than the others. There are few national matters in Australia; the way Australians see Australia is largely the way they see their own States. State differences and State conflicts run through almost every national institution – the political parties (even the Communist Party), the trade unions, the big pressure groups, the Churches, and private firms. As in the U.S.A., it is not possible to understand national politics in Australia without knowing something of the differences in style between the State political parties and where the different pressure spots lie. During the long period of disunity that the Labor Party has suffered, only a knowledge of the controlling factions in each State can make sense of a process that seems otherwise to be merely a perverse neglect of P.R. and 'image'. Small regional party machines have stronger power than in the U.S.A.; unlike the American party Conventions, where the population of a State governs its number of votes in the Convention, in the Labor Party the smallest State has the same number of votes as the biggest at a Federal Conference. In national Cabinet-making in Canberra each State must be represented in almost exact proportion, sometimes making the choice of dunderheads quite unavoidable.

It is obvious enough that the central government has grown enormously in power and importance since 1901, with much less constitutional change than might have seemed necessary. However residual State powers still hold up national planning. Or they might do so. This question has not been put to the test for some years because not much national planning has gone on. Perhaps more could be squeezed out of the present set-up than is attempted. In 1959 there was joint party agreement that the central government needed stronger powers to engage in adequate economic planning; but the Government did not choose to take up this option and put the matter to a test at a referendum. The question of Federal powers generated much heat in the more ideologically inclined 1940s but the heat has gradually gone out of it since a referendum asking for 14 more powers was lost in 1944. There are still Unificationists and State Righters, but with a Government that does not want to do more than it is doing, their weapons have grown rusty. One fears that if they are ever needed again – on both sides – they will prove to be dangerously old models.

Frustrated though they are by Commonwealth control of taxation and loan-raising (and loan-spending), the State Governments are nevertheless the single most important pressure groups in Australia. State issues (particularly regional questions of employment) may decide Federal elections and at every Premiers' Conference and Loan Council Meeting the Prime Minister sees not only State Ministers and their officials but the people of Australia, cut six ways and intensely regionalised in their economic interests. In a book this size, State politics are indescribable. Each State party has its own style and problems. There is one characteristic however, once they gain office, that they all share: they tend to hold on to power by re-arranging constituency boundaries strongly enough in their own favour to sustain any but the biggest swings in voting. Sometimes an entrenched State government is unseated not by voting, but by party schisms.

The six State Governments hold many powers that immediately and obviously influence the ordinary Australian's life – the education activities of his children, control over the criminal code, control over traffic, shopping, leisure activities, decisions on all kinds of urban and rural development and many of the other most significant matters in day-to-day living. And since local government is weak in Australia, the State Governments also set the tone for most of the activity in Australia's 1,000 or so local government units. (Local government in Australia was largely invented by the States at the beginning of this century: the States forced a weak version of it on to a people who still seem largely indifferent to the idea of local independence.) What is supposed to happen to the State Governments – at present blessed with many powers, but not with the power to raise their own money – is one of those questions that might finally be taken up again in Australia some day.

## From Britain – Parliaments

It is hard to escape the conclusion that in Australia Parliaments are now mainly of ritualistic significance and that the significance of the peculiarly parliamentary part of Australian democracy is quite slight. A political leader achieves leadership through his party and normally he then uses his position and power of patronage to dominate, or attempt to dominate his party machine; and rebels work through *the party machine* to try to affect the policies of the leaders. In this power situation Parliaments are subsidiary; it is through the *parties* that political changes are effected – if they are effected at all.

Power within the parties is not gained by any significant appeal to mass membership. There isn't a mass membership. Party branches are small and, with exceptions, moribund. Power within a party is usually gained by secret contrivance and manipulation. Except in the sense that the rival party machines have to submit themselves to regular Parliamentary elections the idea that Parliament represents the people is simply one of the fictions of Australian public life – as is the idea that Parliaments have any particular relation beyond a ceremonial one to the administration of the Commonwealth and the States. All that happens is that the people have a veto; they can keep one of the party machines out of office – at the cost of putting the other party machine into power. And when a party gains power it uses its Parliament as its legislative and propaganda instrument.

The checks on an Executive's arbitrariness are mainly non-parliamentary (although considerable): there are checks within the party machine itself, there are checks from pressure groups, there are the checks of publicity and exposure (here Parliaments are of some significance, but of perhaps less significance than the Press), the checks of regular elections, the checks of the Constitution and of conventional standards of behaviour. There is no lack of checks on Australian governments – although a better informed and more active legislative body such as the American Congress might provide greater checks because of its ability to acquire information through committees and then act on the information. What seems to be almost altogether lacking in Australia is a channel for the invigoration of the political parties. The political structure tends to ossify.

Parliaments are all but useless for the invigoration of the parties. With one of the party machines in control of Parliament and with the Executive in control of the party machine there is no prospect of Parliament – as Parliament – having any effect on administration, unless – as sometimes happens – a rival party machine controls one of the Upper Houses. But again this is not a parliamentary check – it is a party machine check.

The sheer dreariness of parliamentary life – its lack of political meaning and its old-fashioned rituals – repel many of the kind of people who might make good members of an Executive and also the kind of people who like to acquire information and to probe into the processes of government (and would make good parliamentarians). An able man in the prime of life is not usually prepared to make the sacrifice of listening day after day to speech after speech of almost complete drivel. The friction that Parliaments are hotly debating whether they will pass a Bill, as if they were still made up of eighteenth century squires, combined with the demands of party discipline and the general poverty of parliamentary candidates have produced a banality in 'debate' that is of world class. It is doubtful if there are any parliaments anywhere in the world where the standard of speaking is lower than it is in the Parliaments of Australia.

Apart from the windbags who get a sense of relief from opening and shutting their mouths life can assume useful meaning for an Australian M.P. only in his constituency.

Here he performs a useful if rather menial job of getting telephones, or jobs, or pensions for constituents, and, in general, trying to pull strings in government departments. Sometimes he corrects an injustice; more often – by gaining a privilege for a constituent – he may create an injustice for others.

There is one simple fundamental weakness in the Australian Parliaments: they haven't got enough to do. And there is a fundamental weakness in the system of providing an Executive from the ranks of the parliamentarians: most of them are not good executives. The kind of man who is prepared to sit through years of boring ritual in parliamentary sessions before he is rewarded with power in Executive office is not likely to be a good political leader. And the kind of man who is likely to be a good leader finds it impossible to break through quickly into public office – so he doesn't try.

There is still some current of discussion in Australia about constitutional reform but most of it is concerned with the relations of the Commonwealth to the States. Hardly anyone discusses radical reform of the parliamentary system. Assuming that at some time or other in the future Australia must declare itself a republic one can at least hope that by then there will also be some debate both on how it can be governed better and how it can use its Parliaments more democratically. The American system of Presidential government is one that might be considered.

An Australian Prime Minister who gets firmly in the saddle and can manipulate his party has a kind of power an American President lacks; he has the legislative machine completely in his grip. (Although he does not have the same powers of patronage.) The main difference is that in theory an Australian Prime Minister is in the control of his parliamentary party but in practice this is not always so and in any case it is arguable if this is an advantage to anyone except the factions struggling for power within a party. It might be of advantage if he were appointed to office as an American President is and told to assemble a team of men to run the government. This would take him out of the control of his parliamentary party but it could place him – to some extent anyway – within the control of a Parliament that had the duty to inform itself on all public issues, legislate on some of them and act as a conscience.

There are no ideal 'solutions' in politics and this one has dangers too: but it would allow breakthroughs into political life and an invigoration of administration by the appointment of good administrators from outside Parliament to the Executive; and it would allow Parliament to play a much stronger democratic role than it can possibly play when it is so tied up with the Executive. Imagine the effect on government in Australia if the Chief Executive could choose able administrators from all over the country to act as Cabinet Ministers and if Parliament were able to examine in detail what the Executive was doing and begin to exercise its now fictional legislative powers.

One of the difficulties of political life in Australia is that the processes of policy-making tend to gum up. A leader more or less controls both his parliamentary party and the bureaucracy and that's that. Political systems need ways of recognizing what issues there should be decisions about and ways of formulating alternative decisions but this process moves slowly in Australia – and often it does not move at all. If new Executives could move into office with a President this might galvanize the Canberra bureaucracy by introducing it, as it were, to some of the men who knew what was happening out there in Australia, and if Parliament had something to do this might draw attention to the kind of things governments should be concerned with.

## Australia's four-party system: The struggle for the Labour Movement

Australia does not have a two-party system. At times of Labor Party unity it has a three-party system. At times of Labor Party schism (in the 1930s, and again since 1955) it has a four-party system, with two Labor Parties. The other two parties – now the Liberal and Country Parties – normally form partnerships but sometimes the tensions between them make this impossible.

The schismatic character of the Labor Party has proved to be one of its significant characteristics. It has suffered four main explosions. In two of them there was a parliamentary split in which Labor leaders joined a hastily renamed conservative party, and led it; in the other two explosions separate parties were formed out of some of the fragments thrown out by the explosion.

The normal state of the Labor Party has been one of schism, or impending schism, for a complex of reasons. One of these comes from the kind of tension that is also found in the British Labour Party: a fundamentalism about maintaining principle finds itself in conflict with a desire to compromise and enjoy the challenges of power. The party is not fully 'legitimate', in that it contains elements whose beliefs lie outside the general concensus of values among the people. However it is more in Australian Labor's differences from the British Labour Party than in its similarity that the reasons for its fissiparousness are to be found: the union-domination of the party, its federal structure and the greater importance of both Communist sympathisers and Catholics in it.

The real machine men of the Labor Party are almost all of them union leaders, entrenched in their own State Executives. At some of the State Conferences as many as 85 per cent of the delegates are from the unions. When the prevailing group of union bosses in a State puts up its ticket for the State Executive it knows it will win because it has the numbers. Some non-unionists will be put on the ticket, but they are there by favour of the group of union leaders who run the State branch; 'in the interests of party unity' they may even put on their ticket a few representatives of their opponents; but they all know who runs the branch. This means that six different prevailing cabals of union leaders run each of the six State branches. The natural tendency of these powerful union groups is to try to discipline the parliamentary party in each State. Their main interest may not be that the Party should engage in the compromises of office but that they, the party's union bosses, should keep their own power in the party machine.

The fact that the Party is organized on strict federal lines, with the real power in each of the States, means that on the Federal Executive (with each State enjoying equal representation) the six cabals get together and if four of them can agree, they try to enforce their policy on the Federal Parliamentary Party (and this will cause tensions within that party): if they cannot agree the party is split. There is no strong central organisation at the Federal Party's separate disposal, to give it strength of its own. Even when a State group wishes to see the Federal party in power it is often so oriented to State politics that it lacks touch on Federal issues.

Catholics have been peculiarly powerful in the party, overall providing at least 50 per cent of its leaders; in some of the State Tammany machines of the past there were sometimes very few Cabinet Ministers who were not Catholics. At the same time Communist influence in the unions (much stronger than in Britain) has added a much stronger communist influence to the party. Unions that are communist-led have 'captive' Labor Party officials who are sent along as delegates to State Conferences and try to form dominant State machines. They are likely to find allies among radical and syndicalist union leaders who, for various motives, prefer to join the Communist-influenced than the Catholics. Often this is the choice.

Perhaps the extraordinary thing about the Australian Labor Party has not been so much that it is so subject to schism as that it has enjoyed periods of effective unity.

The long political success of Sir Robert Menzies can hardly be understood without first considering the multiple civil war that ravaged the Labour Movement during most of the period of his power. With its complicated involvement of Catholics – even to the extent of issues being referred to Rome – this story, even if told very briefly, gives something of the unique flavour of the Australian Labour Movement.

It is not the kind of story that really begins at any particular time (it grows out of Australian history) but if we begin arbitrarily in the mid nineteen forties we see that by 1945 Communists controlled most of the transport, fuel, power, heavy metal and engineering unions, four State Labor Councils and the A.C.T.U. Congress. Earlier they had even captured the New South Wales Labor Party (but they had quickly been expelled). They were about to embark on a policy of political strikes that was later to cause the Labor Federal Government to freeze their funds, gaol some of their leaders, order a raid on their headquarters and smash a coal strike by sending in the troops. This strike policy (as much as 2,000,000 working days lost in a year) was the Australian Communists' contribution to Stalin's policy of armed insurrection in Burma, Malaya, Indo-China, Indonesia and the Philippines. (The Australian Communists could not fight guerilla actions from the hills so they organized strikes on the coalfields.)

To this background of Communist adventurism a Melbourne law graduate, B. A. Santamaria, had persuaded the Catholic bishops to give moral and financial help to a body known informally as 'The Movement', a secret organization which would organize Catholics to fight communism in the unions, in association with anti-Communist union leaders, not all of them Catholics. By 1946 the Labor Party had begun to form Industrial Groups to fight Communists (perhaps at the instigation of 'The Movement'), and 'The Movement' worked with 'The Groups'. The leaders of the Groups were not all Catholic but the mass membership was almost completely Movement-directed. In New South Wales and Victoria the Groups became a 'party within a party'; they raised their own funds; a Group hierarchy corresponded to the Labor Party hierarchy; F. P. McManus and J. F. Kane, the leaders of the Victorian and New South Wales Groups, also became Assistant Secretaries of their State Labor Parties. Not until 1954 was the name Santamaria mentioned in the daily newspapers. The whole manoeuvre was carried out in complete secrecy – a decision that Santamaria himself considered a mistake, because of the extra suspicion it caused.

These tactics helped the Labor Party recapture the Labor Councils, the A.C.T.U. and some important unions. But the Movement became giddy with success; it began to operate outside the Labour Movement and by the early 1950s there was considerable community resentment against what looked like an outburst of Catholic ambition – although few outsiders knew what was really happening.

Within the Labor Party there was also fear that the Groups were running wild. The Groups had begun to operate in non-Communist unions and in Labor Party branches and it looked to some as if sooner or later they would take over the whole show. In particular the Australian Workers Union, a huge influence within the Labor Party, suspected the Groups. And the Movement's attempt to make *all* Catholic Labor men 'toe the line' alienated some of the most powerful figures in the party. For several years one of the Movement's main interests in Victoria seemed to be to strip the Catholic leaders Kennelly and Calwell of party power. There was also opposition from secretaries of non-Communist unions who were concerned for their jobs, from Masons and anti-Catholics, and, of course, from the Communists and the Communist-influenced. In 1951 the South Australian State Executive disbanded the Groups in South Australia. The New South Wales and Victorian Groups – perhaps in a panic – then used their numbers in 1952 to take over their State Executives.

The Groups' political policies, strongly reflecting Movement ideology, now became part of Labor Party debate. Whatever hard-headed empiricism it had displayed in office, to Labor the sudden emergence of so many new policies was an affront to its traditions. Joint consultation in industry, the relating of wages to productivity, incentive payments, decentralization, development of the North, increased migration, closer rural settlement, pro-

Americanism, some anti-Britishism and a strong concern with foreign policy, defence and strategic planning – however admirable some of them were in themselves, policies like these were too much of a mouthful to be swallowed in one go. They required a whole new language in a Labor Party that was largely stuck with an older rhetoric.

However, despite all the tension within the party, the Groups still flourished until 1954, not least because Dr Evatt, the clouded and tragic figure who led the parliamentary Labor Party, was working with the Groupers. He asked Santamaria to help him write his 1954 election policy speech and said he would put Movement men in his Cabinet if he won. When Evatt lost the election (mainly because of astute use of defection to Australia of Petrov, the Russian spy-diplomat) Evatt seemed to lose all sense of balance. He decided that the Groups were among those who were out to 'get' him. According to his private secretary, he was determined to 'get' the Groupers before they got *him*. On 5 October 1954, he made the first of a series of denunciatory attacks on the Movement.

Evatt's attacks released the opposition towards the Movement and the Groupers that had been gathering for several years. All the bitterness and ruthlessness of politics came on to public show. Evatt emerged from his battle of telephone calls, press statements, telegrams, attacks and counter attacks and called on the Federal Executive for support. By seven votes to five* the Federal Executive dissolved the Group-dominated Victorian Executive. The Federal Conference due in Hobart in January was postponed until after a special Victorian conference in February had sacked the Victorian delegates already appointed to the Federal Conference and appointed new delegates who would vote the other way. (To get the kind of conference it wanted the Federal Executive had ruled that delegates to the Victorian conference need not be Labor Party members and that unions disaffiliated from the Labor Party could reaffiliate

* Mr Kim Beazley, a right winger, was overseas. His substitute provided the majority for Evatt.

with no questions asked. Kennelly and other Victorian 'moderates' who had asked for Federal intervention expected that they would dominate the conference but the 'leftists' beat them to it.) The Hobart Conference that followed then disbanded the Groups. A walkout of Grouper politicians in Victoria defeated the Cain Labor Government, and, frightened by this, the Federal Executive moved more cautiously in New South Wales. It later dismissed the Executive, prohibited the holding of that year's State conference and appointed a 'Caretaker Executive' of thirty-two, but included twelve former Groupers. The New South Wales Labor Government survived, but the split vote defeated Labor Governments in Queensland and Western Australia as well as Victoria and defeated Evatt in Federal elections in 1955 and 1958, and Calwell in 1961 and 1963.

This long, dismaying history of chaos and bitterness has produced many versions of what it was all supposed to be about, in which one side judged another's motives by the effects of its actions. However in this kind of warfare once men are engaged in action it is not their motives, but the demands of action that tend to make their decisions for them, and the effects of the decisions are not predictable. The Movement's greatest mistakes seem to have been its excessive secrecy and its hounding of non-Movement Catholics and other anti-communist Labor men who did not belong to the Movement. And its political policies were too precise and rigid; they were an affront to the muddle of politics with its ceaseless shifts, expediencies, and compromise. Brilliants organization went into the Groups; as an anti-Communist operation they were of world class; but as a political manoeuvre they attempted too much in a too doctrinaire way. Of its opponents, the collaborators with the Communists are beneath contempt; the others have often been too cautious or too moved by old hatreds. To clean up the mess a Gaitskell was needed but in the Australian Labor Party it would be hard for a Gaitskell even to win pre-selection. To discuss the Labor Party over this period of disorder without discussing it in terms of its inner power struggle can be completely misleading. (This is why so much nonsense is written about it.) In losing a significant part of its Catholic support the party was fractured.

After the split communists regained control in some unions; 'unity tickets' between A.L.P. men and Communists were revived; the A.C.T.U. developed a Communist-influenced tone; and at successive Party conferences foreign policy resolutions were written into the party platform that, in Asian terms, were of a neutralist kind. A 1930s kind of United Front atmosphere flourished in Victoria and for a time the Victorian Executive seemed to lead the party; their opponents laid low and concentrated on the power they enjoyed in their own States. The party seemed to drift away from prevailing community values. In N.S.W., where a right-wing Labor Party held parliamentary power until 1965, party membership dropped from 37,000 to 20,000. In Victoria it dropped from 28,000 to 5,000. The embittered right wing made several forays; but it was still losing. One of its problems was that the ordinary right winger was used to compromise and 'deals'; the more doctrinaire left wing remained implacable.

All had not been lost of the Movement. The bitter debate within the Catholic Church in Australia was, in 1957, referred to the Commission of Cardinals in Rome. As a result, official connexion between the Church and the Movement was broken; the Movement itself had broken into several fragments, the strongest of which became the National Civic Council, a lay body, with Santamaria as secretary. The Australian bishops were divided into three groups: some supported the National Civic Council; others dissociated themselves from it (although they sometimes kept their own version of the Movement going in their dioceses in opposition to the N.C.C.); others tried to stay neutral. N.C.C. Groups continued to operate, strongly in Victoria, less effectively in other states, and they still controlled some unions. The expelled Labor Party men and those who resigned from the party formed the breakaway

Democratic Labor Party, which began to contest parliamentary elections, leaving the unions to the N.C.C. It was strongest in Victoria but nationally, as a veto party, its voting strength and propaganda were often credited with keeping Menzies in power. The D.L.P. was still dominated by the N.C.C. and the remnants of the Movement. There were some tensions within it between the minority who would have liked to build it into a broadly based political party and the majority who continued to see it as a temporary guerilla operation designed to modify Labor policy, gain re-entry into the Labor Party, and perhaps later gain control of it.

The reality of Labor's Power Men was the arithmetic of party struggle, the manoeuvre of party position. This situation revealed how stupid men can become when they calculate too narrowly. There was no more cynical politician in the world than an Australia Labor 'fixer' out to 'get the numbers' in a party squabble. But in the broader horizons of the Australian people his cynicism and assurance disappeared: he didn't know how to 'get the numbers' in this broader field.

Power within the Labor machine can become a satisfaction in itself; activists are more concerned with keeping their position in the machine than with winning elections. In this way they can enjoy a feeling of importance and exercise power and at the same time preserve their emotional security (their 'integrity') by never testing their 'policies'. The extreme conservatism of some of their spokesmen can make them appear way-out. Thus when a spokesman says that capitalism is an enemy of equal rank to communism, to many younger people he simply appears insane. To them to talk about 'capitalism' and 'communism' is oldies' talk, some word trick.

Whatever the emotional involvement of the minority of the 'leftists' who put the Labor Party out of action, the view of most men in the Labor Party was not 'socialist'. Australia was the country of *socialisme sans doctrine* and probably most (not all) Labor men, if they obtain power, would pay as little attention to the ideologues of 'socialism' as, in power, Menzies paid to the ideologues of 'free enterprise'. It might be that the view of most men in the Labor Party is nothing much at all: they simply want place and power. Under other circumstances this could be a good thing. Skilful opportunists, stimulated by events and fed good ideas, can become great reformers.

After leading his party into its eighth successive defeat, Arthur Calwell retired. His successor, Mr. Gough Whitlam, a generation younger than Calwell, gave some promise for the future. He seemed to understand that not only the Labor Party, but Australia as a whole, needed a psychological reorientation, a new tone and style to make it adaptable in the modern world. The problem was whether he could re-create a party with a sense of legitimacy about it, something that looked like a real alternative government. The fundamentalists were dying off, but it remained to be seen if he could manipulate the leftists off the centre of the stage.

## The four-party system: Tensions of the coalition

The Liberal Party was created by Menzies in the 1940s and had life in it until it – or perhaps Menzies – had grown too used to power. Some of the life it sang with now seems corny – 'hundred per cent freedom of enterprise', 'the socialist is merely a communist without guts' and so forth. But there was more to it than this now unacceptable rhetoric. It was also an expression of an Australian's desire to be left to himself, to enjoy life as he chose to enjoy it, and the feeling that there was nothing wrong with this. It represented a liberation from the post-war puritanism and touches of megalomania of the Labor Party and the confusion of economic planning with mere wartime regulation. In the same way the Labor Party's earlier impetus towards welfare and planning had represented a desire to avoid the dreary horrors of the 1930s and to be more expert and up-to-date. But no new enthusiasm re-oriented the Liberal Party in a contemporary direction. All that was left in the older men were the impossible dreams of 1949 and a sense of betrayal. (If any political outfit keeps up old ideas too long it is bound to have a sense of betrayal: political ideals never work out in detail; they simply point in a direction. If the party changes its direction it necessarily disappoints some of its supporters, although others accept the change.)

Of these ideals the belief in 'free enterprise' remained a principal obsession. As in the way with politics, this was partly obsessive ideology, partly a racket. To the Australian manufacturer 'free enterprise' meant that the government should help him make money without destroying his illusion of control over his firm or – more reasonably – without mucking him about in too much detail. They were really supporters of a partly planned economy in which governments laid down the guide lines and businessmen filled in the details; but few of them recognized this, or admitted it. Considering the notorious lack of enterprise in Australian businessmen, their reliance on overseas innovation and government support, it was a tribute to the power of ideology that their beliefs went so strongly against their economic interests. Perhaps it was part of the guilt of most Australian *élites*: they are not really very good according to the standards they have read about but they have a profound need to believe that they are. However this may be, businessmen try to be a powerful influence in the Liberal Party and their narrowness of view, their mixture of obsolescent ideology and keen self-interest, is one of the things wrong with it. They are interested in very little except their myth of 'free enterprise'.

The entire East-West confrontation, for instance, for some of them seemed to be a matter of the Australian Communists following strike policies; when the Communists went easy on strikes many of the businessmen lost interest. What the party needs is a body such as the Conservative Central Office that is encouraged to work out new images of the times and to keep the party up-to-date, thereby interesting its leaders in the new. This kind of job requires intellectuals and, for reasons that are partly the fault of the Liberal Party and partly of the intellectuals, few intellectuals would now be seen dead inside the Liberal Party. It has to make do mainly with those it attracted ten to fifteen years ago. There is a party apparatus – with more than a hundred paid staff – but many of them are now time servers (there are exceptions) and in any case Menzies's great shadow starved initiative or recognition. The party machine did not matter much under Menzies.

The party has greater active support among young people than the Labor Party. (Some Labor Party branches have no young members.) Its 'Young Liberal' branches are sometimes mainly an excuse for having a good time but some of them show a lively interest in politics that is not evident elsewhere in the party. There are great potential tensions within the Liberal Party between the enthusiastic young and the timid old men, sometimes on policy (the immigration laws are an example), even more fundamentally on style and approaches to life. Young Liberals sometimes have a mildly social-radical flavour: they would like Australia to be more with-it in administrative style; they would like to modernize Australia. Perhaps they represent the 'westernising influence' in Australian politics.

The other party in the Coalition, the Country Party, may be best thought of as the most powerful pressure group within the Government. It can demonstrably control votes more directly than any outside group. It shows a special and at times ruthless skill in bargaining that provided the only continuing, effective opposition to Menzies's domination of policy. Since political parties are normally, above all, concerned with surviving, the Country Party's greatest single interest must be to keep itself alive by maintaining an electoral system that will give a special weight to country votes. In 1963 it put pressure on Menzies to collaborate in something of a gerrymander (his first) to offset the decline in country population by giving extra weight to country votes. A long procrastination in keeping his bargain followed on Menzies's part. Many Liberals would like to eliminate the Country Party.

The Country Party may best be considered as an instrument of personal power and policy. It has had only three leaders since it was founded after the First World War and two of them, Sir Earle Page and John McEwen, have used the party as a means of influencing policy on subjects far beyond the kind of subsidising of farmers and provision of public works that would be expected of a party that purports to represent uniquely the rural interest. Page used his position to change the financial relation between the States and the Commonwealth and the control of the Commonwealth Bank; he pioneered a medical benefits scheme; and introduced other reforms that had nothing specifically to do with rural areas. McEwen ran a general economic policy that conflicted with other parts of Government policy; this was the policy of 'all round protection', in which manufacturing was protected against competition by high tariffs and farmers were then protected against the resultant rise in costs by subsidies. He may have had ambitions to found a Third Party on a national basis, not specifically devoted to the rural interest. He showed considerable skill in attracting business interest, as well as that of the farmers, by building up his Department of Trade into a portmanteau department that took over, in effect, some of the role of economic planning from the Treasury.

## The bureaucracy

The new forms of the bureaucracy of the Federal Government were first thrown together in the Second World War. There was a thin line of officials before then, carrying out what were, before the war, the comparatively small tasks of government, but the need to fight a modern war caused a bureaucratic convulsion. Men were assembled from all over the place and given desks and the strange tasks of wartime official life. Before the war the bureaucracy had been recruited largely from veterans of the first world war; it was a way of giving veterans jobs. The possibility of recruiting university graduates and men of some education had begun to be exploited just before the war. During the war and in the exciting early post-war period when dreams of 'planning' were strong, the educated men took over the bureaucracy. Most of those now in charge, and those immediately under them, represent the first generation of the occupation of Canberra by educated men. These are the men who saw themselves as the answer to the nation's problems: their expertness and intelligence would put everything right. Hard workers and at first dedicated to change, they were determined to introduce standards of expertness and professionalism. They were reformers who were going to show Australia how it should be run. The period of the businessman was to have ended.

They are still efficient and they still work hard but the excitements of the 1940s have now been revised. Things didn't turn out as was intended. Apart from the fact that things rarely do turn out as intended, there were many other reasons for this disappointment. Impetus ran down when the Federal Government failed to get all the powers it wanted for efficient national administration. The change in government from Labor to Menzies took the kick out of some officials. There is a natural tendency for men when they get older – if left to themselves – to think more of their families and the self-importance of their jobs and less of a sense of achievement. Living in Canberra seemed to solidify the old arrogance, but take the practical meaning out of it. There is a lot of make-believe in Canberra and a tendency to look down on the rest of Australia as crude, self-interested, troublesome and ignorant. Only officials are believed to be well informed and capable of expert decision; the rest of Australia is a distant interruption. Men who have lived there for some time admire the development of Canberra (with its sixfold increase in population since before the war), their own increase in knowledge and importance and what they see as their own increase in sophistication; but their isolation prevents them from realizing that there are parallels to this experience in the State capital cities. They tend to think of Australia as it was when they left it. Australia has been developing as well as Canberra, in some ways and in some places more quickly than Canberra. Some officials compare Canberra with an Australia that no longer exists.

The heads of departments gained quite extraordinary power under Menzies and, with a lethargic government little interested in policy-making, the itch to power sometimes extends not in policy but in the display of power within Canberra. There is a dismal lack of experts in Parliament likely to keep officials on their toes; most Ministers remain remote from their departments; and some of the outside 'advisory boards' are stocked with stooges. With government becoming partly the business of maintaining the prestige of departmental heads, relations between departments are worse than usual. At the same time some of the snobberies of Canberra can acquire a fascination – the Canberra club life, the smaller diplomatic parties. Officials may see themselves as important national figures when in truth hardly anyone in Australia has heard of them. (There are probably fewer accepted important figures in Australia now than in earlier periods of its history. Some of the Menzies business knights thought it strange that he should waste so many knighthoods on unknown government officials!)

Perhaps the most deadening of all the characteristics of the present bureaucratic generation is its over-concern with the subtleties of administrative finesse. To the men in Canberra, self-taught in practicality, it seems that they alone are privy to the subtleties of action. The old vigour of the forties is now seen as naïve. Style becomes a thing in itself, divorced from action. But style can be the enemy of originality in policy. The conformism and conservatism of this style may avoid even the simplest of new tasks. For the generation in power in Canberra who had built their careers around Menzies the sense of the 'possible' is very narrow. That which might entail legislation or new administrative patterns is considered to be impractical. The 'possible' tends to mean simply that which can be performed without any change. Usually this is nothing.

In the business of running the economy there is the usual kind of confusion. The Treasury and the Department of Trade and Industry have for some time been in rivalry in attempting to influence Cabinet on major economic policy; the activities of the Departments of Labour, National Development and Immigration also directly affect economic planning; a number of primary producers boards also have differing degrees of responsibility; and the Tariff Board, the Arbitration Commission and the Reserve Bank all make important decisions.

In all this the Treasury is supposed to be central. Its leadership is highly qualified and highly responsible, although there is a gap in competence between the top men and the lower ranks. Its general style is cautious and conventional, Canberra-proud, academic, remote. So far as the national economy is concerned it pays more attention to internal matters such as inflation, credit control, the circulation of money and employment than to trade. Its members do not often meet businessmen and have little feel for practical affairs outside government business. (They are sometimes proud of this.) Above all, the Treasury is for stability.

The style of the Department of Trade and Industry is one of get-up-and-go; there is high morale and a desire to deal with businessmen, and to take on the world. The Department's direct business is with increasing exports relative to imports but through bodies such as its Manufacturing Industries Advisory Committee and the Export Development Council and through its own Industries Division it can state a case on many matters of internal interest. 'Treasury' tends towards indirect fiscal methods; 'Trade' towards direct control. 'Treasury' is academic and Canberra-bound; 'Trade' loves the bustle of practical affairs and keeps its eye on the whole globe. Its staff recruitment is perhaps the most eclectic of any Government Department. Above all, 'Trade' is for development, protection –

and high costs. And therefore an impediment to the policies of the Treasury.

The Department of Labour deals with the A.C.T.U. and seems to take it more seriously, that is to say, agree with it more, than happened with the Chifley Government with its many links with the A.W.U. It is concerned with technical training and acts unofficially as a diplomatic agent between management and unions. The Department of National Development has a good staff and research work, but has languished for many years. As has been already suggested, the Arbitration and Tariff Tribunals make economic decisions according to a logic of their own, without reference to other planning bodies. The Reserve and Commonwealth Trading Banks play a more constructive role. They implement a lot of Treasury policy and thereby become a clearing house of ideas; they have to interpret the Treasury to businessmen and businessmen to the Treasury, to the advantage of both. They provide a useful conservative factor in internal planning: they have to smooth off the sharp edge of policies to make them work. Their very real concern with trade (as well as dealing with exporters and importers they actually keep the books) helps offset the Treasury's selective concern with the internal economy. All of this, combined with a fairly independent position and the fact that they have their own Research Department, perhaps gives them a rounded view of economic problems in the administration and makes them an admirable vehicle for a knowledgeable second opinion on economic policy when one is called for.

It will be seen that there are a number of quite mature agencies for economic planning in Australia, all of which – with the exception of the Arbitration Commission – could be brought together to carry out plans if there were any plans. The overlappings and power-pushings are just part of the nature of things and if they were operating to some more general purpose they might be beneficial. Policy formulation is usually associated with conflicting power blocs. But there is no policy formulation. There seems to be some reason to believe that in economic matters one can be more positive than this: the old idea of the perfect 'plan' is discredited but it seems possible now to get things moving in more or less the same direction. There has been little attempt to do this in Australia. To quote from an article I wrote in the *Bulletin*, attitudes to planning are reminiscent of the Victorian approach to sex: it's all right in its place, but you mustn't become expert at it, or even talk about it.

In foreign policy, there are also conflicts. The Departments of External Affairs, Trade, Immigration, Territories and Defence appear to proceed with little direction from Cabinet as to what they are supposed to be up to as a whole. The External Affairs Department is particularly unfortunate. Although it has had several good Ministers, Menzies – who on the whole seemed rather bored by Asia – intervened, at times with a heavy hand, and no Minister proved able to stay him. The department has no sense of diplomacy as propaganda, although this could be fruitful as an approach in Asia. And there is little successful dramatization of Australia's position in the world to the people of Australia. (The standard of discussion on foreign policy is appallingly naïve.) This failure has been accompanied by a rather narrow professionalism within the department, as if foreign policy were a private expert matter. Like the Treasury, many External Affairs Department officials suffer grievously from their isolation from Australia, made worse in their case by long periods of absence overseas on diplomatic duty. There is a danger of regarding the rest of Australia as a nuisance that interrupts the professional as he goes about his arcane tasks. At the grand level, foreign policy may perhaps be handled best by those who are experts on life, not merely experts on foreign affairs. The expansion of the External Affairs Department under Dr Evatt was so hectic that it is understandable that a more orderly period with a quieter and more predictable approach should follow. But it has gone on far too long; too much attention has been placed on mere professional subtlety. A little of the robustness of a developing country might have sometimes achieved better results. Within the narrower field of professional diplomacy the Department does well – but you can't achieve all that much these days by pure diplomacy.

## The pressure groups

There is corruption in Australian politics but it is not possible to measure it. By the standards of most of the rest of the world (perhaps not those of Britain) politicians in Australia are relatively honest. However in some of the State Governments there have been notorious periods of minor corruption in liquor, gambling, licensing, government contracts and so on. During the war there was minor corruption in the federal administration (some of it the kind of corruption that sometimes helps to get things done). Federal administration is now almost completely free of corruption of the financial kind. Such finaegling as goes on comes more from favouritism or horsetrading but there is more conspiracy and blackmail – even if it is not corruption – than most people imagine. At what stage this becomes respectable enough to describe merely as 'tough pressure group tactics' one cannot say. There are powerful persons who seem to get most of the things they want, but with no other evidence one cannot say more than that.

It is also difficult to differentiate between pressures on politicians and corruption. Some State politicians make extra money by representing special interests but normally Federal politicians react to pressures of a more subtle kind, some of them merely human, some of them part of their business of representing electors. It is usually easy enough to get a politician to take up a question in the House. A great number of questions and speeches are put into politicians' mouths but most of this is simply part of the democratic process. It is impossible to estimate the effect of contributions to the campaign funds of political parties. All parties draw secret revenue from business firms. Many firms contribute to all parties, as an insurance. But whether they get their money's worth is a matter that even many political leaders could not answer. Campaign funds are tightly controlled and very secret.

Short of corruption – and sometimes one has to draw a very fine line to make the distinction – one can say that the operations of pressure groups on governments, parties, and government officials are one of the ways of running Australia as they are in any other country, and that there is not necessarily anything wrong with that. At their most polite their interventions provide the government and the bureaucracies with information about what is going on; they break down some of the isolation of departments and give officials more of a feel for the realities of policy-making. At their most forceful they set up that conflicting play of demands that is one of the features of democracies; governments sort out policies partly in reaction to the pressures that impinge on them; in this mess they look for areas of possible action, not forgetting whatever is left of their own wishes about how things should proceed. However pressure groups are more 'naked' and obvious in Australia than in some countries because Australian politicians are usually particularly inept in rallying political strength to carry out economic or strategic policies that may go against the special interests of some pressure groups but are believed to be in the general interests of national prosperity or sovereignty. Australian politicians tend to become so absorbed in handling pressure groups that they are slow in developing policies in areas where the groups have little or no interest; they just keep things going, with little creative thinking about general problems that are too diffuse to be the business of any particular group.

So far as the big public pressure groups are concerned – those that aim not at personal but at group advantage – it is relatively easy to assess their significance. The supreme test of their power is *votes*.

Although relatively there are not many of them, the wheat farmers dominate enough constituencies for it to be said that the party that holds the wheat seats holds the

Treasury benches. Its lobbyists operate directly, and through the Wheat Board. It was Menzies's refusal to give wheat farmers special treatment during his early wartime Prime Ministership that lost him some support. War or not, they campaigned against him. In the same way, although it contradicted government policy at the time, the early sales by the Wheat Board of wheat to China went through unchallenged; no one would have been game to challenge the wheat farmers. The representatives of dairy farmers are also treated with considerable deference. Politicians are not likely to argue about subsidies to the dairy industry; there may be constituencies to lose that way.

The sugar lobby is a more private matter, since the industry is largely controlled by the Colonial Sugar Refining Company, one of the world's top hundred companies and one of the few big companies in Australia that is Australian owned. The C.S.R. is said to be skilful in sophisticated top level representations but it could be unskilful and crude and still gets its way. Favourable treatment of the sugar industry is built into Australian politics because so much employment in Queensland depends on it and because, like other export industries, it helps the balance of payments.

The wool pressure groups are less successful. Although wool is still Australia's staple export, wool growers do not congregate sufficiently strongly in key electorates for the wool groups to be able to hand over votes. Unless a government went off its head it must pay keen attention to wool; but it is not so concerned with the prosperity of wool growers. Past campaigns to put more money into their own pockets have failed. These were the men who were once one of the most powerful groups in Australia.

Churches are traditionally said to be powerful pressure groups, but their strength, particularly that of the repressive 'wowser' vote, may be exaggerated. There is no doubt that they have influence but their influence may be based mainly on bluff. The fuss they made about gambling and drinking held up reform but on each occasion when State governments edged in more liberal measures they got away with it.

The Catholics do not join in this agitation. Bookmakers and hotelkeepers are often Catholics and to help finance their schools – one of the principal concerns of Catholic administration – Catholic parishes often organize local gambling of a community kind. The Catholics however have had periods when they put pressure on State Governments to increase censorship laws. The technique of the 'carbon campaign' in which activist Catholics write off more or less identical letters of protest has been used in their occasional repressive campaigns. Editors are likely to worry if they receive one letter of protest from a Catholic on a moral issue. Sir Garfield Barwick won an interesting victory in liberalizing the divorce laws; he moved firmly, explained his case expertly and ignored the Catholic opposition.

The Returned Servicemen's League is one of the most skilful pressure groups. With a quarter of a million members and many other non-R.S.L. ex-servicemen, most of whom hope to get something out of the government at some stage of their lives, the R.S.L. speaks to any government in the language of the ballot box. It deals with a sub-committee of ex-service members of Cabinet. It is the only pressure group that has formal access to Cabinet in this way. In fact it has better regular access to Cabinet than the Service chiefs. Its huge influence can only be understood to the background of 'repatriation benefits' in Australia. Under this system if any ex-serviceman develops a chronic disability the onus is on the Government to establish that his condition was not due to war service. Any ex-serviceman who develops tuberculosis, for example, can get a pension no matter how long after his war service he becomes infected. In August 1964 Labor politicians attacked the Government for not accepting cancer as a war complaint when it occurred in ex-servicemen (even forty-six years after their service had finished).

The newspaper managements might be considered as a series of individual pressure groups. Between them the four big newspaper groups control eleven daily newspapers, five Sunday papers, the most important magazines, a number of radio stations and the larger part of the metropolitan TV stations. Unless it is on some matter affecting their industrial interests (and not always then) they rarely speak with one voice; but normally one individual in each major company sees himself possessed of the power to help make or break governments. This belief may be illusory, but he acts as if it is so and often makes close contact with one of the political leaders and sometimes helps in a party campaign. This intervention can come from the usual variety of motives that throws people into politics, ranging from pure policy to pure private gain. The fact that all the major newspaper companies have interests in television stations and that these stations exist on Federal Government licence has introduced a new relation between newspaper managements and governments.

A huge outfit such as the Broken Hill Proprietary heavy industry complex plays such an important part in the prosperity of the nation that its senior officials of necessity develop regular relations with senior officials of government departments. As with the C.S.R., governments pay considerable heed to it, because its activities affect economic prosperity and therefore votes. Lesser firms do not necessarily get such sympathetic hearings.

The Chamber of Manufactures is noisy and aggressive in public and pushes a lot of special barrows in private but it is probably the least influential pressure group with government officials. (The Chamber of Commerce is said to have a more subtle touch with the Departments.) The demands of the Arbitration Court, the Tariff Board and of private restrictive practices also bring manufacturers together in sub-groups. The most publicly temperamental of these is the motor trades group, which declared Menzies its enemy in 1940-1 when he quite sensibly restricted petrol usage because there was a war on, and again in 1960 when he cut back the economic boom. This latter occasion was marked by dramatic sackings and stand-downs that were interpreted as attempts at pressure and by most intensive private lobbying against Menzies culminating in a group of Melbourne businessmen supporting Calwell in the 1961 election. Manufacturers also tried to put pressure on Menzies from within the Liberal Party. It may be of significance that the most desperate major pressure group in Australia is one that is dominated by firms that are overseas owned or overseas controlled.

The influence of unions in the Labor Party machine is of greater significance than the influence of businessmen in the Liberal Party. Union leaders pretty well own the State Labor machines and when Labor Governments are in power in the States the unions put enormous pressure on them. Union influence on the Federal Labor Party is much more diffuse. So few men (only two from each State) are on the Federal Executive or even the biennial federal conferences (six from each State) that normally they simply vote State tickets; they represent the machines of each State. They exercise influence more as party bosses than as union leaders. To add complication, Labor politicians, including party leaders, must also pay attention to the party bosses of their own States as well as to the Federal Executive majority. This means that the policies they must pay attention to may be in conflict.

## What's in it for him?

To those who are used to nations where much political debate is carried on in terms that hide special interest and which usually is concerned with areas of more or less general interest Australia seems a crude kind of place. The crudity was never clearer than in the ugliness of self interested agitation against Menzies during his wartime Prime Ministership. In addition to the quite legitimate criticism of administrative sluggishness and extremely uninspired leadership, special interests conducted agitations of a kind that are rare in wartime. Import restrictions were attacked by importers, petrol restrictions by motor car interests; there were a lot of strikes and the wheat farmers were out for a bigger cut. The kind of intellectual and emotional effort needed to develop a wartime psychology seemed to be beyond Menzies's or the nation's capacity. Some of the outbursts in 1960 and 1961 against efforts to correct the boom also reached a crudity that seemed to suggest that a generation later there was still an inability to smother special interest in politically powerful generalizations. It was true that Menzies was particularly inept at doing this. But it is also perhaps a reflection of the general intellectual and conceptual climate in Australia, and of its parochialism and lack of imagination.

It may be that what really drives most men into politics is the craving for excitement or status (or, if they haven't got much money – money); that their policies are most often the product of faction rather than coherent belief; that it is a necessary feature of political activity, once power is achieved, that it is essentially absurd, that it can usually not achieve its public aspirations, except by accident; that even 'believers', when exposed to this inner hollowness of power, necessarily become cynical and fraudulent, determined first on the preservation of their own power, with policy as an optional 'extra'; that the best one can hope for is that they will apply whatever values they have wherever they can, whenever the accidents let them. I do not know whether these are the inner secrets of politics or not. (Nor – yet – does anyone else.) But it is certainly the belief of many Australians that politics is essentially a fraudulent activity engaged in by self-seeking crooks. Even public rhetoric amongst Australian politicians is extremely dour, pragmatic and short range; in private they often excuse their participation in politics by boasting of their cynicism. It is as if it would be unmanly and un-Australian for a politician to confess to a serious interest in public affairs.

The public emptiness of Australian politics comes from its lack of intellectual strength. Not only, as in the United States, are intellectuals normally deprived of access to top policy decisions, when elsewhere in the modern world they have considerable influence on political events; they also lack the enormous range of opportunity, available in the

United States, for at least being hangers-on to those who decide top policy, ghosting speeches, testing opinions, and so forth. Australian politics does without these frills; if intellectuals wish to walk down the corridors of power in Australia they must leave their intellectuality at home. As in business, to pretend to some stupidity is safest. However there is some reason for believing that some intellectualisation of issues in Australia now would not only interest people's imaginations in the problems they must face: it might even win votes.

In both political parties, during the Age of Menzies there was an archaic flavour in political affairs, a sense that much of this might have been happening at some earlier period in history. Even for Australia the deadness was remarkable. Politicians seemed pompous and out of touch. They seemed to be conducting a political debate that they had read about in an old book. There was little sign of a breakthrough that could, in a contemporary idiom, dramatize Australia's new challenges. Politicians did not project the symbols of modern life. This may be partly because men of the Menzies-Calwell generation became virtually exiles in their own century; and partly because the distrust both parties have for intellectuals cuts them off from much analysis of what the world and Australia are now supposed to be about. Australian politicians – especially the old and powerful – do not keep up with their reading.

Parties, like human beings, need some 'philosophy', some sense of purpose and identity to keep up their interest in their environment so that they can react to events in a contemporary way. In both parties in Australia a contemporary sense of identity has been lost. That is why a whole younger generation of Australians of the kind who normally might now be revitalizing political life are more likely to despise the whole set-up.

# 8. THE AGE OF MENZIES

## *The great survivor*

WITH his record reign of sixteen years as Australia's Prime Minister, Sir Robert Menzies became one of those people after whom one might name an 'Age' – until time passes and later generations forget why any of it mattered. What follows is an attempt to estimate Menzies's importance in the eyes of history. This is how things looked at the time of writing although this estimate might yet prove to be wrong.

It was a feature of Menzies's long rule that little of what he did seems to matter much. His great talent was to preside over events and look as if he knew what they were all about. His few active interventions proved mainly failures. He was a determined survivor – and even here he was really helped by the split in the Labor Party. It was a feature of his rule that most of the things in which he seemed to believe when he regained office in 1949 did not happen. His general posture in 1949 was one of 'free enterprise', support of British policies, anti-Communism, an interest in defence.* In his period of rule he had to adopt many of the mechanisms of planning, if in a piecemeal way; the American alliance was strengthened and the British connexion was weakened; externally he followed policies opposed to the expansion of Communist regimes in Asia, but, after a false start, (when he seemed to be making political capital out of it) there was less practical concern with domestic Communists than there was under Chifley; the proportion of national income spent on defence declined during most of his rule.

* His promise to develop the North in 1949 was so unfulfilled that he was able to make a similar promise in 1963 – and again do nothing about it. The North is like that.

The positive characteristics of his 'Age' – the spread of affluence, the considerable relaxation in social styles, the increase in national self assurance, the continued migration programme, the beginning of an interest in Asia and the growing tolerance of Asians resident in Australia, the demands of technology, the increasing power of overseas investment in Australia, were none of them the kind of thing that Menzies has 'stood for' and some of them are the opposite of what he said he hoped for before he came to power. When even Menzies appeared to be losing belief in the British connexion (from the time of the Common Market crisis) it is doubtful if he believed in anything anymore – except in himself. His attitude became largely nostalgic; he regretted much of what he saw of Australia in the 1960s. However he stayed in power.

He seemed to believe that only he could run Australia. He presided over meetings, gave martinis to visitors, got in and out of planes, watched papers pass across his table, made speeches. He shared his power with a small group of Ministers and a small group among the heads of Government departments. With the exception of John McEwen he had most of his Ministers bluffed. Most of the men who came into power with him in 1949 went (he helped some of the more independent minded ones go), and the new men lay in his shade; most of them hesitated to decide anything themselves and Menzies himself was not usually a quick decision maker; things piled up and, in the nature of things, some of them disappeared. With policy-making slowing down and sometimes stopping the permanent heads of the government departments got on with the job of administering their departments in a way that would not cause trouble. It was one of the ironies of political life that in the 1940s some of these men were the instruments of Labor's new deal in the government bureaucracy; but they became attached to Menzies and increasingly he regarded them, rather than his Ministers, as his agents in running the nation.

Within his party he soon cut off from power or silenced all those who disagreed with him; he regarded them as mere time-wasters. His private conviction was that disagreement was mere 'grizzling', an expression of 'ignorance'. Party meetings were stage managed so that opposition was not often expressed, and when it was expressed it was often made to look foolish. Of course, he showed charm and guile in maintaining support. He could use the 'old boy' technique effectively. ('There is much substance in what you say, old boy.') And in a political party which contains many ex-officers he knew how to appeal to a sense of obedience and how to isolate the 'disloyal'. He treated all disagreement as serious and from time to time did not hesitate to suggest he would resign if part of one of his few plans was criticized. (Menzies himself was disloyal to Lyons and Hughes when they were his party leaders.) In personal encounter he could prove charming and much more subtly witty than his public performance might suggest. In public he was usually a ham. He revealed different sides of himself to different people but it seemed to be only among his family that he relaxed; with his colleagues he maintained an atmosphere of aloofness and a little mystery. He would unbend a little here, a little there, thereby fooling scores of otherwise sceptical and hard-headed men throughout Australia. They were delighted with a ration of condescension.

He was a great actor. He could amuse with his imitations and clowning but he showed little interest in seeking the company of his intellectual equals; in his off-duty moments he seemed to prefer company in which his remained the superior intellect. He was lazy in his reading and – despite the projection of an image of learning and culture – the truth is that he was not particularly well-read, as little interested in things of the spirit as his fellow countrymen, and in so far as he did have intellectual or artistic interests they were extremely provincial and old hat. He was essentially arrogant, although courageous, with a scorn for most other men (perhaps all other men). He used his power to little purpose.

John Pringle hit it on the head in *Australian Accent* when he described Menzies as a politician rather than an administrator, a man who enjoyed the battle of politics, loved making speeches, but often confused speech-making with the implementation of policy; who was lazy and complacent in power, preferring an easy shot to a hard one; 'a supremely skilful politician – ruthless, adroit, cunning – whose special device is to pose always as a statesman.' This did not particularly fool the Australians. There was a period in the late forties and early fifties when Menzies seemed to believe in what he was doing, and it may be that at that stage, in his defence of 'liberalism', he was really saying what he thought. But for the most part ordinary Australians have held him in little regard: his elevation to the Order of the Thistle was treated as ludicrous; he was widely considered old-fashioned and had always been considered insincere. In personal image, where Menzies really scored was against the even greater decrepitude in image of his opponent, Arthur Calwell. Time and again one heard young Australians say that they had no regard for Menzies but that Calwell with his ancient Labor rhetoric seemed even more antediluvian – some relic of Early Man.

The people's distrust of Menzies seemed to be reciprocated. He did not open his heart or address the Australians as if they were trustworthy human beings. In his first disastrous term as Prime Minister when he almost lost the wartime election in 1940 he did not seem to respect the people sufficiently to dramatize the war for them, and seize their imagination by making demands. It was as if he just wanted to run the whole show without bothering to get anyone's confidence; he even failed to get the confidence of his party and in 1941 they 'did him in', forcing his resignation, after public brawling that had lasted for some months. He made the same mistake in 1961 when, at a time of economic recession, he insulted the people by standing on his records; only Santamaria saved the election for him. And although the decision to call an election in 1963 was his own it was only after a lot of pressure was put on him (by N.S.W. party bosses) that he condescended to show enough interest in the people to gain their votes by promising them something. The truth was that he was a master of adroitness in the political infighting in his party – he cleaned the board – but as a public man fighting for office he was helped more by luck than good management. (Perhaps he was a true Australian in this!) He capitalized on the reaction against Labor's post-war austerity quite skilfully in 1949 and 1951; after that the Labor Party gave him election after election by being stupid – and in 1954 by being unlucky.

Menzies's lack of interest in doing anything much with the power that the Labor Party thrust on him would not have mattered if, as is the case with some politicians of his temper, he had concerned himself not only with the thrill of battle and the delights of office but had also used the talents of able men so that they could exploit events in successful administration. He seemed to prefer to frustrate talent, to surround himself with a firebreak of mediocrity. In this he was of his generation. He was a country boy who made his way in the world with nothing but his own talents to guide him; in his particular environment his talents were exceptional; he was a State Minister before he was thirty; and Prime Minister (in 1939) at forty-four. (He made his first trip overseas at the age of thirty-nine.) Men of this kind and of this generation in Australia rarely respected anyone except themselves. The last thing they would do would be to look for others like themselves; they wouldn't trust them. In Menzies's case the bitterness of his humiliation by his own party in 1941 (which was largely his own fault) seemed to make him decide that it was better to survive than to govern well.

In judging statesmen one can take a reasonable view and judge a man by the possible, by the extent to which he associates himself with the likely and perhaps guides it, reforms where he can, crystallizes ideas and images, galvanizes the bureaucracy and seizes events and incidents to make policy out of them. By this modest view of statecraft one can say that for sixteen years Menzies saw few of the potentialities of the age; that his reactions were most usually those of an old-fashioned man guided by the vanishing standards of an earlier, more rural community. In some ways at times he had seemed to reflect not even the standards of his own generation, but of the one before him. Perhaps when he was a young man making his way in the world those he admired most were the Australian politicians who cherished the English connexion. These were the real provincials: Melbourne gentlemen who adopted what they took to be the standards of the far distant metropolis. Throughout his long career Menzies stressed 'loyalty', by which he did not seem to mean loyalty to Australia but to the British connexion, and to the Monarch (when he was not referring to loyalty to himself). He seemed always to have associated himself with 'loyalty' and the Labor Party with 'disloyalty'; even when the Curtin Government was defending Australia against the Japanese, in some of his speeches Menzies seemed to be doubting its 'loyalty', by which he meant not its conduct of a war to save the Australian nation, but its attitude to the United Kingdom. If this interpretation is true it means that throughout a period in which Australia was in need of orientation towards Asia and towards technology it was governed by a man who had deeply absorbed the provincial standards of Melbourne at the beginning of the century.

## The Age of Menzies

It was the habit of Menzies's apologists to give him credit for anything they liked about what had happened in Australia since 1949; even when they could not demonstrate his connexion with it; even when he did not take credit for it; or even when it was something that he would wish had not happened. But they didn't keep to the rules of this game: they were not prepared to blame him for anything they did *not* like about what had happened in Australia since 1949. For these things more often than not, they blamed 'The People'.

According to his supporters, Menzies was to be credited with Australia's 'industrial revolution' and rapid economic growth. (As will be seen later, this was even given as an excuse for his failures in rearmament). In considering this defence of Menzies one does not even have to consider the relation of his policies to events. The alleged events did not happen. It is ridiculous to claim that an 'industrial revolution' started in the early 1950s and false to claim rapid economic growth for Australia since then.

The 'industrial revolution' began in Australia in the nineteenth century, sooner than it did in most parts of the world. Australia 'took off' not all that long after it was founded. In one of the more specific tests, the foundation of heavy industry in Australia was laid as long ago as the beginning of the twentieth century. After that, from the beginning of the First World War to the Depression manufacturing production went up by 70 per cent; and in the thirties, despite the Depression, *it more than doubled*. The most significant impetus was given during the Second World War when Australians engaged in splendid improvisation: they quickly produced a whole armaments industry, providing the weapons and vehicles of war. When the war ended, in another spectacular improvisation, and with encouragement from the Chifley Labor Government, Australian and foreign-owned companies turned the skills, machines and factories that had been thrown up during the war into private manufacturing industry. The process of increasing the proportion of consumer goods that are manufactured in Australia was already in operation when Menzies took over. Even the establishment of Australian factories in which foreign manufacturers make motor cars for Australians (a key piece of evidence for the 'industrial revolution' claim) was first encouraged by the Chifley Government. (Menzies's indifference killed L.J. Hartnett's attempt to start an Australian-owned car manufacturing firm.)

Despite all the rhetoric about 'Australia Unlimited', Australian economic growth since 1949 has been comparatively low. Australia's comparative affluence – its prosperity compared with that of other countries – is declining. It would be more accurate to say of Menzies's Australia that it was during his Prime Ministership that Australia became a comparatively less prosperous country.

In general social reform, few claims are made for Menzies, and, other than the health services scheme, since 1949 there have been no new concepts in social welfare. However it was in his almost perverse neglect of the defence forces that Menzies was curiously vulnerable. He did not pretend to be a social reformer, a welfare state-ist or an economic planner; he did claim to be a realist in the conduct of foreign affairs, and a patriot. Yet there was no coherent Australian defence force – only some bits and pieces of a defence force. Only about 6,000 soldiers could be put into battle at once, but there were no assault craft to take them to a battle area, not enough transport aircraft to fly in even one battalion, no *effective* air strike force to give them support; there was no effective Fleet Air Arm (nor for that matter, an effective navy; the navy became mainly an anti-submarine force); and on the mainland the radar and ground-to-air guided weapon defence system was quite inadequate. In the early 1960s expenditure on defence ran as low as 2.7 per cent of G.N.P., lower than any prosperous country except New Zealand. Pressures from his own colleagues – and from the Americans – finally rushed Menzies into a defence expansion which brought this figure up to about 5 per cent.

Producing this figure does not tell the most significant part of the story. Sweden spends less than 5 per cent of its G.N.P. on defence and has what may be the fourth or fifth best air force in the world. The Swedes use their *brains* in their approach to defence problems: they have simplified their super-structure, worked out policies that suit their own needs and designed most of their own equipment. Menzies ran five ministries to the Swedes' one; he seemed to lack the intellectual capacity to think about defence coherently; and his rule seriously threatened to destroy the morale of the men who were supposed to run Australia's defence forces. Whatever sense of initiative and desire for achievement they had possessed became eroded; their status was that of courtiers to Canberra officials. Throughout Menzies's period of office Defence Ministers were peculiarly weak. Menzies's Cabinets would muck around with a series of attempts to work out a relation between the defence chiefs and Cabinet, but none of them would work. What happened was that the services were still administered piecemeal, mainly by civilian officials. Despite his conservatism, Menzies was an unmilitary man: he would avoid direct contact with his service leaders – unless, in effect, they turned into civilians. For most of his rule the accountants in the Treasury set a (low) ceiling figure and told the service departments that this was all they could spend: there was no coherent planning from the needs of the situation; just annual improvising. This is now changing.

The emaciation of the defence forces soon left Australian diplomacy with an impossible task. In itself, diplomacy cannot achieve much, unless there is a capacity for propaganda and bluff – and one certainly did not find this in Canberra. Even then, some show of strength may be needed to convince allies that one is at least trying. As Professor B.B. Beddie has said: 'While officially we undertook a major defence effort in order to secure and carry influence in our alliances, in reality we relied upon our alliances to relax our defence effort.' It should be remembered that in gross terms – without even worrying about dividing G.N.P. by population – Australia is by far the wealthiest nation in South East Asia. If its leaders had the brains to develop a defence force of the quality of the Swedes' it would have by far the best defence force in South East Asia. In strategic terms it would be a power in South East Asia; this would provide a base for stronger diplomatic action.

Put down baldly, what Australian policy was under Menzies in facing the new power situation in Asia was this: Menzies entered into a number of commitments and then made no attempt to meet them. He bluffed – and those who were aware of it hoped that if his bluff was called the United States would slip some good cards into his hand.

One of the things a democratic political leader is supposed to do is to apply his values and ideologies to policy-making and then to try to interest people in what he is doing. Menzies had obsolete and irrelevant values and ideologies. His view of the world did not give him a real feel for the problems of the age and of Australia. Unable to formulate the right issues, he did not formulate any issues; or he formulated issues in the wrong way. For instance, when he sent an Australian battalion to South Vietnam he did not try to excite people's imaginations as to why this was necessary; he despatched the battalion off-hand, as if they were assassins sent off secretly into the night by a great prince to do his dirty work for him. After this action such rhetoric as he finally summoned for the occasion was mainly undergraduate Union Night polemic, directed against his critics. To his supporters – on the evidence, most of the people in Australia – he did not address himself in a straightforward and meaningful way. In his attitudes to Asia (which never really caught his attention) Menzies has been a giant obstruction to a natural trend. He has held things up. Spender, Casey, and Barwick, his first three External Affairs Ministers, all realised how Australians should reorientate their thinking to the fact that their island adjoins Asia; they tried to interest Australians in this. Menzies frustrated their efforts – his eyes were on London.

Menzies's lack of feel for contemporary problems and lack of interest in dramatising them applied beyond Asia. He probably had the same contempt for business activity as for Asia yet in this field, as in foreign policy, a political leader can – by making speeches, dramatising issues and displaying styles – affect changes in attitude that may be more profound than changes attempted by legislative action. No one could legislate Australian businessmen into more contemporary approaches; it might be possible to talk them into it. What Menzies should have told the Australian people was what they wanted to hear: that the elites who, in various fields, run the country's affairs should all smarten themselves up. As it was, one of the characteristics of the Age of Menzies was a running down of enthusiasm, a deadening of approach to problems, a retreat.

In a review in *Quadrant* of the first edition of *The Lucky Country* Irving Kristol said: 'In a democracy, *if there is good democratic leadership*, the people are capable of creating better than they know – and of truly appreciating this supra-popular creation. Without Abraham Lincoln and John F. Kennedy, the American democracy would not only be far poorer in its self-definition than it is today – it would be blissfully unaware of its poverty. With them, and others like them, one can discern a promise and a potentiality that is becoming (one hopes) an integral part of American democratic life.'

This view of the role of a democratic political leader opposes everything Menzies has stood for.

## After Menzies

Nothing befitted Menzies better than his going. Perplexed by a changing world offering strange problems to which he could not be bothered offering a solution, he modestly slipped out of office, as satisfied with the Lord Wardenship of the Cinque Ports as a head clerk who goes into retirement carrying an engraved gold watch as a token of the firm's esteem. He left his litter behind him but he spared his successors advice as to what they should do with it.

When Harold Holt replaced him as Prime Minister there was almost at once a greater recognition of what was important to Australia. One of Holt's first acts was to announce some slight changes in the immigration policy, changes that were perhaps more important because of the promptness with which they were made than their substance, but which, by re-definition, have at least allowed greater administrative discretion. Holt went to Vietnam, and to other countries in South-East and East Asia, dramatising by his presence there what it now meant to be an Australian. He announced that, so far as Vietnam was concerned, Australia went "all the way with L.B.J." and followed up the startlingly successful visit of President Johnson to Australia with the visit of Premier Ky. Later he visited Cambodia (then neutralist), throwing light on one of the little known subtleties of Australian policy, that Australia is friendly with nations that hold themselves differently. In the rhetoric of Australian foreign policy he added the idea of social revolution to that of stability: Australia saw Asia not only in terms of a Communist threat but of the necessity for its peoples to break their way through to the material progress and freedoms that Australians themselves enjoy.

Holt surprised his own followers with the boldness of some of his decisions and he fought an election on the Vietnam War with a courage that even some of his critics recognised. But he seemed slow to start that bonfire of Menzies-ism that his success would have allowed: his government continued to show many of the characteristics of its predecessors. The contradictions in Holt lessened his effect on Australians' imaginations. In Parliament he could still show the pettiness of an old parliamentary windbag, with only his little touches of spite enlivening the tedium of his long, disorganised speeches. Yet there was something in him – idealism, opportunism, or both – that made him seize on Australia's relations with Asia as one of the central lines in government policy. Unlike Menzies, his political sensitivity was contemporary, feeling out towards what now mattered, liking it for that reason, and exploiting it for political purposes. Unfortunately he conveyed this sense of what mattered with the words of a mayor opening a new child-minding centre, delivered with the indestructible grin of an old tap dancer.

However there was hope in his very opportunism, combined with what did seem to be his belief that there was nothing to be ashamed of in being an Australian, and perhaps his hope that Australia's neighbours might some day enjoy some of Australia's privileges. One got the impression that, unlike Menzies in his period of decline, Holt was at least still interested in his job.

# 9. FORMING OPINIONS

*Censors*

THROUGHOUT the century, where other democracies have censored badly Australia has censored worse. It has always been out of the main stream and, in the liberalization of its censorship on questions of sex, it is still behind other democracies. The sudden liberalizations of elsewhere have been reflected only in part in Australia. In 1965 an edition of *The Trial of Lady Chatterley*, banned for import, was set up and separately printed in Australia. The Federal Government accommodated itself to this challenge and lifted the ban. Shortly after it lifted the bans on *Lolita*, *Borstal Boy* and *Lady Chatterley's Lover*. Perhaps it was afraid that someone would print Australian editions of these, too. This new method of defiance gave considerable hope to those Australian intellectuals who had been deriding their country's censorship for some years. They looked around for new ways of making an ass of the law.

None of this banning greatly impedes the reading of books. It is the regular thing for anyone with the slightest interest in books to smuggle banned books into the country when returning from abroad and to pass them around. What disgusts is the joy with which politicians can associate themselves with book banning; this regular reminder of a troglodyte past affronts those who consider politicians to be poor judges of what is of human value.

Film censorship has become less prudish about sex, but more concerned about violence. In re-censoring old movies for showing on television all kinds of phrases and episodes that have some relation to sex are now restored; but other phrases or episodes that have some relation to violence are cut out. New movies are censored with a light hand, but cuts are still more prudish than in most democracies.

In the mid 1950s, as a result of Church pressure, mainly Catholic, new censorship laws against popular reading matter were introduced. Licensing systems were set up in some States, censorship boards in others. Except for the Queensland Literature Board of Review, which proceeded to make a fool of itself with great haste and a lavish hand, nothing much happened after that. The Queensland Board, which claimed to be defending 'the civilization of the West' and to be protecting youth against 'the fiery darts of the wicked' appeared at first to have almost completely arbitrary powers of banning without giving reasons. However a number of court actions inhibited its activities. It is of interest that intellectuals – who almost universally oppose censorship of the kind of books that they themselves want to read – hardly ever deplore the censorship of ordinary people's reading matter, and sometimes even support it.

## Schools

Australia's economic growth is impeded not only by lack of research and boldness at the top but by a shortage of trained technicians in the middle range and of skilled workers in the lower middle range. The statistics tell some of the story. Although Australia is one of the most prosperous countries in the world it runs very badly in percentage of G.N.P. spent on education, and since its forward education programmes were scrappy and behind those of many other countries it fell behind in the race to produce the technocrats. There is little planning to train a new kind of person as part of the process of economic development. There is mainly belated scrambling around the mounting slope of crisis. In some secondary schools only half the teachers are University trained. Comparative figures suggest an unusually high wastage of talent. The shortage of technicians is even more serious than the shortage of graduates. Sometimes engineers, for instance, spend only a third of their time on work at a professional level. The rest is spent doing work that could be done by technicians. In the

Universities the student/staff ratios are too high. The proportion of students who take higher degrees is proportionately small compared with other industrialised nations.

The apprenticeship system is still tied to its medieval
past by the shortsightedness of managements and unions,
and by the lack of vigour in governments. Usually there are
no tests of skill at the end of a five year apprenticeship in
which a young man has been indentured to one firm. There
are no national standards; apprenticeship is a 'State matter',
with the Federal Department of Labour and National
Service trying to improve it by federal diplomacy. Appren-
tices are not always given the kind of broad general background necessary in an age of quick technological advance
and quick obsolescence; there is no training in flexibility.
To make sense this would require a longer period of secondary education.

The whole structure of the State Education Departments
is authoritarian. It was inevitable, given the vast distances
of Australia, the sparse population and the weakness of
local government that the State systems of education should
be centralized around the State capital cities. Children
are supposed to be taught the same things in the same way
throughout a State; headmasters and headmistresses have
little discretion; decision is by decree from the Department
rather than by local decision. Experiment is almost impossible. School teachers are shunted around as unpredictably
as officials in Stalin's Russia. The whole tone of the departments is regulatory and disciplinary, to the extent at times
of bleak administrative cruelty. The primary school
teachers, who are not University educated, set the tone of
discussion within the teachers' unions. The tone is almost
completely non-professional. University-educated teachers
are tied to their Departments for a period of service and
sometimes humiliated by their masters while at the
University.

The schools, run by remote control from the Departments, are often isolated within their own social communities. Because of all the shunting around of staff, teachers are

often strangers within their environment or, at best, friendly transients. Participation of the community in school activities is limited to fund-raising and providing amenities. In Victoria when the mothers of Eagle Point started making cocoa with free school milk the Department told them that free milk must not be issued in any form other than straight milk; after a public fuss the Director of Education amended policy to allow small schools to make cocoa with free milk provided they made application to do so and the applications were approved. When the Victorian Federation of Mothers Clubs then assumed that this meant that schools might also make hot soup with free milk they were sharply corrected: 'This idea has not been considered by the Department and will not be considered by it'. It is a tribute to the endurability of the human spirit that so much of education has survived in Australia despite this dreadful system.

Not only because democracy becomes fraudulent if minority views are not protected, but in the interests of education and of human decency, the greatest single reform that seems to be needed in Australian education – and one of the most important reforms that could be made in Australia – is its decentralization, to allow teachers to become members of the communities in which they teach, to allow principals of schools greater initiative, to develop a sense of professional responsibility amongst teachers, to allow variety and experiment, and to allow more community participation. This reform could even be carried out in conjunction with a constitutional reform granting the Federal Government the financial control of education, a general setting of standards and an adequate planning department.

## Images of life

What kind of a world is presented to children in Australian school rooms? Except for the Catholic schools there is little presentation of a religious view of life. In most schools there is no glorification of militarism. There is certainly no worship of the State. Here and there, mainly in the fee-paying non-Catholic schools, there are left-overs of the English ideology of service; but it is a poor thing, divorced from community and home life. Love of country is some-times purveyed, but often it is mainly a literary and historical affair that has little meaning to young minds that are already becoming sceptical; there is no longer available the folk-patriotism that was so confident earlier in the century. The British Empire has naturally disappeared as an article of faith although there is still some adulation of the Monarchy and some attempt to extract meaning from the 'Commonwealth of Nations' idea. A sense of curiosity and wonder is rare. The field in which this could be most easily aroused might be in science (with its materialism and new scepticism about even itself the teaching of science could make a natural impact on young Australians) but the schools are weakest in science teachers; the teachers of the humanities, often not really aware of what they defend or what they attack, lend an anti-science bias to much high school teaching. There is a resentment against science; its civilized values do not require the demagoguery of 'development of personalities' and so forth.

There is certainly no worship of rugged self reliance or of acceptance of the ideology of 'free enterprise'. Apart from the irrelevance of much of this ideology in an Australian context, schoolteachers often have an animus against practical affairs. They may become so demoralized that their main active belief is hatred of 'The Department' that employs them. In so far as they have attitudes to the practical world they are feelings of alienation and opposition; there is a feeling that the practical world is inimical to cultural values (so very often are teachers, but they are stuck with a public defence of them); there are feelings of envy about the better money earned 'outside'. Practical affairs seem so different from the gentle, boring round of school life that they *must* be wrong. (As any observer of them knows, practical affairs have their gentle, boring rounds, too.)

However there is a concern that children should 'get on' – usually in a good white collar job. 'Getting on' is not the get-up-and-go of economic progress but a quiet gaining of respectability in an easy-going job that does not make many demands but provides sufficient leisure and money for the enjoyment of family life and sport. It is not a question of being efficient but of getting jobs with good provision for retirement and of learning to keep one's nose clean. Theoretically the Catholic schools should provide some contrast to this but in practice they often offend most. In this case there is concern not only for the child, but the good name of the Church in urging that children 'get on'.

Living lives that seem inadequate by their own professional standards (such as they are) or by those of the community, many teachers seem to identify themselves with weakness in personality. Subconsciously this kind of teacher might prefer sensible, conventional, well-behaved and only medium-witted children. The spirit of philanthropy that now pervades educational thinking may be connected with this identification with weakness. The weak lead the weak and in these terms 'education for democracy' becomes a degenerate travesty of democracy; belief in majority rule becomes belief in mediocrity; egalitarianism and fraternalism become conformity; liberty becomes salvationary – others have suffered that we might do what we wish, as long as it meets the wishes of most other people. A 'satisfactory life' becomes one that is the same as everyone else's. No new ideas are needed. There are to be no more experiments. We shall go on being the same. Someone or other will look after us.

Fortunately there are counterbalances to this, otherwise Australians would by now be a race of idiots. There are teachers who prefer excellence, and delight in cultivating it: there are children who fight battles of the intellect for themselves. There is considerable distrust of teachers, especially in the higher grades. However, the fact that Australian children are taught by people who are often in a state of mild despair, who are dissatisfied with their material and social lot and are alienated from both practicality and the real values of the culture they purvey must be of great importance. It is in the alienation of both teachers and pupils from the values of the culture they are forced towards that one seems to get near the heart of the problem of Australians.

### 'The Academics'

Before the Second World War Australian universities were of what might be called high provincial standard. They were a reasonably faithful copy, if a dull one, of minor universities in England and Scotland. Even then there were strong criticisms of them for being little more than 'degree shops'. There were a few dazzling exceptions, but on the whole university teachers had not managed to produce universities which transformed the products of the schools. Normally there was little about a graduate that distinguished him from other reasonably successful people in the community. Then for a while the increased demand from the increasingly larger younger generations and the demand for a higher proportion of skills seemed to shock and demoralize those responsible for decisions about universities. There was poor leadership in the universities and some of the new class of university 'administrators' seemed to be managerially illiterate. Then there began to be improvement.

The general tone of university life, especially among those engaged in the 'humanities', is not invigorating. (There are plenty of exceptions of course.) It is a matter of record that the academic issue that arouses the most steady lively group interest among the nearly 7,000 full time and part-time teaching and research staff of the universities is money. This is associated with envious myths about what everyone else is earning. I have heard 'academics' complain that the 'working class people' they meet pity them because they earn so little money. The 'so little money' is several times as much as average weekly earnings. Professors on $14,000 a year feel that businessmen are earning much more than they are, but this – apart from the men at the top – is not so. There is a feeling of self-pity and alienation which extends even to attitudes to students: they see students mill in and out of lecture rooms, resent their numbers and their demands, but have little individual knowledge of them. And among the non-scientists there is an impotent unease, perhaps envy, about the successes of science.

The one field in which comparative earnings make sense is science. Here one can describe a salaries market quite specifically. In the humanities, with exceptions, one cannot, except to hazard a guess that at least some of the humanities men would earn less money outside. (This is not a criticism of them.) However, again with exceptions, the science faculties cannot put in competitive offers and raise their rates to attract new talent, any more than the Education Departments could pay science and mathematics teachers more than the others. Usually the non-scientists are in control and market rates are determined by the price for professors of Latin.

With exceptions, the non-scientist 'academics' in Australia have been rather undistinguished. The middle ranges are adequate but there is nothing much at the top. Even the occasional brilliant man sometimes gets away with it too easily for him to maintain excellence. He suffers from the Australian lack of competition, lack of interest in excellence, and a certain amount of conformist envy or sheer misunderstanding. Vincent Buckley gives a convincing picture of the Australian non-scientist academic in *Australian Civilization*: 'They are institutionally absorbed and job-conscious, they are suburban ... they take questions of salary and promotions as seriously as any trade unionist ... There is no nonsense about an intellectual's existence to think and to make other people think: on the contrary he exists to "work" in a "job" ... As one lecturer in literature (of all subjects) has said, "The only sensible thing is to see it as a nine-to-five job" ... As every idealistic schoolteacher knows, a man who lets his life work be reduced to the status of a "job", with increments, working conditions, and all the rest of the weary defensive mechanism, soon becomes cynical about the very job he has been so avid to fill ... At "work", one sticks to the "job"; the rest of the time is for gentle living. The Smiths visit the Joneses at predictable intervals, drink a little red wine decanted from a flagon, eat French salad off wooden platters, chat about the car and the kids and the holidays.'

Before the Second World War the general line of belief of the most influential Australian academics was, on the whole, conservative. Some were reactionaries tied into the crude conspiracies that then tried to run the capital cities. There is still some of this conservatism left, although it is necessarily changed in style, but on the whole Australian academics now hold orthodox Australian liberal opinions: they are critical of censorship, licensing laws, hanging and the police; in politics they would tend to distrust the Liberal Party, hate the Democratic Labor Party and worry about the Labor Party; usually they would feel detached from party politics; they detest anti-semitism but often are suspicious of all Catholics; they fear McCarthyism, a term that they often wrongly apply to spirited discussion of communist influence in trade unions. A few of the older men, who learned their politics in the Spanish Civil War or in hatred of Hitler, still see things in terms of the 1930s; there is sometimes a streak of hysteria in the fears and manipulations, and an old-fashioned flavour about their language that can make the subject they are talking about unrecognizable.

Some academics consort with businessmen and some with politicians or government officials, but the attitudes of most to practical affairs reveal the frustrations of the social fragmentation so strong in Australia. Often the academics' discussion on public affairs is no better informed than any-one else's: where it *is* better informed, as with economists, it is sometimes not thought out thoroughly enough to be intelligible to an educated audience.

There is a very strong sense of difference, and of moral superiority. Most academics would not disagree with the

Sydney lecturer who said academics were 'more fair, sensitive and unselfish than the greater part of mankind.' There is a distrust of any intellectual activity that is not carried out by academics, as if contributions to a 'subject' could not sometimes be made by a person outside a university, or as if 'subjects' covered the whole field of intellectual discourse. This specialism goes with a quite frequent indifference to literature and the arts: these are treated either as specialist subjects or as un-academic. There are not many Australian academics whose conversation shows awareness of the main intellectual dilemmas of the age. (These are nobody's specialty.) Some of them seem to take the ordinary Australian view: the main intellectual dilemmas of the age have nothing to do with us. Yet they often try to arrogate more honour to themselves, compared with the rest of the community, than university people do in countries where membership of a university means more than it normally does in Australia. In particular, those who consider themselves intellectuals often consider intellectual life to be coterminous with academic life.

The prevailing tone is perhaps one of isolation and of self-pity rather than of academic responsibility; it is passive rather than active, even in the running of university affairs. The universities meet the demands of the age with a reserved resentment; lectures are delivered, exam papers marked. That's that.

## The press

Complete independence is something that no man can achieve but given less idealistic definitions of independence one can say that there are not many men of independent position in Australia who regularly discuss public affairs with a sense of audience and in some depth. The professional classes have become more or less commercial-minded; there is no cultivated leisure class; with exceptions, members of the universities are silent; and there are very few independent-minded journalist-publicists who write with considerable knowledge, originality and style. There are no 'quality' daily or Sunday newspapers of the standard of those of London, New York, or Western Europe, and no journals of record and opinion as independent, as strongly established, as well-staffed and as well provided with contributors as the 'quality' periodicals of Britain and Western Europe. The casting up of new concepts of how things are going is very rare; even regular background information and interpretation is hard to come by; there are few possibilities for sustained and rigorous debate on new problems; few journalists can take the time to involve themselves in a field to the point at which they can give an interpretative, related account of it, to follow a story to the point of significance. The result is that images of Australian life usually fall into crude stereotypes. Decision-makers and intellectuals get so used to reading about Australia in oversimplified terms and they so lack information that their discourse becomes brutalized when they talk about Australia. There is an irascible ignorance, impatient with complexity, and a failure to understand that policy making involves the analysis of alternatives.

In Australia people get away with things that would be exposed in a more sophisticated nation. In other countries some of our politicians would be satirized so successfully that to survive they would have to acquire a better public style. Discussion on public affairs in Australia has become very solemn; it takes the principal performers at their own value and perpetuates their pomposities. The traditions of cheekiness and scepticism have all but died. The ordinary people know that politicians are often clowns and that powerful men are often power racketeers, but writers no longer tell them so, although once there were Australian publications that gave an almost Brechtian view of the world. One of the reasons for the distrust by ordinary people of the Press may lie in the false note it often strikes: it almost always presents the mediocre men of Australia as if they were to be taken seriously. To ordinary Australians public affairs now seem spurious and remote. But the tiredness and cliché-thinking of opinion-makers is unable to capture the scepticism of the people. It is almost a conspiracy of tiredness of the spirit.

The ordinary Australian intellectual or decision-maker often lumps all the blame for this on to the daily newspapers, as if they could provide all the expertness and complexities of an intellectual community. The popular newspapers sell their 3,500,000 copies a day at less than cost to ordinary people to reach a circulation high enough to attract enough advertising revenue to make money. They cannot be expected to provide a capsule of intellectual life, taken once a day, like a pill before breakfast. Intellectual life needs many regular forms of expression. The weakness or absence of forms of intellectual expression is probably a more important factor than the inadequacies of the daily newspapers in the infertility of much discussion on public affairs in Australia, in its sheer inexpertness and naïvete.

One fair way of evaluating Australian newspapers is to compare them with the local newspapers of the U.S.A. In general, in coverage and interpretation of local news, Australian newspapers do not come out so well in this comparison; in coverage and interpretation of overseas news they come out better. In Australia coverage of foreign affairs is usually scrappy, without background or depth, but often ahead of American coverage. Newspapers already devote more space to foreign news than mere motives of profit-making would suggest as prudent; they are not likely to increase the proportion. If Australian intellectuals or decision-makers want to know what's going on in the world they must supplement with overseas publications. On local news, Australian newspapers lack the vigour and cynicism and the detail of American newspapers. They don't often go out and get stories. Many of these stories might help to sell newspapers but stereotyped attitudes to what is a 'story' mean that whole areas of Australian life remain unexplored. One gets a narrow and freakish view of Australian life that excludes detailed reporting of, say, migrants or even – with the exception of Alan Reid – of the union movement.

The established part of the Australian Press, very largely, has stayed in a rut. On his return from six years in London John Pringle said: 'My first impression on returning to Sydney ... was how little the press had changed since I left six years before. The type and make-up were the same. Very often the stories themselves seemed the same ... I couldn't find a single new feature or single new writer – though some of the writers, of course, had changed papers ... I couldn't find a new columnist, a new cartoonist or even a new comic strip. Oh yes, one new comic strip bought from England.' The rewards for being a good writer can be comparatively low; an ambitious journalist often gets out of writing and into administration – or out of the industry altogether.

Some journalists are nothing more than hired hands on call for odd jobs. There is little attempt at cultivating a sense of joint professional involvement; the journalists' union provides no professional initiative. The status of journalism and its attractiveness as a way of earning a living have declined.

Australian newspaper managements have not reduced their papers to the kind of comics that in London tell everything except the news, and most of them do not trump up stories with ridiculous sensationalism. They are usually proud of their products and are affected by considerations other than profit-making. However they are far too sensitive to attack. Men who dish out criticism with considerable verve can become very cross when someone attacks *them*. Almost any criticism is seen as an attack on the freedom of the press. There is not enough criticism and such criticism as there is is often wild, or self-interested. Newspaper people sometimes take themselves far too seriously, reaching out for all the honours associated with the written word. Like so many other Australian Top People they seem to wish to be given a great deal more credit than is their due: history rests heavily on them and generates unease. If they would only confront the world with a more open manner, with less pretence of disinterest and more

Australian humorous self-denigration they might not be so unpopular.

However there have been some new developments in Australian publishing – first in periodicals and now in a 'national newspaper' – and three of the four main mass media groups can take credit for most of this. The fortnightly intellectual review the *Observer* was started early in 1958, with Australian Consolidated Press paying the bill, and this was followed later in the year by *Nation*, produced by a group of individuals. These two magazines achieved larger sales than those who despised the Australian potential had thought possible and they gave Australian general intellectual life a kind of substance that had previously evaded it. The *Australian Financial Review* (produced by the *Sydney Morning Herald*) began to assume a more general appeal and its cover of management and economic affairs also added to informed discussion. The takeover of the *Bulletin* by Australian Consolidated Press and its transformation by people connected with the *Observer* dramatized this minor publishing revolution. The *Bulletin* was a symbol of the old Australia, an Australia that started to die fifty years ago, and suddenly this relic of old attitudes was ripped to pieces and replaced in a few dreadful months in 1961 (dreadful for the victims of the change) by something that bore the image of contemporaneity. When the News Limited Group launched the *Australian* in July 1964, another element entered the situation. The *Australian* is Australia's first national newspaper, printed simultaneously in Sydney, Melbourne, and Brisbane. It represents the first attempt to produce a 'quality' newspaper in Australia (mixed with elements of more popular appeal). In the same month the *Canberra Times* (bought and refurbished by the *Sydney Morning Herald*) was also transformed into a quality-type paper.

What has happened in Australian publishing is that while the main newspapers simply stood still, the field for experiment moved into *new* publications, produced by University-educated men and bringing new kinds of people on to their staffs. There is more change going on than is evident from a glance at the news stands but these changes had no immediate effect on the main newspapers, even though all of these new publications (except *Nation*) had been published by groups who also controlled the main newspapers. In association with their publishers, a very small group of journalists effected this change.

## The intellectuals

So far the word 'intellectual' has been used without being given any clear meaning. This seemed safe because whatever meaning is given to the word, in Australia, as a strong and publicly influential type of person, 'intellectuals' do not exist. This makes Australia one of the oddest countries in the world. People who might be described as intellectuals are assuming enormous importance almost everywhere in the world except in Australia. It seems unlikely that such a situation will last in Australia. In fact it is now changing. There is a developing middle class of the intellect and taste, although it still lacks leaders, self-confidence and established forms of communication and influence.

By 'intellectuals' I do not mean only creative thinkers. Creative thinkers display curiosity about their environment, either systematically or by insight; or they make patterns; or they both examine some of the mysteries of existence and also try to make patterns of them. Other intellectuals are simply their conducting medium. An intellectual community may be the force by which a new vision is conducted into general attitudes. Or it may be an insulating medium, of the conservative kind that may stifle creative intelligence, even making it look foolish or wilful. There is no necessary relation between creative intelligence and universities; indeed the conservatism that is necessary to most academics in their monastic tasks of maintenance and transmission or their tasks of elaboration ('research') often stifles the creative intelligence. All of these processes have occurred in Australia: there have been creative intelligences, and their new visions have been conducted into general attitudes; or they have been frustrated in a society whose structure does not allow for the concept of originality. There have been Australians who have entered the world's intellectual community: Sir John Eccles and Sir Macfarlane Burnet became Nobel Prize winners because they extended the boundaries of a field of inquiry. Australian radio-physicists are doing the same. Australian writers, painters and philosophers give visions of which some part of the world takes note.

Where Australia has been weak, in matters of High Intellect, has been in a determined lack of serious consideration of human destiny, or in prolonged consideration of the Australian condition. Australian intellectuals tend to shelter from the major challenges and ideas of the twentieth century. It is usually not possible to conduct in Australia the kind of conversation that would be immediately acceptable among intellectuals in Europe, or New York.

What is even more remarkable is weakness in matters of Middle Intellect. There is a lack of a general class of educated persons who are familiar with the history of human thought (at least in outline), and see their connexion with it, who are familiar with analytical, categorizing and generalizing approaches, who work in many different fields in which the only common characteristic is a 'relatively high degree of abstraction or of ordering of some common experience', who can apply knowledge and curiosity to the things they are interested in and who, despite their occupational differences, can communicate with each other, as equals, in sustained and rigorous discourse on the affairs of the day. It is a lack of this kind of class that may present a danger to the future of Australia. This is the main meaning I have been giving the word 'intellectual'.

A 'new' country may need urban living (as distinguished from suburban) to develop this kind of person and more communication between occupational groups than exists in Australia. It needs regular reading matter in which there is information and a knowledge of what ideas are doing the rounds. It has been the Australian style to deny the intellect; sometimes its only social acceptability seemed to lie in some professor clowning on a television discussion panel, displaying his ordinariness. This suppression has meant that one thing wrong with many individual Australian intellectuals is that they rust away, or freeze into postures that are years out of date. A self-pitying loneliness becomes the intellectuals' style. They contract out.

There has been a growing cafe culture, of a sort. Coffee shops and espressos are popular meeting places for migrants; during the day for occupation groups (barristers or advertising men or hat salesmen); and for the young. For a few years young people might lead the life of an intellectual in-group in espressos or pubs, then it all peters out. As they get older they retreat to the suburbs. There is not much intimate conversation or sharing of opinion between the young and, say, people of forty. If a man of forty started a round of the young people's espressos they would probably decide he was looking for a pick-up.

The most flourishing in-groups are usually of the literary or arty kind, whether old bohemian or new beat, where dispossession is a virtue and alienation a matter of principle. Australia has its share of 'writers' who don't write and 'painters' who don't really paint, for whom to be a 'writer' or a 'painter' is more a matter of a way of life than of creative activity. These groups are often anti-intellectual. Even among those who write or paint well, the normal tone would be anti-intellectual. They are 'feelies', as Peter Coleman put it, rather than 'thinkies'. To be a 'thinkie' is to be academic.

Central among Australia's problems is that some of the values of the culture it has inherited from Europe are in conflict with the realities of Australian life. As A. A. Phillips said in *Australian Civilization*, a belief in easy achievement of happiness is basic in Australia, yet it has not become ingrained in people's temperaments like the joyousness of the Polynesian; cultural influences in Australia reflect the sense of dissatisfaction of European culture. The notion of people getting their deserts is strong in European culture, yet it is an inaccurate picture of Australian society. (Australians get more than their deserts.) The European novelists' obsession with the class system is as interesting a study in its own right in Australia as the study of ant colonies, and about as relevant.

This position in which a Europe-derived society has developed aberrant characteristics but is expected to judge itself and see itself totally in terms of European culture, not even of contemporary European culture, but of European culture as it has been, may be responsible for some of the extreme anti-intellectualism of many educated Australians. They are baffled by what seems to be the irrelevance of what is held up to them as true. Some of it is obviously not true, but those who do the holding up are not themselves thoroughly familiar with the values they purvey: they sell the whole job lot, throwing doubt on the relevant by including with it the obviously irrelevant. The humanities teachers know there is something wrong; the society in which they live does not follow the prescriptions they have learned by heart. They become angry with society; it becomes an unimportant, freak society rather than a challenging one which they might try to interpret. One finds even left-wingers lamenting affluence and alleging that moral fibre declines once the economic struggle lessens, when all they mean is that there has been a change in the rules.

What is lacking among Australians is a real feel for the history of the human race, and a sense of belonging to a long-lasting intellectual community that reaches its great moments when it seeks out in wonder towards the mysteries of its environment, that has concerned itself with more momentous problems than the nature of Australia but whose present members could well take this question up in the light of the history of human knowledge.

Australians 'learn' their culture. They 'learn' it as if it described their own life and attitudes, when in part it does not, and this process seems to make the relevant in the culture they 'learn' also unreal. This sense of unreality can affect even those who have 'learned' their culture very thoroughly: they cannot detect the difference between their own society and the societies of the culture they have 'learned'. But some of the valuable parts of the culture they 'learn' – its awareness of horror, failure, inadequacy – can also seem unreal. Yet it is Australians' failure to understand the tragic (or the comic) in life that may place them at a disadvantage in a world in which happiness is largely still hard to achieve. It is as if a 'cultured' Australian rejects the Australian concept of happiness because it is not in the culture he has 'learned'; at the same time he is still sufficiently a 'happy' Australian not to absorb the reality of horror and tragedy in the culture he has 'learned'. He is *déclassé*, unable to talk to other Australians of the culture he has 'learned' because he lacks a real feel for both it and his own society. To rational, pragmatic, happy Australians the conduct of foreigners seems either crazy, or they seek rationality where it may not exist: the 'cultured' Australian is not able to make real the concept of ideological irrationality in the foreign conduct. The problems of a culture that is 'learned' are not unique to Australia, but it is in Australia and several other countries that they reach their strongest forms. Throughout the developed nations new qualities of life are emerging, largely mysterious and undescribed. In some ways there are already new kinds of people living in new societies; one of the fascinations of Australia is that it may be one of the first of these societies to emerge.

Presumably the alienation of intellectuals both from their own people's ways of life and from the culture they have 'learned' accounts for some of the weakness of intellectual life. The Intellect becomes a precious thing. It is learned and transmitted, but beyond some minor elaborations it is not dynamic. You don't use it. It's not part of the affairs of the day. It was this problem that I had in mind when I said in the first chapter: *Is Australia really inimical to ideas? Or has there been something wrong with the ideas presented to it?*

Whether it comes from this alienation, or their own addiction to happiness, Australian intellectuals often lack stamina. After years of wondering some collapse into silence; others, who do engage in intellectual performance, do not usually seem fully extended. They don't try very hard; they seem to lack the impulses of excellence. Discussions on public affairs often become shouting matches; nobody has much detail. Either they think too big or they think too small; they shout without knowledge or they wilt, overwhelmed by detail. Those who understand the need for a rigorous examination of alternatives often get lost in the examination and come to no decision; those who come to decisions do not always comprehend the possibility of alternatives or that decision-making is a realistic practical-ism that examines alternatives and possible effects but nevertheless still reaches decision – if partly without belief.

It is a characteristic of intellectuals anywhere that some of them prefer obscurity in style but this is of particular interest in Australia. Among those who have 'learned' culture there can be a distrust of clarity. Closed systems of beliefs on public affairs are also common. Subtleties of argument are ignored (unless it is a professional matter); intellectuals react for or against their 'image' of an article, without making any investigation of detail. Detecting one argument, they assume others. It is as if they reject the possibility that there could be subtlety or unpredictability in any article outside a professional publication or by any author other than a specialist. And if an article is by a specialist it has the sanctity of being within a 'field'.

However there is more development or organized intel-lectual life in Australia now than at any other period in its history and there is some understanding among some prac-tical men that intellectuals can be recorders of change, transmitters of new problems and new attitudes that can be of immense importance in practical affairs. Half the Cabinet does not read *Encounter*, as Kennedy's Cabinet did, but a few of the better ministers are reading what is available; some of the younger businessmen and professional men are now also doing some reading.

The emergence of new publications referred to earlier

was accompanied by the development of a new style of 'little magazine', socio-cultural rather than old style literary; and there have been influential pamphlets. In book publishing there are now books of intellectual interest; in history there has been a period of diffuse re-examination; there are some beginnings of a detailed examination of Australian society; there is an increasing number of conferences and seminars. However before diagnosing a 'renaissance' one must also note that while a country of small population such as Australia may need proportionately *higher* intellectual activity than larger countries, Australia has not yet achieved even a proportionate share; that the provision of interpretative information is still patchy; and that one could not yet really say that there was any competitive sharpening of ideas. To get rigorous, continuing discussion with standards of excellence is not yet possible in the new magazines.

It became the vogue to find two main strands in this new intellectual activity: that of Melbourne, with its emphasis on social improvement, Australianism, a belief in the perfectability of mankind, and a sense of high morality; and that of Sydney, with its emphasis on high culture, cosmopolitanism, acceptance of the inadequacies of life, political indifference and a sense of scepticism and gaiety. For one the Putney debates was required reading; for the other Plato's account of the trial of Socrates. At Melbourne University: a feeling that the English Puritan Revolution was still being fought (if in social terms), a continuing concern with moral affirmation and sincerity of motives, and a belief in the implementation of eternal righteousness. At Sydney University: an avoidance of 'illusion' and 'confusion', a destructive analysis of practically everything and the consolation of feeling oneself one of the elect. For the one, Professor Max Crawford: for the other Professor John Anderson.

However, these comparisons became a bit old hat. Intellectual life has become more diffuse as people are working through old positions.

# 10. THE LUCKY COUNTRY

*Living on our luck*

AUSTRALIA is a lucky country run mainly by second-rate people who share its luck. It lives on the other people's ideas, and, although its ordinary people are adaptable, most of its leaders (in all fields) so lack curiosity about the events that surround them that they are often taken by surprise. A nation more concerned with styles of life than with achievement has managed to achieve what may be the most evenly prosperous society in the world. It has done this in a social climate largely inimical to originality and the desire for excellence (except in sport) and in which there is less and less acclamation of hard work. According to the rules Australia has not deserved its good fortune.

The rules may be wrong. It is already becoming obvious that the belief in hard work may become one of the impediments to happiness in the future technological societies: some way will have to be found in which most people will work less without suffering comparative economic hardship. Australia has been one of the pioneer countries in cutting down hours of work and increasing holidays. In this sense Australians may be more progressive than the world thinks – in the very field about which they feel guilty. And however hard it is to imagine that a feeling for originality and excellence is not necessary for continuing prosperity, some people might say: if Australians can get away with it, good luck to them; after all, in a commercialist society, much of the originality and feeling for excellence is absorbed in matters of immense triviality – a new knob on a TV set, a new way of slicing beans.

Others raise the question that I have excluded from this book: What is the sense in there being an Australia at all? When it looked as if the Japanese might conquer Australia early in 1942 Vance Palmer wrote in *Meanjin* 'The next few months may decide not only whether we are to survive as a nation, but whether we deserve to survive. As yet none of our achievements prove it, at any rate in the sight of the outer world ... we could vanish and leave singularly few signs, that, for some generations, there had lived a people who had made a homeland of this Australian earth ... There is very little to show the presence of a people with a common purpose or a rich sense of life.'

Then Palmer gave his own answer to this question: 'If Australia had no more character than could be seen on its surface, it would be annihilated as surely and swiftly as those colonial outposts white men built for their commercial profit in the East – pretentious façades of stucco that looked imposing as long as the wind kept from blowing. But there is an Australia of the spirit, submerged and not very articulate, that is quite different from these bubbles of old-world imperialism ... sardonic, idealist, tongue-tied perhaps, it is the Australia of all who truly belong here ... And it has something to contribute to the world. Not emphatically in the arts as yet, but in arenas of action, and in ideas for the creation of that egalitarian democracy that will have to be the basis for all civilized societies in the future. That is the Australia we are called upon to save.'

This was an unusual outburst of rhetoric even in a wartime Australia that feared it might be destroyed. (And in which sardonic idealists in some of Sydney's water suburbs sold out cheap, afraid that their houses might be shelled by the Japanese.) However the perils of war showed – on the whole – how, being laconic, Australians can take surprise in their stride. The very scepticism of Australians and their delight in improvisation have meant that so far Australia has scraped through. On the face of it Australia has had gamblers' luck. Even to use the phrase 'gamblers' luck' can be misleading; it suggests a knowledge of risk and insecurity, when it is a feature of Australian life not to take insecurities into account. The saving Australian characteristic – and this has some of the gambler's coolness about it – is the ability to change course quickly, even at the last moment, and seek a quick, easy way out. This can happen almost without discussion or dramatisation of the change. Australians have good nerves. They hate discussion and 'theory' but they can step quickly out of the way if events are about to smack them in the face.

## Will the luck last?

However there are two fields where reliance on luck and last-minute adjustment are not going to work; these are the fields of Australia's strategic environment and of reactions to the demands of technology. So far as the first is concerned, it is just remotely possible that events in Asia will pass Australia by, but it seems insane to trust to luck that they will do so. So far as the second is concerned, there does not seem to be even a remote possibility of luck coming to the rescue; Australia will not be able to maintain its prosperity in the new technological age without profoundly changing its life patterns. It is because these two demands cannot possibly be evaded that I suggested earlier that Australia has now completed the first chapter in its history. Things are going to change so deeply that some new kind of Australia is emerging; either that, or they will not change, and the present kind of Australia will go under anyway.

In the next few decades one can see such possible catastrophes in Asia that Australia might be overwhelmed whatever it does. There are all kinds of catastrophes less than total victory that could change the world for the worse for Australia. There are also several crises in South-East Asia, that, although not directly related to communism, might also wreck things for Australia, if only, in the first place, in scaring off migrants and overseas capital. Australia can never have the strength to affect the results of the grand game; but it can play its part, and in some of the smaller games it could play an important part. The more its economic growth and population increase the greater that part can be. When the present ruling generations go, will the rigidities and obsolescence of Australian public life change quickly enough for Australia to accept its connexion with events? It is easy to talk about increases in population, in economic development and in military strength and about making changes in attitudes to Asia. These may be necessary (though not sufficient) for Australia to survive, let alone to play a more important part in Asia (or actually play the part it has written for itself). But will they happen?

Will Australia be able to accept the wonderful opportunities for greater participation, and sometimes initiative, in the world in which it lives? Will it rid itself of the belief that it is a dull country, that nothing happens to it, that it is safe from the unpleasantness of history? Perhaps Australians are too modest, capable of more than they attempt, believing that as a nation they are not old enough or important enough for great events; too concerned with happiness to understand the possibilities of tragedy, projecting their illusions on to others.

The demands of technology will be less dramatic than the demands of Asia, but of immense economic and social importance. Australia is playing for a high stake: maintenance of a general level of prosperity higher than almost anywhere in the world. That is why the standards one applies to the people who run Australia's economic affairs must be high. There is no point in comparing them with the economic masters of some small country that is just struggling along. We're at the top. We must apply the standards of the top. The answer to the question, *Can we keep our standards of prosperity and our present way of life?* or to put it more bluntly, *Can the racket last?* appears to be *NO*. That is to say, that if things go on as they are Australia will slip down the per capita national income scale. (It may be worth noting that since I wrote these words in the first edition of this book, according to one set of estimates, Australia dropped from fifth to tenth in the list of the world's prosperous countries – in one year.)

It has had its material success because its ordinary people

were educated enough and adaptable enough to work in modern ways; because they were eager to buy enough consumer goods to keep the whole show going; and because their masters, although not usually of high calibre, were skilled enough, with government protection, to decode the instructions they got from overseas. Now something more than that is needed. It does not seem likely that in this new age material progress can continue at the highest rate unless society jumps into new life with higher standards of training, with an increasing proportion of scientists, technologists and technicians, with a greater emphasis on administrative and managerial capacity and an absorption of the technocratic approach into ways of thinking. All the industrialised nations are now reacting to this problem, but few of them are doing it as slowly as Australia and in few of them does it represent quite such a change in social pattern. In most industrialised countries cleverness and skill are part of the national ethos, even if they share it with contradictory elements. In Australia they play no part in it. Even if more and more of Australian enterprise is run directly by overseas firms, there must be enough Australians able to decode the new instructions and carry them out. It is unlikely that enough skilled migrants can be acquired to do the whole job for us. And given the present inadequate training programmes it is likely that this crisis may become apparent at a time when it would take up to a decade to meet it.

When most Australians think of their economic growth they think that people should work harder. This leftover from puritanism may be the opposite of the truth. It may be desirable for the 'workers' to work *less*: what will be needed will be a great deal more thinking, training, organization and cleverness. But we are now getting only about half the vocational results from our education system that we could be getting out of it and the position may become worse. It's easy to say that more money should be pumped into the infrastructure – into education, research and development – and that talent should be sought out and given power and prestige. So it should. But it should be realized that to do this involves a social revolution, something that will change parts of Australian civilization beyond recognition. It is such a social revolution that now becomes necessary in Australia if the standards of material prosperity are to remain the tests of policy.

That a revolutionary change in attitudes towards life is needed to further material progress does not mean that this change will necessarily be achieved. A politician, government official, union leader or company director who does not wish to change his beliefs and the habits that give life meaning for him will simply not change them; they are more important to him than the further material progress of the nation. Normally, people prefer their ways of life to material progress: it is one of the reasons why most nations are 'under-developed'. What is advocated is a radical overthrow and destruction of the prevailing attitudes of most of the nation's masters. If this does not happen there is likely to be a general demoralization in Australia; the nation may become run down, old-fashioned, puzzled, and resentful.

One can go on advocating until one is black in the face but the concept of social revolution is nonsense if there are not the people to make it. The ordinary Australian people seem adaptable; it is a matter of the people on top. Here one can draw some confidence in the possibility of change (for better or worse) from detecting a difference between the generations. On top there is a stiff-necked carrying on of old ways based on enervated wisdoms. One has only to watch a top person on television to sense in the lowered eyes, in the inability to reach towards the camera and generalize, in the lack of excitement about the problems of the modern world, in the meticulous muddling around with trivia, that these are the symptoms of a lost generation. What Bagehot said of generations in politics is true of generations generally: 'Generally one generation ... succeeds another almost silently; at every moment men of all ages between thirty and seventy have considerable influence; each year removes many old men, makes others older, brings in many new. But sometimes there is an abrupt change. In that case the affairs of the country are apt to alter much, for good or for evil; sometimes it is ruined, sometimes it becomes more successful, but it hardly ever stays as it was.'

Australians do not take easily to the concept of one generation taking over from another. There has been hardly any study of the process, and none of the journalistic labelling that goes on in most developed nations. Among writers this lack of interest may have come from the obsessive desire to define Australian characteristics in terms of the upsurge of the 1890s instead of as a dynamic process or from the opposite desire (in rebellion against this one) not to find any Australian characteristics at all. There is a desire to maintain traditional standards of what 'Australian' should mean instead of finding out what it does mean. (To admit that generations can change would be to admit that a static concept of an 'Australian', based on the writings of the 1890s is false.) And the continuing dominance of old ideas and ageing men has led to a lot of imitation or appearance of imitation in younger generations. Geoffrey Dutton said in *Nation* that there are probably more old men of thirty in Australia than in any other country in the world. Among some of the younger generations there is an obsession with 'maturity'. As Dutton says, 'A sure way of discrediting anyone whose opinion you disagree with is to tell him that it's time he grew up.'

However, beneath the pretence of sameness one can detect difference. One can make some guesses, at the same time qualifying generalization by recognizing that men are often born out of their generation. In general the remains of the Menzies-Calwell generation is antediluvian, nurtured in a backwater, strongly provincial. They are of the post-Federation generation, proud that the Australian States had federated; they developed their theories of the world in a context of British power. They can be more old-fashioned than men of the same generation in Britain because their imaginations have not been fundamentally stirred by any of the cataclysms of the last fifty years. The men who came of age between the two World Wars see themselves as the innovators and men of iron will – the one-man shows who in their brilliant improvisations changed the face of Australia. Often the changes they made represent the dreams of the thirties rather than the demands of the sixties; though still believing supremely in themselves they have no trust in the men underneath them (often their problems of succession are their own fault); they trust in their own intuition (which is sometimes just luck), will-power and the handling of men. The wartime and immediate post-war generation understands the demands of the age better and sees life in more complicated terms than the men they are now beginning to replace. They understand the need for expertness and co-operation more. They are the New Generation, the men who see Australia in more sophisticated terms. Some of them have imitated the Men of Will. Others already seem tired. Some of the best may have been so long frustrated by the amateurishness of the Men of Will that they may have lost their punch. But they are Australia's immediate hope. The younger generation than this seems fresher, but it is still full of mystery, not defined. It is condemned as hedonistic and stupid. Yet some of its apparent stupidity may be indifference to the bogus view of life that is presented to it and some of its hedonism an expression of a strong Australian characteristic that is now less confused by puritanism. It may be a genuinely rebellious generation, developing its own style. It may be the generation that changes Australia.

Why is there no longer any sense of importance in Australia, no feeling that great events (except catastrophe) can still occur? Small nations usually have histories to sustain them or futures to enlighten them. Australia seems to have lost both its sense of a past and its sense of a future. In making appeals, in attempting to make policies 'rational' there is nothing to appeal to, no sense of purpose; yet people need some sense of definition to which they can

relate their actions as an individual needs a sense of identity:
a sense of having had a history, of having reached a particular point in it and of facing a certain kind of future.
It may be that all this is because Australia sees itself as a
dependent nation. It doesn't develop ideas; it looks overseas for support and recognition; it doesn't adopt policies
because it has only a small area of decision. This is the way
it may seem to the older successful men who are baffled
about what they are supposed to do next. Among the more
active younger people there is a feeling that Australia can
resume its history, but in a different direction. They are
fascinated by the idea of Asia. This fascination, combined
with a greater concern for education and cleverness, could
prove the creative, liberating element in Australia – if
there is to be one.

It is in dealings with Asian countries that Australians
might regain a sense of confidence and importance. In
different ways different kinds of Australians can feel more
at home (and more important) in different parts of Asia
than they do in their often unsuccessful and sometimes
humiliating attempts to keep up the family relationship
with Europeans. To take some examples: Although Japan
is a great industrial power and Australia is not, in Asia
they are the two countries that have achieved economic
take-off; they are familiar with the world of industrialisation and they are both big trading nations; they can distinguish themselves from the rest of Asia. They are in
business together. When a party of Japanese arrived in
Australia in 1963 after a tour of 'developing nations' they
said they felt more at home in Australia. Japanese take
Australians seriously. In one sense more seriously than
Australians take themselves – they see Australia as the
'great power' in Oceania, thereby showing more perci-
pience than Australians. Another example: The kind of
'Asian intellectual' from a developing country who is lost
in rhetoric is lost in a similar kind of rhetoric to that of a
certain kind of Australian intellectual; they both have an
obsessional usage of the word 'Asia' (without much know-

ledge of the subject); they are both making up their own 'nationalism'; they both see signs of cultural breakthrough from even the most insignificant art product; they both speak the language of anti-colonialism, under-development and foreign exploitation. For a third example: a Harvard-educated Filipino sitting in his air-conditioned office trying to avoid the rhetoric that stifles Manila, and get on with at least one practical thing in one small field, is likely to appreciate the kind of Australian expert who is not a rhetorician. The pragmatic, sceptical Australian can walk through the rhetoric of Asia like a blind man avoiding bullets. There they are, out there in Asia, advising on pest control, credit policies, irrigation, language teaching, some of the thousand and one little things that help civilizations survive the radiations of their own bombast. They are oblivious to all the generalities. They want to get on with a bit of detail. Their ability not to generalize, simply to get on with the job can open the hearts of practical-minded Asians.

Despite distrust caused by the 'White Australia' policy, the link with Britain, the great prosperity and the plain fact of being of European origin it should be remembered that there are so many differences and fears between the peoples of Asian countries that Australia is not usually high on most people's hate lists. Amendment of several traditional policies could even produce a rush of goodwill. When Australia was reclassified as an Asian country by ECAFE in 1963 many Asians were pleased. This was one up for them. What they want is for Australia to get off its high horse, be one of the crowd, express confidence in its own style. They want to cease being insulted. To do this – to be 'one of the mob', to accept one's environment and get on with the job, to be friendly with one's neighbours – these are notable Australian characteristics, part of the Australian genius. If Australians would 'be themselves' nationally tensions with Asian countries not based on power conflicts, (which are a different matter) would lessen.

People in Asia may envy Australian material prosperity

when it is poked offensively under their noses; but they can respect it and acknowledge that it was achieved without exploiting a subject people. Many consider it a miracle. (*But how did you become so affluent? Why are you so much more successful than us?*) Many Asians respect Australia's relations with the United States. They see this as a 'special relation' that means Australia should be taken seriously. (Confidence and respect is not necessarily gained by appearing weak.) The old Commonwealth links still have meaning in Asia; Australians can sometimes get on well with the people of Pakistan, India, and Malaysia because of this. The new anti-communist links can make Australia respected in the Philippines, Thailand, Taiwan, Vietnam. Trading connexions can increase esteem everywhere, but particularly in Japan. And to the neglected peoples of Oceania Australia is potentially a great and powerful friend.

Educated Australians share some problems with those educated in universities in India, Malaysia, Hong Kong, or Manila: they are all getting second-hand products. A greater concentration on Asia might liberate Australian intellectual life from its narrowness and frustration. Australian intellectual life has a potential 'style' of its own, but it frequently lacks the confidences to express it and falls back into imitation. Concentration on the many new fields available in Asia and the explosion of new imagination that could come from sensitive cultural interchange could make Australia an important intellectual centre in Asia, and therefore the world.

Acceptance of the changes of technology, involvement with Asia, the shock (when it comes) of declaring Australia a republic: these possible events could set things moving again in Australia. Something else seems needed: accommodation on top to some of the values of ordinary Australians. It is among the younger Australians, less puritanical and less anxious to compare themselves with Europeans, that this may be developing: a greater acceptance of pleasure; an acceptance of the fact that all that one can see of the world is man and his environment; a concern for extreme ease in human relations; the ability to act without fundamental belief, to give it a go. Australians have for long both understood the inadequacies of action and at the same time enjoyed action. They know how to be heroes without a cause; to suffer ordeal sardonically; to accept rules in which they do not finally believe. Ken Inglis said in a paper to the 1964 A.N.Z.A.S. Conference that, in the commemoration of the dead in the Anzac monuments, the appeals are not to Christianity but to the stoic view of life as a heroic ordeal. In economic planning, for instance, this attitude could carry Australia along the way; a plan imposes morale and pattern; it leads to action; some of the action does not follow the plan; one improvises, changes the dogma; one then proceeds to further action with equal disbelief. One is both sardonic observer and cheerful participant. Nothing finally works but one proceeds with action as if it did. Such is life.

Everywhere one goes in Australia among sensitive, intelligent people of the middle generation – once the conversation reaches a certain depth – one meets a sense of desperation: What is going to happen next? In the younger generation it reaches a sense of outrage that public images of life should remain so freakishly irrelevant. Those who love their country, or (in the more restrained Australian idiom) are worried about the life their children will lead, or are simply wondering what is going to happen next ... none of these can imagine the future. It is usually seen as a political problem: in the form of Menzies and Calwell the images of obsolescence stood there, improbable but apparently immovable; succession was seen simply as replacement by the same kind of thing. Among those who are frightened by this perpetual state of Stand Easy – and it is an emotion breaking through political party loyalties – there is a feeling of distrust for their own nation; a fear that responsible, clever people will just not be found; that there will be no breakthrough of new men; things will just go on; no one will do the job. This sense of hopelessness may prove to be an accurate forecast. The conventionalism of Australian elites may prove so strong that it breaks men who have new views of the possible; the desire to preserve certain beliefs and ways of going on may conquer all attempts to react to new demands or define reality anew. There are plenty of good people around but the conventions of the institutions by which power is reached stifle them or repel them. The nation that saw itself in terms of unique hope for a better way of life is becoming reactionary – or its masters are – addicted to the old, conformist.

All the same something is going to happen. The demands of the age will destroy the present conventions – sometime. As Bagehot said of a sudden change in generations, things are not going to stay as they are; the results may be good or evil, success or ruin. It is time in Australia not for consideration of minor change, but for broad, general views of change. These must be based on some sense of reality, but not merely on the practicalism of what is possible for the moment. Very little is possible for the moment. But the time might come when broad views of change that now seem impractical will seem sensible and to the point. A reformer must forget the present occupants of power; they are unteachable. In the irrelevance of the present, he has to look to the future, perhaps produce ideas that may prompt action at some later time. In this situation, to be impractical may be the only way of being practical.

One can hope that events will liberate what is good and progressive in Australians, not perpetuate what is bad; that the relaxation and ease of life and the prosperity will grow; that the ideal of fraternalism will gradually extend to include the Asian races (as it appears to be doing among the young) so that ultimately – but perhaps not for some years – Australia's population problem will be solved in what may be the only way it can finally be solved – by large scale Asian migration. Then, assuming huge advances in science that will make development possible where it now is not, Australia might really claim the name of continent, a continent in which for a second time, but more successfully than in the U.S.A., a new nation will be created with values that have some relation to ordinary human aspiration.

For the present one sees only the impossible. But here again there are Australian qualities that can be liberated. The change in generations may meet some of the demands of technology and already there have been the beginnings of a breakthrough for the intellect and, more successfully, the arts. The talent in empiricism might add a new and practical dimension to economic planning, and save it from the doctrinaire. The laconicism and courage of Australians are waiting to be drawn on to face the world outside Australia: this reserve of Australian stoicism has not been summoned for many years but it still seems a feature of the existential young as it was of their fathers and grandfathers. The good qualities of Australians should be described and admired and brought into play. Their non-doctrinaire tolerance, their sense of pleasure, their sense of fair play, their interest in material things, their sense of family, their identity with nature and their sense of reserve, their adaptability when a way is shown, their fraternalism, their scepticism, their talent for improvisation, their courage and stoicism. These are great qualities that could constitute the beginnings of a great nation. This nation should be impelled to display its talents in a sense of reality. Many problems threaten the future of Australia. But we might have good luck. It's worth giving it a go.

# EPILOGUE

## *Seven years later*

*The Lucky Country* was published in December, 1964. A lot more has changed since that time than most of us recognise, although, naturally, much more has remained unchanged. Even revolutions often leave a society with many or most of its earlier features still in existence, and Australia certainly hasn't had a revolution. What is likely to make Australians feel that *nothing* has changed is that the principal inventors of what Australia is supposed to be like – the politicians, the commentators – don't seem to have wanted to recognise change, either because they don't see it, or because they don't want to see it – in some cases because the changes are not what they wanted, in other cases because the changes have not seemed fundamental enough. I would belong among the latter, but things *are* moving and during the 1970s they might add up to the kind of changes that we will all have to recognise.

The most obvious of all changes and the one most commented on has been the sudden expansion in the discovery and export of minerals and metals. In itself this is not going to throw up new economic classes big enough to change Australian society directly – and in any case so much of what goes on is off in such remote parts of the continent that Australians see them only when a television crew goes to them for a documentary. But minerals are quickly changing the pattern of Australia's exports: while the exports of some rural products will continue to be important, the exports of minerals and mineral products are quickly becoming more important, both positively (there are more of them) and negatively (markets for some rural products are ceasing to expand, or are contracting.) Whether this means that the cost of treating farming as something sacred becomes much higher, or whether Australian governments scale down the attention they have traditionally given to the rural industries remains to be seen. Perhaps one, then the other. What is undeniable is that Australia has enjoyed an extraordinary stroke of luck – a second chance to shape its economy. The increased receipts from exports of minerals and metals during the decade can mean that Australia can afford to 'restructure' those rural industries whose markets are going, so that some holdings can be turned to something else, others can amalgamate into more efficient units and some (one hopes) can join together in national parks, to meet some of the demands of the new conservation lobby. At the same time Australia can begin to dismantle the system of over-protection of some of its manufacturing industries and import what can be produced more efficiently elsewhere.

This leads to an even more important result of the mineral boom. In *The Lucky Country* it is suggested that Australia might begin to lose its place in the international prosperity ratings. Minerals or not, unless it becomes a more advanced technological society, it will do so. But, if it hadn't been for the extra revenue from mineral exports, there would have been balance of payment crises, import restrictions and so forth and these might by now have depressed an already timid sense of enterprise. Once again, there is a second chance. Something seems to be happening – whether it will be good enough or quick enough is not yet known. There is a change of generation in business and a rapid expansion in colleges of advanced education and other forms of tertiary education that might be more related to the art of running things than the existing universities, and, at the time of writing, there seems a chance that the apprenticeship system might at last be replaced with a system of technical training more in touch with the times.

Perhaps the most important of all the middle distance effects of the boom in metals and minerals might prove to be that it is throwing Australia into the arms (or tentacles – according to your viewpoint) of the Japanese technocracy.

When *The Lucky Country* was first written Australia's main customer was still Britain, although Japan was moving up to replace it. Now Japan is buying more than twice as much from Australia as Britain (which, as a customer, runs a rather bad third, with prospects of declining further in importance to Australia with entry into the E.E.C.). Australia is now increasing its purchases from Japan more rapidly, and if Britain goes into the E.E.C. Australian purchases from Japan may jump up higher than now predicted. During the 1970s the Japanese are likely to become interested in increasing Australia's capacity as an industrial society.

Japan might do something more than prove to be an important agent of technological change in Australia; views of its importance are already re-shaping Australian views of international politics and relations with Asian countries. The idea of Britain as a world power has now pretty much vanished in Australia, with the decision to get out of Malaysia and Singapore. Faith in the United States as a universal provider has been weakened by events in Indo-China. To some Australians these two changes in attitude have seemed to be a prompting to greater independence; to others, addicted to the idea of Australia as a faithful parasite, to a suggestion of a greater dependence on Japan. It is not going to work out like that – the Japanese see Australia as a power with strength of its own – but a period of greater co-operation in regional affairs between Japan and Australia seems the next thing coming up, and it is hard to see how, given this, Australia will not assume new attitudes to its role in the world.

When I wrote *The Lucky Country* there was an image of Australia as the most urban nation in the world, but this still seemed a bit surprising. Now it is becoming a basis for action. The last dreams of a rural Australia have gone, and the drop in the importance of rural exports and the increase in importance of mineral exports will keep it so. Australian rural industries can only become more efficient by even further depopulation of the countryside (bigger

236

farming units, with fewer people working them); the only real possibility of getting more population in country areas now comes from the idea of new mineral towns, some of which might later develop into industrial centres that do some of the processing of minerals. This is what the long awaited 'development' has proved to mean – not more expensive dams to encourage the growing of foodstuffs for which there is no market, but the growth of new industrial towns.

But the most significant of all 'development' is now seen to lie – or is now beginning to be seen to lie – in the big cities. How these cities can become more efficient – and better places to live in – is now what matters to most Australians. The New South Wales and Victorian Governments have not yet really got around to redefining their task as being primarily to concern themselves with planning for the future growth of groups of interconnected cities, but there are fumblings and jostlings towards this conception of government. One of the several new horizons opened up by Federal Labor Leader Gough Whitlam as to what Australian politics should now be about is that it should be concerned with the development of the cities. (He should know: he's been living in one of the new parts of Sydney's sprawl, where they all haven't got the sewer on yet.) Ripples of interest in town planning spread wider. The rumpuses in the older nations about pollution, traffic congestion and so on, get a ready echo in Australia.

With varying degrees of hesitation the Australian cities are now beginning to adjust themselves to more permissive living. There have been further reforms in drinking laws, betting laws and other matters since *The Lucky Country* was written. *Hair* plays to full houses in Sydney; *The Boys in the Band* has reached Adelaide. Censorship of films and books continues to irritate, but by the simple passing of time it becomes more liberal, if still behind most other prosperous societies. And so far as at least the provision of money goes, there has been progress in the performing arts. The Australian Ballet and the Australian Opera are now

well established; the Australian Council for the Arts is
handing out money; at last there are attempts to subsidise
a film industry. Status surveys show university professors and
scientists in the top rank of popular esteem (along with
doctors and lawyers); over the last ten years the general
level of what is provided by the press has risen (partly by
the arrival of some new publications, partly by the reform
of some old ones); ideas from other countries flood in;
there is more discussion of Australian conditions; a small
but growing number of university people are applying
themselves to matters of the day; at long last the rigidities
of the system of secondary schooling look as if they are
beginning to break up; the Catholics are fast rejoining
the rest of the community.

All these matters affecting city life – its material planning,
its leisure side, its intellectual and artistic side – have a
direct relevance to Australia's future immigration programmes in a way that to some seems obvious enough, but
that certainly has not sunk into the heads of the State Governments. The immigration figures have stayed high – in the
case of British immigration unexpectedly high – but there
are shifts in content: as the northern countries of Europe
become more prosperous there seems less incentive to
emigrate to Australia; the proportion of southern European
immigrants increases, but there are fears that for them
emigration to northern Europe (or in the case of the
Italians, to northern Italy) may become more attractive
than emigration to Australia. New immigrant markets are
opened up – Turks, Egyptians, Latin Americans. There are
hopes that a big emigration from the United States might
break loose – from those who are fed up with the failures of
the United States cities. But in all of these cases, whether
the figures are up or down, the big point is that it will be
the quality of Australian city life that will increasingly
decide the future of Australia's immigration programme. As
prosperity spreads, sheer economic need ceases to be an
impetus to emigrate: the desire to find a better kind of
place to live in takes over. Along the coasts of Australia –

especially along its eastern coasts – there is still an opportunity to build some of the most attractively positioned cities in the world, with breathing spaces between them, connected by new fast transport. If these cities are planned so that they are without the frustrations and perils of the world's present big cities, and if the life in them has sufficient of the ease and plentitude of the modern style, then Australia is likely to get so many applicants for immigration that it will be able to pick and choose whom it accepts. But there is not for the moment any planning for this. Projections of the expansion of Sydney and Melbourne are based on hopes for a successful immigration programme, but unless Sydney and Melbourne, and the new cities to be built, are turned into something that will attract immigrants, these projections may not prove to be true. The present attitude is like a firm that expands its plant without having a marketing program.

So back to the politicians. *The Lucky Country* was written in the Age of Menzies, when nothing seemed to move. Now things seem to move – it again makes sense to put up plans – but where are the politicians to give them a sense of direction? As Prime Minister John Gorton played a curious role in this. For the first two years of his Prime Ministership he made practically no new decisions, but his very inactivity – his long silence, his off-the-cuff outbursts, his ditherings – seemed to shake things up; and break some old ways. Still with no particular point to it, he continued his career of destruction in his third year; he put on a terrible show in the 1969 election campaign, but he trailed a lot of promises, the implementation of which swished a few more breakables off the shelves in 1970. With a stubbornness that seemed to be coherent only when it came to hanging on to his job or shoving his weight around he cleared a lot of ground in which those with more creative attitudes may later be able to plant new policies.

Many of his shakings-up were quite deplorable — particularly the demoralization of the public service that came from his do-it-yourself style and the collapse of idealistic attitudes towards Australia's relations with South-east Asia. History may suggest that his more creative role was to destroy his own party in such a thorough but slow way that it gave the Labor Party time to put itself together again and look like an alternative government. But even his underminings of public service confidence and of attitudes towards Asian countries might end up doing some good (now that he has gone) because they did clear away a lot of rubbish. His rule may be remembered negatively, like that of a barbarian invader, but it did mean that great parts of the Age of Menzies as I have described them in *The Lucky Country* are now destroyed.

His rule may be best thought of as an interim period. Of course all periods are interim periods – what I mean is that it was unlikely that anyone was going to spend much time characterising the Interlude of Gorton, however long it had lasted, because, even in a transitory world, it seemed remarkably transient.

On the face of it events since 1964 have moved Australia nearer a fuller recognition of itself as a nation appended to the islands of South-east Asia, both as regards internal racial prejudice (the Aborigines) and external racial prejudice (immigration policies) as well as general lines in foreign policy and broad social contacts between peoples, even if some of this change has been most tentative.

So far as Aborigines are concerned, the most remarkable event was the referendum of 1967 when, by a ten to one majority the voting people gave the Commonwealth Government extra powers to deal with the Aborigines, a vote that can surely be interpreted as a general expression of good will, if a vague one. Government reactions to this were slow to start, but it does now look as if all remaining civil discrimination against the Aborigines in those States that still practice it is on the way out. Not that this does not leave a lot more to be done. It was early in the short Holt Ministry, in March 1966, that there was at last a change in the policy of special discrimination against non-European immigrants, so that restrictions were slightly eased. In the three years after that a backlog of 4,687 non-Europeans who were already resident in Australia on a temporary basis were given permanent residence and 3,373 other non-Europeans – spouses and children of residents – were allowed into Australia as residents. Over the same period 3,767 new non-Europeans immigrant were accepted. It now looks as if up to 3,500 non-Europeans are now being allowed in each year and there are indications that the government will let this figure rise a bit more. And then?

Events are also moving in New Guinea. (Ignore that screech you hear in the distance – it is simply the Australian government still trying to put on the brakes.) New Guinea will not only rule itself in this decade; it will also become a fully sovereign nation. Perhaps more than one nation, since whether it can hold together is at present unknown. That as an independent nation it will be governed by the system of parliamentary rule seems very unlikely indeed. The removal of Australian colonial rule in New Guinea is merely the biggest event in the general de-colonisation of the islands of the South Pacific. Fiji became independent in 1970; the British will now unload themselves of the Solomons; only the French possessions are likely to remain colonies. All this may also twist Australia around in new directions, perhaps providing a greater sense of co-operation with New Zealand.

The Australian decision to leave military forces in Malaysia and Singapore after the British said they would go took Gorton a long while to agree to, and even when he did he followed it up with an act of bad grace. But it was a significant decision, taken by those who supported it as an affirmation of Australia's right to act as an independent regional power. If Gorton had followed what seemed for a while to be his own urgings – pull the troops out and back to fortless Australia – this might have created a chain reaction in Australia towards that position to which move (in effect, if not in intent) the extremists of both right and left: an isolationist, selfish Australia, ignoring the opportunities of its geographic situation and slowly submerging itself beneath its own tattiness. As it was, the budget for economic assistance to Indonesia increased, (if not sufficiently); in 1970 Australia joined the Jakarta conference on Cambodia just like any other regional power; and in other ways the push of events made it look a bit more 'Asian'. Here Gorton's destructiveness was useful: the idea of Australia as a regional Asian power did not enter his rhetoric, as it did, if not altogether satisfactorily, the speech-making of Harold Holt, but Gorton seemed to have some distrust of the old Liberal-Country Party use of fear – the downward thrust of Communism – as a political weapon. The phrase 'forward defence' began to be replaced by the phrase 'regional involvement'. At the same time Australian military planning began to move, if slowly, from the ridiculous position described in *The Lucky Country* towards something that appeared more rational and efficient.

In the epilogue to *The Lucky Country* I suggested three types of useful shock therapy for Australia – the act of becoming a republic, the acceptance of the changes of technology, and a greater involvement with Asian countries. To these I added, as a kind of soothing balm, the idea of more accommodation by their leaders to some of the values of ordinary Australians. What is the clinical report in 1971 on this treatment recommended in 1964?

Balms first. It seems to me that in certain ways Australians are more confidently 'becoming themselves'. Unfortunately it would take a book to explain what I mean. It doesn't mean that they are going back to the old rural ethos – they are not insane – although perhaps certain selected parts of the old ways are spreading more pervasively through urban life, if in somewhat changed forms, easiness of manner most notably. It has something to do with the beginning of the dismantling of the colonial imitations of British snobbery and of the appalling traditions of provincial British mid-Victorianism. (Thus the idea of swinging, permissive Britain becomes an ally in the destruction of the relics of 19th Century provincial Britain.) There seems a bit more self-assurance in those who follow the intellectual or artistic lives, especially among the young. But intellectuals continue to distrust their fellow countrymen, and therefore miss some of their targets. For example, what could worry people in Sydney most of all about pollution would be the possible ruining of the beaches, (a process said to be only thirty or forty years away from completion on present estimates), but this does not get quite the emphasis needed: they don't have suburban beaches in New York.

Britain. Queen Elizabeth and party came and went in 1970 in a way that made one almost feel sorry for them. Why on earth did the Australian government have to invite these celebrated Londoners out here to spend five weeks displaying themselves in the glass box of their special car? They tried a new, more 'democratic' line, quite sensible from their point of view since, so long as Australian politicians go on requiring this service, the Queen and her family are properly determined not to make fools of themselves. They don't want a flop. But are they ever going to spend as long as that again? (If so, why? Do they really want to hang on to us?) Other than this use of Queen Elizabeth and her family as celebrities, it is mainly the idea of London as a culture and fashion centre (is there a difference?) that lasts. There are still a few left of what Denis O'Brien called in the *Bulletin* 'ancient grovellers', but not much sinew remains to support their grovelling: the old sacred connexion of trade has loosened very quickly, and the strategic importance of Britain is about to disappear. For a few months John Gorton became an Australian nationalist, but he didn't seem to know what to do with it. There was no republic in sight, but there was no real sign that the sense of apathy towards Britain was not still growing and much of the old Britain-worship was dissolving into a more diffuse reverence for 'overseas' in general. Those of us who want to see Australians choose their own head of state now have our eyes on Canada: they might do it this decade, and that might set Australians going.

Technology. The idea that Australia should become a more talent-oriented and reason-oriented society seems to have got a lot more support in the last six years, although it has not yet acquired much political stimulus. There seems to be some truth in Professor Encel's suggestion in *Equality and Authority* that Australian politicians have been slow to recognise that since 1939 they have had a bureaucracy which can enlarge their scope for action. The most significant development seemed to be an extra concern that rationality should be applied not only to manufacturing but also to those other activities that can make life a bit more worth living. Ideas shot in and out of the newspapers, although there is considerable doubt as to whether Australia yet has the people who could carry some of these ideas out – or, if it has, whether it has the leadership that can release their energies. Here John Gorton represented an alarming symbol of backwardness: he seemed to see himself as an old style Man of Destiny who didn't really need a bureaucracy. He could do it all himself.

Relations with Asia. In the Age of Menzies one could see a small but growing sense of idealism (often healthily backed by general considerations of self-interest) expressing the hope that, by its relations with Asian nations, Australia could become a different – and unique – kind of country. The old man himself had nothing to do with it, of course, unless his very obvious irrelevance gave this sense of a new kind of future some of its force. But one had the feeling that when he went, things might follow more a 'natural' path. So they did, in a limited way, under Holt. But this was followed by a rather dispirited period. One could see the old isolationism both to right and left. For some, the movement against the war in Vietnam became a transcendant obsession – as if 'out now' were a policy for Australia's future relations with Asia; for others, drawn into an interest in South-east Asia because of what was seen as the downward Communist threat, the American disengagement seemed an invitation to Australian withdrawal not only from Vietnam but also from any real concern with South-east Asia. Neither in the writings of intellectuals nor in political rhetoric was there much sense of excitement or even interest. It became possible to imagine that Australia might refuse its destiny, although since it *is* a destiny it seemed hard to imagine it developing the strength of will to do so.

# INDEX

*Some more Australian Penguins
are described on the
following pages*

# GOD IS AN ENGLISHMAN

DONALD HORNE

'It was the lesson of the sporting fields, the public schools, the cadet forces, the Boy Scouts, the press, the pulpit, that British morality was the backbone of civilization. When they bellowed out *Land of Hope and Glory* the British thanked God for making them mighty and then asked him for more.'

Donald Horne scrutinizes the British predicament with a deadly eye.

# A NEW BRITANNIA

HUMPHREY MCQUEEN

In writing his interpretative analysis of the components of Australian radicalism and nationalism in the nineteenth and early twentieth centuries, Humphrey McQueen has written a hard-hitting manifesto for the New Left. He describes his work as 'a frantic dash from one battlefield to another' in an attempt to demonstrate that nineteenth century Australia was a capitalist society and not possessed by some natural socialist ethos.

McQueen is perceptive and often amusing as he examines what he sees as the essentially racist character of Australian nationalism, our 'siege mentality', the workers' concern for property symbolized by the piano, and the petit-bourgeois nature of the Labor Parties that emerged after 1890.

This book may well be attacked for being extreme but it will generate controversy and force its way into consideration wherever Australian history is being seriously discussed.

# MORRISON OF PEKING

CYRIL PEARL

In 1897 Dr George Ernest Morrison, a young Australian journalist, was appointed to the staff of the London *Times* as its Peking correspondent. He was soon to become the greatest and most influential foreign correspondent of his era.

In his youth Morrison walked the trail of Burke and Wills across Australia and explored unknown New Guinea.

Meticulously and judiciously drawing on Morrison's vast collection of papers and diaries, Cyril Pearl has written an authoritative, full-blooded and often witty biography of an extraordinary man whose life and achievements influenced the course of Chinese history at one of its most crucial periods.

# THE SURVIVOR

THOMAS KENEALLY

The Survivor is Alec Ramsey, veteran of a 1925
Antarctic expedition, now Director of Extension
at a university in the Australian tablelands. His
mounting guilt at the part he played in the death
of the expedition's leader, the horror with which
he faces the prospect of viewing the body when
the grave is discovered, are examined against a
background of provincial academia with all its
malice, soured ambitions and clumsy adultery.

'His tone is often wry, sometimes faintly cynical,
but his purpose is always investigatory . . . It is
a fine and truthful balance. . .' *Times Literary
Supplement*

'. . . the details of the denouement . . . surprise
without improbability and carry a formidable
weight of symbolic truth. Mr Keneally writes a
disciplined and stylish prose. . .' *Sunday Times*

# THE SOLID MANDALA

This is the story of two people living one life. Arthur and Waldo Brown were born twins and destined never to grow away from each other.

They spent their childhood together. Their youth together. Middle-age together. Retirement together. They even shared the same girl.

They shared everything – except their view of things.

Waldo, with his intelligence, saw everything and understood little. Arthur was the fool who didn't bother to look. He understood.